Irene M. Herremans, PhD, Business Administration Editor

Cases in Sustainable Tourism
An Experiential Approach to Making Decisions

*Pre-publication
REVIEWS,
COMMENTARIES,
EVALUATIONS . . .*

"This publication will be a great help to anyone teaching sustainable tourism concepts. Each case has been thoroughly researched and summarized, saving instructors valuable preparation time.

Integrating the authors' suggestions for in-class discussion, role-playing, and debates will assist students in understanding the complexity and ambiguity inherent in sustainable development. By using this book, instructors can easily bring theoretical concepts to life and deepen their students' understanding of sustainability principles. A must-have for any tourism instructor's library!"

Carol Patterson, BAdmin, BA, CMA
Sessional Instructor,
University of Calgary,
President Kalahari Management Inc.;
Author of *The Business of Ecotourism*
and *Saving Paradise: The Story of Sukau Rainforest Lodge*

More pre-publication
REVIEWS, COMMENTARIES, EVALUATIONS . . .

"I have always favored the case study approach for studying tourism, because it provides a richer and more comprehensive learning experience than just textbooks and statistics alone. For more complex concepts such as sustainable tourism, the use of case studies is essential if students are to really grasp the need for balancing social, economic, and environmental dimensions.

The case studies and the package of resources for instructors are based on clear learning objectives linked to current thinking and practices, model questions and solutions, and extensive references and further resources. It deals with the difficult topics in sustainable tourism, such as stakeholders, certification, monitoring and verification, management, finance, and reporting. There are options for updating the case studies using the list of supplementary materials in each chapter, comprising Web sites and other media to support the learning experience.

The most gratifying aspect of this new resource for teaching sustainable tourism is the fact that it actively engages students in their learning experience, through scenarios, Q&A, and role-play designed to prepare them for the opportunities and challenges that sustainable tourism presents. What's more, all relevant areas of sustainable tourism are included: airlines, tours (both terrestrial and marine), protected areas, programs, adventure and educational tourism, as well as a range of accommodation businesses. Students using this resource will be well prepared for the plethora of issues that confront those in the business of developing sustainable tourism.

This resource is a welcome addition to the literature on sustainable tourism, as well as offering a contemporary approach to teaching and learning. I will definitely employ this valuable new resource in teaching sustainable tourism, tourism management, and tourism planning at the undergraduate and postgraduate level as well as using it as a framework for developing a similar experiential approach for teaching and learning sustainable tourism in Australia."

Professor Jack Carlsen, PhD
BEcon, PhD
Co-Director,
Curtin Sustainable Tourism Centre,
Curtin University of Technology,
Perth, Western Australia

"Sustainable tourism is a hot topic and a 'must' course in tourism-related departments. Sustainable tourism books for students are everywhere due to its popularity and importance; however, only a few useful books are available as instructional vehicles for parks, recreation, and tourism majors. In this regard, I was so delighted to review this textbook, *Cases in Sustainable Tourism,* the first casebook in tourism with a comprehensive instructors' manual that covers sustainable tourism issues and addresses the major challenges in that area.

The book incorporates many concepts and frameworks regarding sustainable tourism development, planning, and management classes that include environmental reporting, social and environmental responsibilities, codes of ethics, development conflicts, development plan implementation and evaluation, stakeholder participation, and more. This casebook gives students an opportunity to apply what they have learned about sustainable tourism management frameworks and concepts to real-world examples of environment-related situations, and to develop the analytical and thinking skills necessary to make good decisions in real-world management situations.

In addition, the textbook comes with the user-friendly instructors' manual that directs instructors to hundreds of information sources, including not only additional readings but also videotapes and related Web sites. The authors also provide thought-provoking discussion questions and possible solutions.

As a tourism instructor and researcher, I recommend this textbook for both undergraduate and graduate students who wish to pursue their careers in parks, recreation, or tourism. This text is appropriate both for junior and senior tourism management classes and graduate classes. The textbook is an excellent primer to understanding of the fundamental concepts, issues, and real-world examples of sustainable tourism."

Hwan-Suk Chris Choi, PhD
Assistant Professor,
School of Hospitality
and Tourism Management,
University of Guelph
Ontario, Canada

THHP

The Haworth Hospitality Press®
An Imprint of The Haworth Press, Inc.
New York • London • Oxford

Cases in Sustainable Tourism
An Experiential Approach to Making Decisions

Cases in Sustainable Tourism
An Experiential Approach to Making Decisions

Irene M. Herremans, PhD, Business Administration
Editor

THHP

The Haworth Hospitality Press®
An Imprint of The Haworth Press, Inc.
New York • London • Oxford

For more information on this book or to order, visit
http://www.haworthpress.com/store/product.asp?sku=5486

or call 1-800-HAWORTH (800-429-6784) in the United States and Canada
or (607) 722-5857 outside the United States and Canada

or contact orders@HaworthPress.com

Published by

The Haworth Hospitality Press®, an imprint of The Haworth Press, Inc., 10 Alice Street, Binghamton, NY 13904-1580.

PUBLISHER'S NOTE
The development, preparation, and publication of this work has been undertaken with great care. However, the Publisher, employees, editors, and agents of The Haworth Press are not responsible for any errors contained herein or for consequences that may ensue from use of materials or information contained in this work. The Haworth Press is committed to the dissemination of ideas and information according to the highest standards of intellectual freedom and the free exchange of ideas. Statements made and opinions expressed in this publication do not necessarily reflect the views of the Publisher, Directors, management, or staff of The Haworth Press, Inc., or an endorsement by them.

Illustrations by Sara Mitchell-Banks.

Cover design by Laurie J. Steelman.

Library of Congress Cataloging-in-Publication Data

Cases in sustainable tourism : an experiential approach to making decisions / Irene M. Herremans, editor.
    p. cm.
    Includes bibliographical references and index.
    ISBN-13: 978-0-7890-2764-1 (hard : alk. paper)
    ISBN-10: 0-7890-2764-X (hard : alk. paper)
    ISBN-13: 978-0-7890-2765-8 (soft : alk. paper)
    ISBN-10: 0-7890-2765-8 (soft : alk. paper)
    1. Ecotourism—Case studies. I. Herremans, Irene M.

G156.5E26C37 2006
338.4'791—dc22
    2005024816

I dedicate this book to my parents, Albert and Eleanor Herremans, who were environmentalists before the word became popular.

CONTENTS

ABOUT THE EDITOR

Irene Herremans, PhD, is Associate Professor in the Haskayne School of Business and Adjunct Professor in Environmental Design at the University of Calgary in Alberta, Canada. She has previously worked with business firms through a consultative position with the Small Business Administration and as Director of the Small Business Institute, and continues to do some consulting with selected companies.

Dr. Herremans has taught management seminars and workshops in Cuba, Slovakia, England, Ecuador, and China, as well as international management programs offered at the University of Calgary for managers from various countries. Her research has been published in numerous professional journals, including the *International Journal of Sustainability in Higher Education, Journal of Sustainable Tourism, Journal of Teaching in International Business, Eco-Management and Auditing,* and *Corporate Environmental Strategy.*

CONTRIBUTORS

Marcos M. Borges is a doctoral student in the Department of Recreation, Park, and Tourism Sciences at Texas A&M University sponsored by the Brazilian CNPq, Conselho Nacional de Desenvolvimento Científico e Tecnológico (National Council for Science and Technology Development). He is also founder and director of Grupo Nativa, a Brazilian organization that has been working with sustainable tourism planning and implementation since 1986. Marcos's main interest is in tourism planning for small and rural communities. He worked as consultant for ecotourism planning and development projects in several Brazilian states. He was the coordinator and worked in all stages of the extractive reserves ecotourism case study presented in this book.

Mary Jane Dawson is a principal with the Office of the Auditor General of Alberta, where she is responsible for the completion of a variety of government program audits including those that examine the efficiency, economy, and accountability reporting of the government. Her special interest is in environmental performance reporting. She is also interested in the mechanisms and influences that result in changes in social policy. She received her bachelor's degree in commerce in 1980 from the University of Alberta and became a chartered accountant in 1983. In 1998 she became a Fellow with LEAD International. LEAD International is a global network of individuals and nongovernmental organizations committed to sustainable development.

Marcus Eyre is an environmental specialist with the National Energy Board in Calgary, where his current work is primarily focused on impact assessment of energy transmission projects. Prior to this he worked in socioeconomic impact assessment, as a policy analyst in Ottawa, international development, and for several years as a researcher and park warden in the Canadian Rocky Mountains National Parks. He holds a master's degree in environmental design from the

University of Calgary, as well as undergraduate degrees in zoology and outdoor pursuits.

Sandy Hershcovis is a doctoral candidate in organizational behavior at Queen's University. After receiving her Bcomm from the University of Calgary, she pursued her MSc in management at Queen's School of Business. Sandy's experience as a retail manager and a staff auditor at Arthur Andersen sparked her interest in organizational justice, and sustainability and corporate responsibility. Sandy has published case studies and journal articles in sustainability and environmental reporting in the oil and gas industry.

Simon Hudson, PhD, is an associate professor in the Haskayne School of Business at the University of Calgary. He has held previous teaching positions at Buckinghamshire College and the University of Brighton in England, and has worked as a visiting professor in Switzerland, New Zealand, and Australia. Prior to working in academia, Hudson spent several years in industry, and ran his own successful business for eight years. He has lectured and consulted in many aspects of tourism and has written three books: *Snow Business: A Study of the International Ski Industry; Sport and Adventure Tourism;* and *Marketing for Tourism & Hospitality: A Canadian Perspective.* Dr. Hudson has also published over twenty journal articles and a dozen book chapters.

Tazim B. Jamal is an assistant professor in the Department of Recreation, Park and Tourism Sciences at Texas A&M University, College Station, Texas. She earned her PhD in management at the University of Calgary, Calgary, Alberta, Canada. She also has an MBA, BSc (geology), and BA in French. Her research projects include the study of land fragmentation and diversification strategies of small agricultural enterprises, developing impact assessment and destination management tools for local communities, and stakeholder-based processes for sustainability. She has published in journals such as *Journal of Environmental Planning and Management, The Encyclopedia of Ecotourism,* and *Journal of Sustainable Tourism.* She also authored a book chapter titled "The State of Nature Tourism in Texas: Sustaining the Rural Agricultural Family Enterprise" in *Ecotourism: Management and Assessment.*

Fergus T. Maclaren is currently a senior consultant, Consulting and Audit Canada Sustainable Development and Environmental Management Practice. He was formerly the director of International

Programs and the International Year of Ecotourism with The International Ecotourism Society (TIES) in Washington, DC. He holds a master's degree in environmental design from the University of Calgary and is experienced in all aspects of tourism resource management and development including training, site evaluation, needs assessment, strategic tourism marketing, program design, and evaluation.

Ron Murch has a BMath from the University of Waterloo and an MBA from the University of Calgary. Since joining the University of Calgary in 1985, Ron has worked extensively with the School's IT support team, Executive Development Programs, MBA programs, and undergraduate programs. He has received teaching awards and in 1998 was a visiting faculty member at the Henley Management College in the United Kingdom where he focused on the use of experiential learning techniques in program delivery as well as researched the role of information technologies in the changing forms of work. He continues to bring his interests in both these areas to his teaching in the BComm and MBA programs at the University of Calgary.

Robin E. Reid holds a diploma in recreation and leisure services, a bachelor's in communications, and a master's degree in resources and environment. She is a full-time instructor in the Tourism Management Department at the Thompson Rivers University School of Tourism in Kamloops, British Columbia, where she teaches courses in sustainable development, environmental and cultural issues in tourism, as well as the more traditional tourism courses. Her research interests focus on environmental and cultural issues and she is actively involved in community projects that encourage environmental and cultural awareness.

Sarah Richardson is a faculty member in the Department of Recreation and Parks Management, California State University, Chico. She holds PhD and MS degrees in Recreation Resources Development from Texas A&M University, and a BES (environmental studies) degree from the University of Waterloo in Ontario. Much of her professional and academic work has focused on rural development, particularly in Texas and the American West. Her research interests include community image, identity, and development, and human-wildlife interactions in tourism.

Hanako Saito has a bachelor's degree in commerce in finance and international relations and a master's degree in economics from the

University of Calgary. She specializes in environmental management and international trade. Her master's thesis considers the effects of international trade in wage inequality in developing countries. She has also written a case study on the effects of the oil spill in the Galapagos Islands and an analysis of environmental management systems of tour operators in western Canada. She is currently a conference manager at International Association for Science and Technology for Development (IASTED).

Neil Symington has an MBA with a concentration in environmental management and sustainable development from the University of Calgary. He received a bachelor of arts from the Royal Military College of Canada and a certificate of public relations from the University of Victoria. Neil worked for two years (1997 to 1998) in the whale-watching industry as a boat pilot and in the outdoor industry as a backcountry guide in Victoria, British Columbia. Neil works in the energy industry concentrating on sustainability issues and policy development primarily in alternative energy, climate change, and stakeholder engagement.

Cameron Welsh has a BSc in zoology, a BA in psychology, and an MBA. He is the founder and president of Treadsoftly An Environmental Education Company Inc. where he guides mountain biking, hiking, fly-fishing, and corporate programs. Cameron is also involved in consulting and research in such areas as strategic environmental management, environmental ethics, environmental communications, database development, and Web site and e-commerce development. Cameron has done presentations on environmental management at conferences such as the Summit on Eco-Tourism and Adventure Travel and has written a number of articles for academic and practitioner journals in the areas of sustainable tourism and control systems. In the off-season, Cameron is a sessional instructor in management information systems at the Haskayne School of Business at the University of Calgary.

Agnieszka (Agnes) M. Wojcieszek graduated from the University of Calgary, and has obtained a chartered accountant designation and is currently a manager in the Assurance and Business Advisory Services department at Grant Thornton LLP, in Calgary. Growing up near Okanagan Lake in Kelowna, British Columbia, she took part in various water activities. Her participation in outdoor activities sparked an interest in environmental ethics and awareness and led her to get involved in this project.

Acknowledgments

I thank the Chartered Accountants Education Foundation of Alberta, the University of Calgary, and the Haskayne School of Business who had the foresight to provide seed monies for development of many of these cases. A great contribution was made by many authors and research assistants who provided the material to make this book possible. I am especially grateful to those instructors and authors who tested the cases in their classes to ensure relevancy and usability and to authors who edited their cases and resource guides, many times, to make them as timely and useful as possible. The cartoon illustrations were prepared by Sara Mitchell-Banks and Shivana Maharaj, and Hanako Saito prepared the exhibits and maps to accompany the cases and resource guides. Ron Murch, a valued colleague, inspired me to think of cases as tools for experiential learning. Rookmin and Kailash Maharaj were extremely helpful with final edits and permissions. I am deeply indebted to Hanako Saito, who checked details, used her creative abilities to prepare exhibits from my rough sketches, prepared maps, and worked without complaint for endless hours in helping to prepare this book. Thanks, also, to the people who contributed photos, which made the cases come alive. In addition to the authors, I received photos from the following people and companies: Leah Adair, Robert Bott, Patti Dolan, Dixon Thompson, Aspen Skiing Company, Canadian Mountain Holidays (CMH), Fairmont Palliser, WestJet Airlines, Paul Gray, Joaquín García Benavides, and Costa Rican Specialties. Through such progressive organizations and individuals, we will be able to work together to achieve our goal of sustainable tourism for everyone.

Part I:
Introduction to Cases
and Environmental Thought Leaders

Gifford Pinchot, John Muir, and Aldo Leopold are a few of the early thinkers who are well-known for putting forth progressive thoughts about the relationship between humans and the environment. Our current initiatives, activities, and programs regarding sustainability can be traced to these forward-thinking and insightful individuals. In the early 1900s, Pinchot declared that "our forefathers bequeathed to us a land of marvellous resources still unexhausted. Shall we conserve those resources, and in our turn transmit them, still unexhausted, to our descendants?" (Pinchot, 1967, p. 3).

Pinchot went on to predict that when a nation exhausts its natural resources, disaster and decay in every aspect would follow. Pinchot's beliefs build the foundation for environmental responsibility based on economic logic. In other words, it pays to be a responsible environmental citizen, whether corporate or individual. Pinchot, notwithstanding his progressive thinking, did not propose guarding natural resources from exploitation but rather advanced the thought of resource conservation based on scientific, intelligent, rational, and efficient distribution in order to eliminate waste. Natural resources were not valuable for their intrinsic worth but rather their value for human consumption.

Muir, on the other hand, believing in the inherent value of nature, would be comfortable with protecting significant natural areas through the watch eye of the U.S. Army. He believed that humans needed encounters with nature and suggested that if people just came to the national parks that they would find "everything is hitched to everything else" (Wolfe, 1978).

Although friends, John Muir and Gifford Pinchot had definite differences in fundamental beliefs as to why conservation was important. Even though both Pinchot and Muir provided advances in our thinking about how humans and nature interact, neither paradigm provided a practical model for peaceful coexistence between humans and nature.

Aldo Leopold's contribution to environmental thought, through his land ethic, provided a workable model for mutual respect of both the environment and humans. His model did not prioritize human consumption over the value of nature as did Pinchot or prioritize the value of nature over human consumption as did Muir. Leopold suggested that quality of life of humans depends on the quality of nature and that humans and nature must live in harmony without one having priority over the other. New ways of thinking regarding our relationship with nature provided new hope for a model of sustainability. Thinking now turned to the functions of the natural landscape as an ecosystem and how humans can learn to live within those ecosystems. What processes would support both human activities and economic interests? In 1987, Leopold explained in *A Sand County Almanac:*

> A system of conservation based solely on economic self-interest is hopelessly lopsided. It tends to ignore, and thus eventually to eliminate many elements in the land community that lack commercial value, but that are (as far as we know) essential to its healthy functioning. It assumes, falsely, I think, that the economic parts of the biotic clock will function without the uneconomic parts. (Leopold, 1987, p. 214)

Thus, the first wave of environmentalism came, and along with it, the first mass discussion about the concept of ecocentric values. Unfortunately, the political and economic climate of the late 1970s and early 1980s made it increasingly difficult for the embryonic ecocentric values developed in the 1960s to take hold and grow. A second wave of environmentalism took hold in 1983. The wave grew in power and size at the request of the General Assembly of the United Nations to formulate a world commission to develop "a global agenda for change." Thus, the World Commission on Environment and Development (WCED) was formed and published its report titled *Our Common Future,* often referred to as the Brundtland Report (1987). The report awakened many to the pending crisis of our planet and the need to take action.

The Brundtland Report defined sustainable development (similar to Pinchot's thoughts) as "development that meets the needs of the present without compromising the ability of future generations to meet their own needs" (Bruntland, 1987).

This report provided the foundation for many industries and sectors to set their own agendas to answer the call for change. Soon thereafter, in 1990, the tourism industry began considering how it could answer the call set forth in the WCED report. The Globe 1990 International Tourism Conference first defined sustainable tourism similar to the Bruntland Report's definition. However, the World Tourism Organization (WTO) now defines sustainable tourism as "an enterprise that achieves an effective balance between the environmental, economic, and socio-cultural aspects of tourism development in order to guarantee long-term benefits to recipient communities" (WTO, 2005).

At the Earth Summit Conference held in Rio de Janerio in 1992, 182 governments adopted a comprehensive program to implement the Bruntland Report. To further the initiative begun by the tourism industry, in 1996 three international organizations launched the tourism industry's strategy and action plan titled Agenda 21 for the Travel & Tourism Industry: Toward Environmentally Sustainable Development. The World Travel and Tourism Council (WTTC), the World Tourism Organization (WTO), and the Earth Council have been active in providing regional seminars to ensure awareness and implementation of the program at the local level.

In the same year, the 1992 Global Conference on Business and the Environment (Globe '92) identified steps necessary for the tourism industry to develop sustainability. Briefly, these steps involved the following activities:

- Develop a long-term strategy and create comprehensive policy and planning structures.
- Protect the industry's resource base.
- Establish partnerships between tourism providers and host communities.
- Use inventory and monitoring systems for the resource base and tourists activities.
- Take advantage of both improved technology and market opportunity.
- Develop standards and implement effective regulatory mechanisms through collaboration.

In addition, initiatives were undertaken to ensure that sustainable tourism is a characteristic of all tourism operations. The WTTC developed a set of environmental guidelines to help companies and governments develop policies that create a clean and healthy environment for all tourism activities. These guidelines have evolved into a Green Globe certification and a benchmarking process for tourism organizations.

In response to Agenda 21, WTTC launched its Green Globe program providing guidelines for more environmentally responsible behavior. WTO has established a set of indicators for monitoring stress and carrying capacity of tourism sites. In 1999, the WTO, through its Global Code of Ethics for

Tourism, synthesized various declarations and codes that had been developed at various times and locations. Article 3, titled "Tourism, A Factor of Sustainable Development," specifically addresses the ecological considerations of sustainability in tourism. Most of the other articles address, either directly or indirectly, the social considerations of sustainability in tourism. Of course, both of these dimensions (the social and the environmental), in addition to the profitability of tourism activities, are necessary to make sustainable tourism feasible.

Tourism 2020 Vision by the WTO (2001) forecasts long-term growth in travel and tourism in spending by 4.1 percent each year. Therefore, to ensure this growth is sustainable, all tourism organizations must do their part in providing socially acceptable, environmentally responsible, and economically viable services and products. As well, tourists must be responsible consumers. If the predicted growth in tourism materializes, it will result in 1 billion arrivals by the year 2010 and 1.6 billion by the year 2020.

The case studies in this book, along with the exhibits and references in the resource guides, provide an enormous selection of materials to bring awareness to a variety of tourism stakeholders: university students in tourism programs, tourism business professionals, employees of all kinds of tourism organizations, and tourists.

Each case is based on a real-life incident; however, some of the circumstances have been changed slightly in order to provide additional pedagogical merit or to provide confidentiality to the organization(s) on which the case is based. The cases have been written so that students can engage in an experiential session by placing themselves in the role of one of the characters in the case. Sufficient information, ideas, and activities have been provided in the accompanying resource guides to make the cases extremely flexible and adaptable for use in many different types of academic programs and many locations throughout the world. In this way, the learning can become self-initiated and pervasive, making it more meaningful to the learner. Local speakers who engage in similar activities as those in each case can bring them alive. Students and instructors can use Internet materials to delve deeper into some of the issues presented in each case. Visits to local tourist areas to investigate similar problems in the local area will also enhance learning.

REFERENCES

Brundtland, Gro Harlem (1987). *Our Common Future: World Commission on Environment and Development.* Oxford: Oxford University Press.

Global Code of Ethics for Tourism (1999) United Nations and World Tourism Organization. http://www.world_tourism.org/code_ethics/eng/brochure.htm.

Leopold, Aldo (1949). *A Sand County Almanac, and Sketches Here and There.* New York: Oxford University Press.

Pinchot, Gifford (1967). *The Fight for Conservation.* Seattle: University of Washington Press.

United Nations and World Tourism Organization (1999). Global Code of Ethics. www.world-tourism.org/code_ethics/eng/brochure.htm.

Wolfe, Linnie Marsh (1978). *Son of the Wilderness: The Life of John Muir.* Madison: University of Wisconsin Press.

World Tourism Organization (WTO) (2001). Tourism 2020 Vision. World Tourism Organization Madrid, Spain.

World Tourism Organization (2005). www.nric_net/tourism/what_is.htm.

Chapter 1

Overview of Cases and Their Use in Experiential Learning

Ron Murch
Irene M. Herremans

EXPERIENCES

You are about to venture into an experiential learning session through the scenarios provided in this casebook. Experiential learning provides you with a basis for your learning. It also allows you to draw from your own work and personal experiences to better understand theories and principles used in traditional textbooks. Using experiences as a basis for learning will allow you to become personally involved, making learning more meaningful and applicable to your everyday life. Putting theory into practice enables solutions or approaches for addressing everyday dilemmas, allowing you to realize how much you really know. Evans (1992, p. 41) states "Most people know more than they think they know if only they knew that they know it."

Throughout your life you may participate in many different tourism-related roles

- as a tourist,
- as an employee or owner of a business providing goods and services to tourists,
- as an employee of a government or its agencies attempting to regulate or promote the tourism industry,
- as a member of a community receiving tourists,
- as a member of an organization concerned with the health of the environment, or
- as a combination of the above.

The World Tourism Organization (WTO, 2000) recognizes that tourism encompasses more than activities for leisure time and vacations. The WTO officially defines tourism as "the activities of persons traveling to and staying in places outside their usual environment for not more than one consecutive year for leisure, business, and other purposes not related to the exercise of an activity remunerate from within the place visited." Therefore, it is highly likely that we will all be tourists at some time in our lives; consequently, we should be aware of the impacts that our activities create in order to make sound decisions. In our dynamic, evolutionary society of the twenty-first century we are required to think differently about organizations' various and diverse relationships to society and the environment. The topic of sustainability was not of grave concern until the 1990s; therefore, we are all students learning how to lead sustainable lives.

All cases are based on real problems that the organizations represented had to resolve. Several cases are written in docudrama format, many with dialogue, to make it easy to relate to and "to get a due sense of [your] own capacity to learn" (Evans, 1992, p. 41). One type of experiential session might include a set of activities and learning elements that occur both in preparation for and as follow-up to a focal, experiential classroom session, class presentation or discussion with a core theme. The expectation is that as a student you will take full responsibility for your own learning and be accountable for that learning. Thus, you are put in a position of wrestling with multidimensional, complex, sustainability issues. It places you, the student, at the center of learning and places more of the responsibility for learning on you as you search for information to help you find a solution to the issues presented in the scenario. These scenarios, when supplemented with imaginative approaches by your instructor and by you, can make a case more realistic by embellishing the situation with local speakers, field trips, newspaper articles, and other props that turn the case into a real life experience. The cases can be easily adapted, applied, or translated to a situation or organization that is local. You could even write your own case by patterning your work after one of the cases in this book and your own life experiences.

You can be placed in the role of one of the case characters to more effectively learn to handle difficult, but realistic, sustainability decisions. This will sometimes require some advance preparation on your part. Some sources for preparation include articles written about the organizations, information provided on the organizations' Web sites, materials, and readings related to the specific theories or constructs that would be helpful in addressing the complex problem. You may be asked to prepare a memo, briefing, short report, or position paper if a speaker will be coming to the classroom in a future class session. Other cases work well after viewing a selected video or movie. Sometimes controversial issues can be discussed via teleconference with employees from another organization or students from another university.

Frequently, you will be asked to break apart the elements of a case in order to more fully analyze certain relationships or dimensions and then to synthesize these relationships or dimensions so that you not only understand the separate parts but also how the parts work as a system. Finally, and most important, you will be challenged to make decisions about what you would do, often requiring you to make informed judgements that are supported with logical reasoning and quantitative evidence. These are the kinds of skills that are extremely important in the workplace.

With this approach and its incorporation of guided practice and experience and with thoughtful follow-up and learning, perhaps we can provide a solid grounding for establishing tourism programs that are *living* and *sustainable*.

MEET THE CASES

Traveling Responsibly

"Implementing Ecosystem Management: Mount
Assiniboine Lodge, Mount Assiniboine Provincial Park"
by Fergus T. Maclaren

This case provides a discussion of a backcountry lodge located in the Canadian Rockies (accessible only by hiking, skiing, or helicopter) and how it addresses its environmental responsibility. It leaves open the issue of whether this lodge is an ecolodge but provides sufficient information for the students to logically come to a conclusion and make suggestions for improvements. In addition, many ideas are presented to give students opportunities to discuss how this lodge or any type of accommodation could lessen its ecological footprint. Students can explore the definition of an ecolodge and view several accommodations located throughout the world that call themselves ecolodges. The discussion can naturally lead to which accommodations qualify as ecolodges and the types of certifications that inform tourists of the level of environmental responsibility taken by an accommodation.

"Flying High: The Airlines and the Environment—
Freedom Airlines, Inc." by Irene M. Herremans

This case introduces students to environmental impacts that airlines and their activities create. Then, it suggests how companies can disclose their impacts and programs to reduce those impacts through an environmental reporting process. Students can access a copy of an environmental report, become familiar with it, and critically assess the communication aspects of the report as well as the environmental performance of the company producing the report. For students with accounting or financial backgrounds, many comparisons can be made to financial reporting characteristics. The case allows for an introduction to the Global Reporting Initiative (GRI), the internationally recognized guidelines for environmental reporting. Students can also determine the potential environmental impact of their next travel plans.

"The Greening of the Fairmont Palliser" by Robin E. Reid

This case discusses the environmental initiatives of the Fairmont Palliser, owned by Fairmont Hotels and Resorts (FHR). FHR started its environmental program under the name of Canadian Pacific Hotels (CP Hotels) but continues to expand its program under its new name. FHR owns, leases, and manages hotels, spas, and resort properties throughout North America and the Caribbean under the Delta, Princess, Fairmont, and Legacy hotel banners. As CP Hotels, it was one of the first hotels to introduce guests to environmentally responsible behavior. The case can be used in several different ways. Simply reading the case can provide a springboard to discuss environmental activities that are taking place in the hotel and hospitality industry. Using the Fairmont Palliser as an example, the process that a hotel must go through to ensure that its environmental policy is transferred into actions can be discussed. Along with some of the supplementary materials suggested, the case also provides an avenue for discussing the economic viability of environmental initiatives and whether they might conflict with other organization objectives, such as customer satisfaction or service.

Sustainable Nature-Based and Adventure Tourism Activities

"The State of the Pacific Northwest Whale Watching Industry, 1999" by Neil Symington

Whale watching is a tourism activity that experienced phenomenal growth over the 1990s. Increasingly, countries worldwide are providing programs to learn about and view whales. Although this activity provides many socioeconomic benefits, problems are also incurred. Whale watching in the Pacific Northwest is the focus of this case. Because of the context in which the industry operates, whale watching in this area was allowed to grow without proper regulations. This situation is affecting not only the ecological conditions of the whales but also the economic viability of the industry and the quality of the social experience. Students are presented with several issues for discussion:

1. the promotion of whale watching as an ecotourism activity;
2. the attempt by an industry to self-regulate its members; and
3. the difficulties associated with regulating an industry and a natural resource that crosses international borders.

"Treadsoftly An Environmental Education Company Inc.—
The Environment and the Business of Backcountry
Tours, Part 1: Understanding Stakeholder
Issues" by Cameron Welsh

This two-part case dealing with a new mountain biking venture helps students to understand the importance of setting up a new company with a sustainable focus even before creating the business plan. Part 1 addresses the need to consider stakeholders' needs when starting a private business and developing the business plan. Determining the context in which the company will operate identifies not only opportunities but also threats that may inhibit the development of the company. Identifying potential threats early in the development stage of the company allows the entrepreneur to avoid costly mistakes later on. Students follow the thinking of the entrepreneur of this company as he develops its mission and direction.

"Treadsoftly An Environmental Education Company Inc.—
The Environment and the Business of Backcountry Tours,
Part 2: Creating Environmental Controls"
by Cameron Welsh and Robin E. Reid

Part 2 of this case continues with the development of the company's policy for sustainable operations. The students must make decisions on how to measure the implementation of a sustainable policy. The case suggests the importance of having both input and output measures to monitor whether the company is truly sustainable. The case also presents the question of how a small tour company can afford to perform an environmental audit and who might be an appropriate person/organization to do the audit. Finally, it presents the issue of how a company continues to grow as an environmentally sensitive adventure tour company.

"Canadian Mountain Holidays: Risk Assessment
and Management" by Fergus T. Maclaren

Tourism as an extreme sport is the focus of this case. The case deals with the social aspect of sustainability by discussing the risks and natural disasters that are created by our environment. The heli-skiing setting not only helps to understand the concept of risk and control but also the joint responsibility of the operator and the participant to manage the risk. The concepts presented in this case are easily transferred to other environmental issues or activities in which the tourist might engage. Awareness of risk is the first step in taking responsibility for reducing it. Various risk perceptions are presented in the case as well as equations for attempting to quantify risk associated with certain activities.

"Ski Resorts: Enjoyment versus Environmental
Responsibility—Does There Have to Be a Choice?"
by Simon Hudson

The case provides an awareness of the environmental impact that ski resorts can have and what some resorts are doing, worldwide, to lessen their impact. It provides information of the criteria that one environmental group used to grade ski resorts in the United States on their environmental responsibility. The case gives students that live near a ski resort an opportunity to talk to the management of the resort to determine environmental impacts. Also, students can question the criteria used in the rating system to determine environmental performance. Those who live near or are familiar with some of the ski resorts that were graded can determine if they agree with the grade given. Those students not living near one of the graded resorts can use the criteria to provide a grade for a resort with which they are familiar.

"Vacations by the Sea: Troubled Waters"
by Agnieszka M. Wojcieszek and Irene M. Herremans

Troubled reefs worldwide is the subject of this case. Even though the case focuses on recreational diving and snorkeling in the Florida Keys and the Great Barrier Reef, it provides insights into the human pressures that are causing ecological concerns in reefs. Students will understand the intricacies of ecosystems and the benefits that reefs provide, which should in turn encourage more responsible behavior when they engage in water recreation activities. Not only does the case provide an avenue for becoming aware of the crisis conditions associated with reefs worldwide but it also provides an opportunity for students to learn how educating tourists about proper behavior can preserve the ecological integrity of tourist destinations.

Wrestling with the Sustainability of National Parks

"Yosemite National Park: Parks Without Private Vehicles"
by Irene M. Herremans and Robin E. Reid

This case illustrates the process of implementing a plan to eliminate private vehicles from a national park in California. YARTS (Yosemite Area Regional Transportation System) is the focus of this case. The organization's objective is to improve the visitor experience in Yosemite National Park by alleviating traffic congestion and its related environmental damage. YARTS works with the outlying communities surrounding Yosemite to design a system that accommodates the stakeholders' needs. Many of the procedures used to change human behavior (concerning use of private vehicles) can be transferred to a discussion of using alternate modes of transportation in our cities. The case takes the approach of identifying the barriers to change and devising a plan to address those barriers. It illustrates the necessity of using the stakeholder approach and providing avenues for input in order to get the necessary support for execution of the plan.

"Grand Canyon National Park: Tourists by Land, Tourists by Air"
by Irene M. Herremans

User conflict and user rights are the subjects of this case. The case contrasts tourists who want a quiet, tranquil visit to Grand Canyon National Park versus those who want a whirlwind tour. The concepts in this case are easily transferable to other situations that create conflict among users, such as hikers, horseback riders, mountain bikers, ATV users, flightseeing, and jetski users. The case helps students understand that as tourist demand grows there will inevitably be more conflicts between users as they visit the same destination for their favorite, but different, activities. It provides a framework to determine whose rights receive priority in a particular setting, what activities are appropriate in national parks, and how our changing lifestyles sometimes do not allow us to receive full enjoyment from the activities in which we participate.

"Addressing Tourism Conflicts in Banff National Park:
The Banff Bow Valley Round Table Process"
by Marcus Eyre and Tazim B. Jamal

This case raises a number of interesting questions pertaining to tourism destinations set in environmentally sensitive areas, such as national parks, by providing a sense of the lived experience and voices of a number of stakeholders in an ecologically sensitive tourism destination. It illustrates the tensions faced by protected areas that are subject to pressures for tourism visitation and growth, whether these pressures are political, global or local. The case demonstrates that national parks are not simple spaces of nature but rather social constructions subject to conflicting ideologies. The diversity of values, opinions, and understandings relate to the diversity and interdependence of stakeholders in the Canadian Rocky Mountains, as well as to the different worldviews and attitudes toward development and preservation held by various groups and individuals. Questions raised by this case encourage students to consider the characteristics of stakeholders, values, and ideological narratives in interorganizational domains, and the mechanisms for addressing conflict over issues of preservation versus use and development.

"A Journey to Define Sustainability: Waterton Lakes
National Park" by Robin E. Reid

The Waterton-Glacier International Peace Park area is used in this case setting. Interviews with stakeholders in the Waterton area provide insight into the difficulty that can arise when different stakeholders place different demands upon the landscape. Through stakeholder interviews, students are introduced to the role of human values and the role of education in achieving sustainability. The interviews provide a social context to examine local values toward tourism in Waterton Lakes National Park and the surrounding area. The concept of sustainability is commonly viewed from three dimensions: economic, social, and ecological. In addition to these three dimensions, this case introduces a political perspective as a possible fourth dimension of sustainability. The political dimension includes government decisions and administrative processes that can affect the rate of human development and the ecological condition of the earth's environment. The case provides an opportunity for students to illustrate with specific examples how the conflict or congruency of the sustainability dimensions can encourage or discourage sustainability. Students are encouraged to provide recommendations of how areas of conflict can be eliminated to move to a more sustainable system.

Land Development and Governance Issues

"Costa Rica: Banana Plantations or Ecotourism?"
by Mary Jane Dawson and Tazim B. Jamal

This case explores the conflict that arises when a banana plantation owner wants to expand onto land that is adjacent to national park land. The expansion of the plantation is opposed by the ecotourism hotel owners and the rafting business owners as it may impinge either on their current business or their plans for expansion. A stakeholder process is convened to address this contentious issue. The case is set up with the following roles: a facilitator appointed by the president of Costa Rica; the mayor of the town adjacent to the park; the biologist from the neighboring turtle reserve; an environmentalist from an international environmental nongovernment organization (IIENGO); an elder from the town; a worker from the banana plantation; a representative from the Ministry of Natural Resources, Energy and Mines; a representative from the Department of Tourism; and the plant manager representing the multinational corporation who will buy the additional production from the plantation owner. The case helps students to recognize the necessity of asking for information and including time to gather and develop a common information base from which further discussion and strategy planning can occur. It offers an opportunity for students to forward a number of alternatives related to ecological and social sustainability and involve the local community more fully in decision making about developments that can impact its future.

"CAMPFIRE: A Sustainable Use of Wildlife Resources?"
by Sandy Hershcovis

This case examines the controversial approach used by the Communal Areas Management Program for Indigenous Resources (CAMPFIRE) in addressing conservation issues. The program, which began in Zimbabwe in 1989, empowers the people of local communities to take charge of their natural resources by putting an economic value on resources such as local wildlife. One of the primary goals of the program is to effectively encourage the culling and hunting of big game animals, such as lions and elephants, in order to prevent poaching and illegal slaughter of these same animals. The ethical challenge that emerges from such a program is whether the practice of killing some animals to preserve others can result in sustainable conservation. The case gives students an opportunity to examine the positive and negative externalities that result from the CAMPFIRE program.

"Ecotourism in Extractive Reserves in Brazil"
by Marcos M. Borges and Sarah Richardson

Extractive industries are the focus of this case. An example shows how a community effort in Brazil worked to change an area that was harvested unsustainably in the short-term to activities that take a long-term sustainable approach. Even though government funding was provided to support the transition, the case highlights the necessity of education and training during the transition period not only to change attitudes and beliefs but to build knowledge and skills about the new activities to ensure economic viability. The students have the opportunity to study the overlap of environmental and economic sustainability by studying the transition from an activity that was sustainable economically but unsustainable environmentally to an activity that is sustainable both economically and environmentally.

OVERVIEW OF CASES

Tables 1.1 and 1.2 provide information about the key elements of each case according to four different classifications:

1. Environmental management system (EMS) elements
2. Behavioral aspects of EMS implementation
3. Type of organizations involved
4. Type of natural resource involved

These tables should be used in conjunction with the case summaries in the Meet the Cases section to determine which case(s) would complement a particular classroom unit of study. An effort was made to place check marks only under the key elements emphasized in each case rather than all elements. The resource guides are excellent sources for determining which of the elements marked can be made the primary focus of the case.

REFERENCES

Evans, Norman (1992). *Experiential Learning: Assessment and Accreditation.* New York: Routledge.
World Tourism Organization (2000). *Basic References on Tourism Statistics.* www.world-tourism.org.

TABLE 1.1. EMS elements and behavioral aspects of implementation.

Case	Environmental Management System (EMS) Element				Behavioral Aspects of EMS Implementation				
	Defining/Designing	Feasibility	Implementing	Measuring/Monitoring	Awareness	Value Differences	Changing Behaviors	Conflict Resolution	Commitment/Capability
Traveling Responsibly									
Assiniboine Lodge	✓	✓	✓						
Flying High: Freedom Airlines			✓	✓					
Fairmont/CP Hotels	✓	✓	✓	✓					✓
Sustainable Nature-Based and Adventure Tourism Activities									
Whale Watching	✓		✓		✓	✓	✓	✓	
Treadsoftly, Part 1	✓		✓						✓
Treadsoftly, Part 2			✓	✓					
Canadian Mountain Holidays	✓		✓	✓	✓	✓			
Ski Resorts	✓			✓	✓	✓	✓		
Vacations by the Sea	✓		✓		✓	✓	✓		✓
Wrestling with the Sustainability of National Parks									
Yosemite	✓	✓	✓			✓	✓	✓	
Grand Canyon	✓		✓	✓	✓	✓		✓	
Banff-Bow Valley	✓					✓	✓	✓	
Waterton Lakes	✓				✓	✓			
Land Development and Governance Issues									
Costa Rica	✓					✓		✓	
CAMPFIRE	✓	✓				✓	✓		✓
Extractive Reserves in Brazil	✓	✓					✓		✓

TABLE 1.2. Organizations and natural resources.

Case	Type of Organizations Involved			Type of Natural Resources Involved						
	Community	Private Business	Public Resources	All Resources	Waste	Air	Water	Energy	Land	Biodiversity
Traveling Responsibly										
Assiniboine Lodge		✓	✓	✓						
Flying High: Freedom Airlines		✓	✓			✓				
Fairmont/CP Hotels		✓	✓		✓		✓	✓		
Sustainable Nature-Based and Adventure Tourism Activities										
Whale watching	✓	✓	✓				✓			✓
Treadsoftly, Part 1	✓	✓	✓						✓	
Treadsoftly, Part 2		✓	✓						✓	
Canadian Mountain Holidays		✓	✓						✓	
Ski Resorts		✓	✓	✓						
Water Recreation		✓	✓				✓			✓
Wrestling with the Sustainability of National Parks										
Yosemite	✓	✓	✓			✓			✓	✓
Grand Canyon		✓	✓			✓			✓	✓
Banff-Bow Valley	✓	✓	✓						✓	✓
Waterton Lakes	✓	✓	✓						✓	✓
Land Development and Governance Issues										
Costa Rica	✓	✓	✓						✓	✓
CAMPFIRE	✓		✓							✓
Extractive Reserves in Brazil	✓	✓	✓						✓	

Chapter 2

UNESCO:
World Heritage Convention and Man
and the Biosphere Program

Fergus T. Maclaren

INTRODUCTION

The World Heritage Convention and Man and the Biosphere (MAB) Program were developed to preserve the world's natural and built heritage. The World Heritage Convention applies a set of criteria to determine whether a site should be designated based on cultural, historical, ecological, or taxonomic data, while MAB applies a prescriptive formula that considers the contextual and protective strata of significant ecosystems.

The World Heritage Convention and MAB have member states as signatories to ratify the terms of both conventions. However, neither has any actual legal status within these member states. These conventions merely act as contextual conservation/preservation frameworks for designated natural and built resources. Hence, the international stature and recognition of designation is valued, particularly for tourism purposes. However, these same sites are under constant threat of development pressures and human incursion.

WORLD HERITAGE CONVENTION

The World Heritage Convention defines cultural heritage as "a monument, group of buildings or site of historical, aesthetic, archaeological, scientific, ethnological or anthropological value" and natural heritage as "outstanding physical, biological, and geological features." The Convention Concerning the Protection of World Culuture and Natural Heritage was adopted in November, 1972 at the 17th General Conference of the United Nations Educational, Scientific and Culture Organization (UNESCO). The convention defines and promotes conservation of the world's heritage by drawing up a list of sites with outstanding values and ensures protection of the sites through cooperation among nations. Member countries to the convention nominate the sites considered by the World Heritage Committee for the list. As of Nov 2005, there were 754 sites that the World Heritage Committee had inscribed on the World Heritage List (628 cultural, 160 natural, and 24 mixed properties in 137 states parties).

To be added to the list a site must be technically evaluated. The International Council on Monuments and Sites (ICOMOS) and the World Conservation Union (IUCN) advises the committee on selection of sites through their independent technical evaluations.

World Heritage Committee

The World Heritage Committee is the statutory body responsible for decision making in the following areas:

- Selecting new sites for the World Heritage List from among the cultural and natural properties nominated by the different countries
- Protecting the named sites by allocating resources of the World Heritage Fund and determining the technical and financial aid to be given to the sites in need

The committee consists of representatives from twenty-one states' parties, elected by the General Assembly of the States Parties to the Convention. One of the main responsibilities of this committee is to provide technical cooperation under the World Heritage Fund for the safeguarding of World Heritage Sites to States Parties whose resources are insufficient.

States' parties can request international assistance under the fund for expert missions, training of specialized staff, and supply of equipment when appropriate; they can also apply for long-term loans and, in special cases, non-repayable grants. Requests must concern work necessary for the preservation of cultural or natural sites included in the World Heritage List or assistance to national or regional training centers. Emergency assistance is also available in the case of properties severely damaged by specific natural or manmade disasters or threatened with imminent destruction.

World Heritage in Danger

As of Nov 2005, there were thirty-four properties that the World Heritage Committee decided to include in the list of World Heritage in Danger. The development and evolution of life, demographic pressure, industrialization, pollution, neglect, poverty, excessive tourism, building development and the resultant culture shock, in addition to natural catastrophes and wars— all these represent serious, ever-present dangers that threaten the world's cultural and natural heritage.

Yellowstone National Park in Wyoming was the first national park established anywhere in the world, and was authorized into existence in 1872 by the United States Congress. Yellowstone was inscribed on the list of the World Heritage in Danger in 1995, over concerns that the values of the park were threatened by the potential impacts of adjacent mining operations on the watershed ecology of the Yellowstone River. Other issues included the impact of sewage leakage and waste contamination; the illegal introduction of nonnative lake trout competitive with the endemic Yellowstone cutthroat trout; road construction; and year-round visitor pressures. A potential threat to the bison population is related to proposed control measures to eradicate brucellosis in the herds. The United States authorities have been addressing these concerns through analysis, mitigation measures, and management plans. Therefore, Yellowstone has recently been removed from the "in Danger" list.

Canada is confronting development issues within its four Rocky Mountain Parks World Heritage Sites (Banff, Jasper, Kootenay, and Yoho). They were designated in October 1984 and UNESCO invited Canadian authorities to continue to ensure that urbanization and heavy tourism did not jeopardize the natural integrity of the sites.

The ecosystem, is threatened by a number of factors:

- The two major east-west highways, the Trans-Canada and Yellowhead, run directly through them.
- The mandate of Travel Alberta and the Canadian Tourism Commission (CTC) is to continually increase tourism numbers in the province, and by extension, the parks.
- The town sites of Banff, Jasper, and Lake Louise continue to expand and develop within the major wildlife corridors and along the rivers that they straddle.

The two most notable parks are Jasper and Banff. Banff was Canada's first national park, established in 1890. Despite a growth management plan recommended by the Banff-Bow Valley Corridor Study in 1996, a number of factors had already compromised the park's status:

- expansion of Sunshine Village's Goat Creek Mountain ski facility;
- the twinning of the Trans-Canada Highway between the Town of Banff and Castle Mountain Junction; and

- increasingly frequent animal-human confrontation in Banff town site and the backcountry.

These developments have led to the threatened removal of the Rocky Mountain Parks' World Heritage status. The site, however, has not yet been designated a World Heritage Site in Danger.

Two World Heritage sites cross the borders between the United States and Canada. One is Waterton-Glacier International Peace Park that is located in the province of Alberta and the state of Montana. The other crosses the borders of the state of Alaska and the territory of the Yukon, and involves the area of the Kluane/Wrangell St. Elias/Glacier Bay/Tatshenshini-Alsek.

World Heritage Information Network

In the year 2000, UNEP-WCMC (United Nations Environment Programme-World Conservation Monitoring Centre) was established even though the work of the Centre was started by IUCN (World Conservation Union) in 1979 in order to monitor endangered species. In 1988 WWF (World Wide Fund for Nature) and UNEP joined IUCN to establish WCMC. Now it is under the auspices of UNEP and is closely linked to its program on Environmental Information, Assessment & Early Warning. UNEP-WCMC acts as a clearinghouse to collect, house, and exchange data with a variety of conservation and professional organizations. Its interactive map service allows access to global conservation information on such topics as coral disease, forest conditions, marine information, world heritage sites, and more. Other information services include a database on protected areas, a virtual library, and the World Heritage Information Network (WHIN). Through WHIN you can search for information on World Heritage sites or subjects.

MAN AND THE BIOSPHERE

The concept of biosphere reserves was originated by a task force of UNESCO's Man and the Biosphere (MAB) Program in 1974. MAB is an interdisciplinary program of research and training intended to develop the basis, within the natural and the social sciences, for the rational use and conservation of the resources of the biosphere, and for the improvement of the global relationship between people and the environment. MAB is a voluntary, interagency effort that operates under the existing authorities of the participants. The purpose of the biosphere reserve program is to encourage voluntary cooperation in the management of the environment and the development of sustainable economies.

The World Network of Biosphere Reserves fosters exchange among the individual reserves in the form of research and monitoring results, experiences, environmental education, and training through a variety of communication avenues and cooperative initiatives. Regional or subregional networks also exist in particular geographic areas or surrounding certain themes.

Each biosphere reserve is intended to fulfill three complementary functions:

1. *Conservation*—preserve genetic resources, species, ecosystems and landscapes
2. *Development*—foster sustainable economic and human development
3. *Logistic support*—support demonstration projects, environmental education and training, and research and monitoring related to local, national, and global issues of conservation and sustainable development

Physically, each biosphere reserve should contain three elements:

1. One or more core areas that are securely protected sites for conserving biological diversity, monitoring minimally disturbed ecosystems, and undertaking nondestructive research and other low-impact uses (such as education)
2. A clearly identified buffer zone, which usually surrounds or adjoins the core areas, and is used for cooperative activities compatible with sound ecological practices, including environmental education, recreation, ecotourism, and applied and basic research
3. A flexible transition area, or area of cooperation, which may contain a variety of agricultural activities, settlements, and other uses in which local communities, management agencies, scientists, nongovernmental organizations, cultural groups, economic interests, and other stakeholders work together to manage and sustainably develop the area's resources

Biosphere reserves are designated by the International Coordinating Council of the MAB program at the request of the state concerned. Biosphere reserves, each of which remains under the sole sovereignty of the state where it is situated and thereby submitted to state legislation only, form a world network in which participation by the states is voluntary.

As of November 2005, 482 biosphere reserves exist in 97 countries. Biosphere reserves are areas of terrestrial and coastal/marine ecosystems, where, through appropriate zoning patterns and management mechanisms, the conservation of ecosystems and their biodiversity is combined with the sustainable use of natural resources for the benefit of local communities, including relevant research, monitoring, education, and training activities.

One other major international treaty concerned with the natural environment is the Ramsar Convention on Wetlands of International Importance. The convention was signed in Ramsar, Iran, in 1971. It is an intergovernmental treaty that provides the framework for international cooperation for the conservation and wise use of wetlands and their resources. There are presently 147 Contracting States Parties to the Convention, with 1,317 wetland sites, totaling more than 111 million hectares, designated for inclusion in the Ramsar List of Wetlands of International Importance. Ramsar sites are also World Heritage sites and Biosphere Reserves.

CONCLUSION

World Heritage Site and MAB designations are intended to recognize and preserve the world's significant natural and cultural resources. However, there are many contentious issues predicated on economic development, and resource extraction and property rights that threaten these areas in North America. The unique status should continue to be salutary and applied voluntarily. Recognizing the sensitivity of ecosystems and cultural resources involved, World Heritage and/or MAB status should be used as a lever, where possible, to maintain that tenuous hold on an area's unique ecological integrity.

APPENDIX: WORLD HERITAGE SITES

In Canada

Dinosaur Provincial Park
Head-Smashed-In Buffalo Jump
Wood Buffalo National Park
Alberta

Anthony Island
British Columbia

Canadian Rocky Mountain Parks

This site is comprised of four national parks: Banff, Jasper, Yoho, and Kootenay, and of three British Columbia provincial parks: Mount Robson, Mount Assiniboine, and Hamber (the last three added in 1990). The Burgess Shale Site, previously inscribed on the WHL, is part of the Canadian Rocky Mountain Parks.

L'Anse aux Meadows National Historic Park
Gros Morne National Park
Newfoundland

Old Town of Lunenburg
Nova Scotia

Miguasha Park
Historic Area of Québec
Québec

Nahanni National Park
Yukon

In the United States

Wrangell-St. Elias National Park and Preserve
Glacier Bay National Park and Preserve
Alaska

Grand Canyon National Park
Arizona

Redwood National Park
Yosemite National Park
California

Mesa Verde National Park
Colorado

Everglades National Park (on danger list)
Florida

Hawaii Volcanoes National Park
Hawaii

Cahokia Mounds State Historic Site
Illinois

Mammoth Cave National Park
Kentucky

Waterton-Glacier International Peace Park
Montana

Statue of Liberty National Monument
New Jersey/New York

Carlsbad Caverns National Park
Chaco Culture National Historical Park
Pueblo de Taos
New Mexico

Great Smoky Mountains National Park
North Carolina/Tennessee

Independence National Historic Site
Pennsylvania

Monticello
University of Virginia Historic District
Virginia

Olympic National Park
Washington

Yellowstone National Park
Wyoming/Montana

La Fortaleza-San Juan National Historical Site
Puerto Rico

In Canada and the United States

Kluane/Wrangell St. Elias/Glacier Bay/Tatshenshini-Alsek
Yukon and Alaska

Waterton-Glacier International Peace Park
Alberta and Montana

Biosphere Reserves

Forty-seven Biosphere Reserves are located in the United States and twelve in Canada. Some World Heritage Sites are also Biosphere Reserves. Information for accessing a list of these reserves is given under online resources.

Online Resources

The Ramsar Convention on Wetlands
<www.ramsar.org/index.html>

UNEP World Conservation Monitoring Centre

UNESCO Man and the Biosphere Programme
<www.unesco.org/mab/>

UNESCO's World Heritage Centre
<www.unesco.org/whc/>

World Heritage List
<www.unesco.org/en/list>

World Heritage List In Danger
<www.unesco.org>

World Heritage Sites in Canada
<www.pc.gc.ca/index_e.asp>

World Heritage Sites in the United States
<www.cr.nps.gov/worldheritage>

Part II:
Traveling Responsibly

Tourism frequently involves traveling via an airline and staying in some type of accommodation. Airlines and hotels are usually not thought of as industries that produce high environmental impacts and degrade the environment relative to manufacturing and resource-extracting industries. However, hotels, and especially airlines, consume energy and contribute emissions that could effect climate change. Airlines also create noise pollution, and hotel and resort development can disturb wildlife habitat and create water pollution.

Both industries have made strides in developing programs to help their members improve environmental performance. A few companies in these industries are leaders in their economic, environment, and social activities and thus are listed on the Dow Jones Sustainability Index (DJSI). The advent of the DJSI, and its strong showing compared to other stock indices, provides evidence for economic performance compatible with social and environmental responsibilities.

InterContinental Hotels Group PLC (formerly known as Six Continents) is one of the leading companies in the Restaurant and Lodging sector of the DJSI with strong performance in all three areas of economic, environmental, and social performance. InterContinental Hotels owns the Holiday Inn and Crowne Plaza as well as other well-known brands. Accor is also listed on the DJSI and owns well-known brands, such as Motel 6 and Red Roof Inn. Although Fairmont Hotels and Resorts, the focus of one of the cases in this section, is not currently listed on the DJSI, it was one of the first hotel companies to develop a green plan while under the Canadian Pacific Hotels name. Some of its initiatives were incorporated in the environmental guidelines provided by the International Hotels Environment Initiative (IHEI).

A number of organizations, such as Green Globe, and Green Leaf Eco-Rating, certify that hotels have attained a certain level of environmental achievement. However, for the consumer, these certifications can be misleading, as some labels are provided for mere membership while others require a high standard of environmental performance.

Another term with an unclear definition is *ecolodge*. Ecolodges have become popular tourism destinations as tourists want to experience natural and unique settings. The implication is that an ecolodge, usually situated in a remote location, has been designed and constructed in an environmentally responsible manner and is operated following a high standard of environmental management practices. In addition, its customers are educated about the local culture and ecosystems in a sustainable manner, and the lodge's operations benefit the local community. Unfortunately, not all lodges that call themselves ecolodges have these characteristics. The Assiniboine Lodge is an example of what it means to carry the label of ecolodge.

The Freedom Airlines case emphasizes the reporting aspect of an organization's environmental process. The case provides an opportunity to investigate various types of environmental reports and to evaluate the credibility of their information. More companies are producing information on their environmental performance through reports or via their Web sites. The Freedom Airlines case, along with the supplemental materials provided in the resource guide, provides a wealth of information for gaining a better understanding of the environmental or social information contained in these reports.

Chapter 3

Implementing Ecosystem Management: Mount Assiniboine Lodge, Mount Assiniboine Provincial Park, British Columbia

Fergus T. Maclaren

Although this case is based on facts, some parts have been fictionalized in order to convey certain theoretical concepts in a setting that is more conducive for instructional purposes.

INTRODUCTION

Jane Webb had recently completed a chef's apprenticeship program through the New England Culinary Institute and was looking for work. A lucky coincidence occurred when friends in Canmore, Alberta, Canada, notified her of a chef's position at Mount Assiniboine Lodge in the Canadian Rockies of British Columbia (BC). After some correspondence and telephone conversations with the lodge's managers, Barb and Sepp Renner, they eventually agreed to hire Jane for the summer season, starting June 1.

To prepare her for her trip from the east, the Renners sent out a package containing a history of Mount Assiniboine Provincial Park and the lodge, as well as the park's Master Plan to give Jane some background on the area and its special status.

Mount Assiniboine Provincial Park, situated in southern British Columbia on the Alberta border, was established in 1922. Mount Assiniboine is referred to as the "Matterhorn of the Rockies" because it reflects a similar geological formation to its Swiss namesake. Canadian Pacific Railway (CPR) constructed the lodge in 1928 as North America's first cross-country skiing lodge and as a starting point for mountaineers who had trekked from Banff to tackle the mountain ranges. Today, the arduous 28 km (16 mile) journey is made easier by telemark skis or helicopter. The park's proximity

Lake in front of Mount Assiniboine.

Hut in Mount Assiniboine Provincial Park (Photo courtesy of Irene M. Herremans.)

to, and interrelated ecosystem with, the Canadian Rocky Mountain Parks (Banff, Jasper, Kootenay and Yoho National Parks) World Heritage Site, resulted in its inclusion to the site in 1990, along with Hamber and Mount Robson Provincial Parks.

In BC, provincial parks are designated and managed to preserve particular places of natural beauty and historical value for the inspiration, recreational use, and enjoyment of the public. The Park Act's dual mandate of landscape protection combined with recreational access is achieved in the following manner: 85 percent of the land base in BC's backcountry parks is preserved in a completely natural state. These wilderness areas remain protected because they are difficult to access and are rarely visited by people.

Facility development, including Mount Assiniboine Lodge, and visitor services are concentrated in intensive recreation zones, or "core areas" of parks, which use relatively small areas of land and have convenient access. At Mount Assiniboine Provincial Park, the core area comprises less than 13 percent of the land base in the park. Within the core, human impact is concentrated within the small circle of service facilities (Mount Assiniboine Lodge, the Mount Shark heliport, the Naiset Cabins and the Magog Campground; see Figure 3.1).

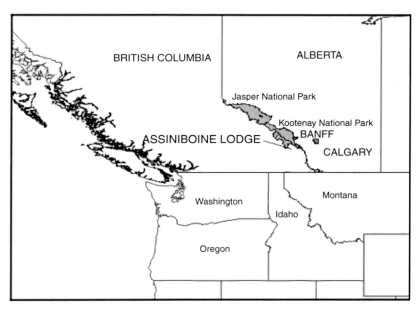

FIGURE 3.1. Assiniboine Lodge (map prepared by Hanako Saito).

When Jane arrived in Canmore, she was taken to the Alpine Helicopters heliport (the other being located at Mount Shark on the Smith-Dorrion Highway south of the town). She and her gear were being transported by pilot Jack Harper on the fifteen-minute ride up to the lodge.

LEARNING ABOUT THE LODGE

JANE: Do you fly every day?

JACK: We fly only on Sundays, Wednesdays, and Fridays in the early afternoon.

JANE: Why is that?

JACK: By establishing and compressing flight times, the Renners have reduced flight access options for guests to both increase efficiency and reduce flights to the park. When incoming guests arrive at the lodge's helipad, departing guests fly out. They handle all aspects of scheduling of lodge flights to ensure that every empty seat is utilized, either flying groceries and propane in, or laundry and garbage out.

JANE: That makes both good business and environmental sense.

JACK: Well, helicopters are their biggest expenditure, at twenty percent of total expenses, and the main way to transport guests. The Renners also recognize that helicopters affect the local environment, and have tried to reduce their impact by

- negotiating with BC Parks to ensure that there will be no day-use helicopters sightseeing over or landing in the park;
- improving insulation in the lodge to minimize fuel flights;
- using a larger helicopter to increase flight speed and efficiency; and
- investigating the possibility of using NOTARS (enclosed tail rotor) helicopters to reduce noise pollution.

Jane saw Mount Assiniboine in the distance as the helicopter descended onto its gravel pad. A group of guests were waiting to be transported back to either Canmore or Mount Shark. Sepp and Barb Renner greeted her and then helped unload bags.

BARB: How was the flight?

JANE: The trip was amazing. I've never seen anything like these massive, wild mountains. When we were landing, I saw the spectacular local scenery and now better understand the Master Plan in regard to concentrating buildings and trails around the core area.

BARB: The area is pretty sensitive around here, given the number of alpine lakes and meadows in proximity. We try to make a conscious effort to ensure that the management of the lodge and the activities of its guests have a minimum impact on the local environment.

JANE: How is that?

SEPP: In this age of continual change, there is constant pressure to develop more comforts and to expand services to meet the demands of clientele. People often demand that the environment change to meet their expectations rather than people altering their expectations to meet the natural limitations that are present in the environment. A conservative management approach is necessary to create a sustainable ecological model. This approach may mean "no more development" in an area, or no more "creature comforts." We believe, however, that the interdependent economic, environmental, and social goals used in managing our business are important goals to also convey to our guests.

JANE: How do you convey these goals to guests?

BARB: When a guest makes a reservation at Mount Assiniboine Lodge, they are sent information sheets, which establish the "expectation level of accommodation" and make it clear to clients what they need to bring. Each guest receives an equipment list (winter or summer) with baggage limitations (15 kg [33 lbs.] per person). The baggage restriction helps to reduce flights to the park. We make it very clear to guests that the lodge is rustic (i.e., outhouses, one shower for thirty-five people in the summer). This advance information allows our guests to adjust their expectations to our operation. We use this information to educate guests on the importance of waste management and recycling in the lodge, as well as the importance of staying on the trails, not trampling vegetation and not agitating local wildlife. We also inform them of some of the special initiatives that we have started here.

JANE: And what are these "special initiatives"?

BARB: That's Sepp's department.

SEPP: Energy use and heating are important conservation areas. As you know, Mount Assiniboine Lodge is located in a high alpine environment where winter conditions prevail nine months of the year. We do not depend on any one single technology to provide heat or electricity. It is important to have backup systems in case a component fails. For example: the living room and cabins at the lodge are heated with propane. Due to the elevation of the lodge [2,200m/7,200 ft.], the temperature is often ten degrees colder than at Banff or Canmore. Propane gels and does not function at –45 degrees Celsius [–25 degrees Fahrenheit]. This is significant, given that there have been many occasions at Assiniboine when the temperature has dropped to –40 and even –50 Celsius [–20 to –30 degrees Fahrenheit], especially during the Christmas period. The wood heater in the dining room and the coal heater in the living room of the lodge are used for backup heat during cold periods and to supplement the propane heating system. We also use the following techniques in our energy conservation program:

- We completed an insulating program to reduce energy output.
- When we are baking in the kitchen, the heat from the ovens helps to heat the dining room.
- When we take guests to their cabins on arrival, we give them a demonstration of how to turn the propane thermostat to pilot when they are not in the cabin to conserve fuel.
- Heating rules are posted in each cabin.
- After the guests go to bed at night, the lodge managers make sure that all of the propane lights are turned off and that the living room propane stove is turned to pilot.
- In the morning, each cabin receives a bucket of hot water from the kitchen for washing. While guests find this an added "luxury," this service is actually designed to reduce propane consumption. If we did not deliver hot water, guests would turn up the propane space heaters to warm water.

BARB: There are also some technical innovations that we use here.

SEPP: That's right. We have introduced on-demand water heaters to replace the old one-hundred-twenty-liter [thirty gallon] tank. They are small, space-saving units that use propane very efficiently and provide hot water only as needed. There are also three types of electrical generation for the Lodge: Pelton wheel, solar panels, and a Honda gas generator for backup. The Pelton wheel generates power up to one-hundred-twenty watts. It is fired by the water coming off the lodge's gravity-based water line at twenty-five kg [60 lbs.] of pressure during optimum periods. The generated power trickle charges a battery bank. These batteries in turn supply power to the lodge's computer, kitchen appliances, and power tools. Electrical power availability has been extended through the installation of energy-efficient lighting and a super-insulated freezer. Solar batteries supply power to the lodge's UHF octophone telephone, while a backup generator is used when the Pelton wheel is out of commission.

BARB: Well, I see a BC Parks helicopter landing over at the pad. Maybe you'd better talk to your new colleague in the kitchen, Marie-Claude, to get started on your work here.

Jane walked through the dining area into the kitchen and saw Marie-Claude preparing food for that evening's meal.

M-C: *Allo bonjour!* You're Jane, the new chef, right?

JANE: Yes I am. Barb said that I should come and talk to you about getting started.

M-C: Well, I am kitchen staff here, which means I do anything from food preparation, waiting tables, scrubbing out the kitchen, changing linen, cleaning guest rooms and bathrooms, and hauling trash.

JANE: That last part sounds exotic.

M-C: Well, there is actually a system here that we use to minimize waste, given that it probably has the biggest impact on the local environment. On a daily basis waste is sorted, recycled, and the subsequent waste is reduced. We buy food for the lodge in bulk and store it in recyclable or reusable containers to reduce packaging waste. Boneless meats are ordered so that there is no animal waste. The food ordering is carefully monitored so that the lodge has adequate supplies in case we lose our helicopter access for a few days due to inclement weather. The system of food ordering is designed such that we do not need to run extra flights if we are missing something, which saves money and reduces helicopter impacts in the park.

JANE: All of this sounds like a great system, but there is still going to be waste.

M-C: That's true. Minimization is only part of the process. We try to apply two other important aspects to the process: recycling and pigs. Recycling means that a product that was originally used as a container will later be reused to store something else. This means that cardboard boxes are used to store things and glass jars are sterilized and used for food storage. Wine bottles and aluminum cans are sent to Canmore to be recycled. Proceeds go toward supporting two foster children, one in Bolivia and the other in India. The pigs are kept in a pen a hundred yards from the lodge. We only use them during the summer months and they consume eight to twenty [two to five gallon] buckets of food waste per day. In the kitchen, the plates are scraped with a spatula before washing. This procedure reduces the amount of water that is necessary for washing dishes, reduces fat collection in the grease trap, and increases the amount of food for the pigs. The pigs weigh approximately twenty-two kg [fifty pounds] when they arrive at the end of June. By the end of September, they weigh more than ninety kg [200 pounds] each! The pigs are then butchered, and the meat is frozen and used during lodge meals in the winter. This experimental program has been carried out over a twelve-year period with great success. To date, the pigs have never attracted bears. This method of waste management has not been officially approved by BC Parks. However, we have been allowed to keep pigs at the lodge for the past thirteen years. The success of this program can be acknowledged by the fact that other backcountry operations such as Canadian Mountain Holidays now have recycling pigs.

JANE: The pig idea is unique, but what about composting?

M-C: Well, the constraints of altitude coupled with low annual temperatures makes composting an unacceptable method of waste management at the lodge. Composts also attract bears, which can lead to ongoing nuisance problems in the backcountry.

JANE: I'll certainly try to be careful around here.

A short while later, Park Warden Carl Malone, on an inspection visit to the area, arrives at the lodge. Barb introduces him to Jane. The two converse:

JANE: What does your job in the park involve?

CARL: Well Jane, the joint goals of park managers are to control access to parks in order to minimize impacts on these landscapes, while retaining high recreational values. Facility and access management in the backcountry parks is an ongoing process. We must monitor the need for changes in park management through extensive public surveys, as well as public and permit-holder input into Master Plan processes and Visitor Services Plans. Park statistics of visitor usage and prevailing trends help guide us in our decision making.

JANE: What does that mean in terms of your job here?

CARL: Mount Assiniboine's resources are under pressure from a variety of sources: hunters [guided and resident]; loss of habitat due to forest encroachment; campers [particularly in the park Core]; dayhikers [Rock Isle basin]; horsemen [guided and private]; and permit holders [helicopters, Mount Assiniboine Lodge, Sunshine Village]. Management of the natural resources must reflect conservation and recreation objectives of the park as well as general BC Parks management policy. Mount Assiniboine Lodge, as a concession operation, is a rarity in the BC Park system, and its interrelationship with the park must be considered in planning. Special management policies are required to ensure acceptable blending of the entrepreneurial philosophy with BC Parks' commitment to resource conservation and public recreation.

JANE: I can see where there may be some conflict between the conservation and human activity.

CARL: Well, ecosystems are incredibly complex and it is unlikely we will ever completely understand how they work. We have, however, learned a great deal. We plan to build on our collective knowledge to develop more tools to measure the health of our forests and rangelands and the plant and animal communities of ecosystems. Such tools are essential in developing and implementing strategies to conserve biological diversity and maintain aesthetic values, while producing needed commodities—in essence, the fundamental premise behind the concept of sustainable land and resource use. We think of ecosystem management as a holistic approach to natural resource management. With an ecosystem management approach, we step back from the forest stand and focus on the forest landscape. We look at the larger environment in order to integrate the human, biological, and physical dimensions of natural resource management. Strategically, we are concentrating our approach to implement ecosystem management concepts on three desired outcomes:

- To enhance protection of ecosystems
- To restore deteriorated ecosystems
- To provide a variety of benefits within the capabilities of ecosystems

The bottom line is that no human [or collection of humans] has enough information to even make an accurate prediction as to the actual outcomes of theories applied to the landscape. In our quest for "management" of ecosystems, we fail to recognize that nothing is better than nature left to her own devices. This could be considered the natural order and balance of humans, vegetation, and wildlife. In recent years, however, this balance has been upset. "Park health" would not be the issue of such grave concern as it is today, were it not for past management activities—virtually all for the benefit of resource extraction and recreation. After years of past mea culpas like, "we don't do it that way anymore," it's time we stopped doing things that way in the first place.

JANE: And how do the Renners fit into this equation?

CARL: They have done a good job in managing the lodge in the context of the park's sensitive environment, particularly when BC Parks' goals are very broad in terms of ecosystem use and management. I can also say, however, that recent trends and the policies instituted by the provincial government would mean that another lodge like this could never be built elsewhere in the park. The "ecological footprint" that it occupies would place too great a strain on the local ecosystem.

With these thoughts in mind, Jane headed back to the kitchen to get started on the evening meal.

BIBLIOGRAPHY

BC Parks (1989). *Master Plan for Mount Assiniboine Provincial Park.* Wasa, BC: British Columbia Ministry of Parks Southern Interior Region.

Coopers and Lybrand Consulting (1995). *Report for the British Columbia Ministry of Environment, Land and Parks: Economic Benefits of British Columbia Parks.* Vancouver: Coopers and Lybrand Consulting, April.

Donnelly, Michael (1995). "Ecosystem Management Cannot Work," *Cascadia Planet,* December 30.

Maclaren, Fergus T. (1996). "Hidden Heritage Threatened: Mount Assiniboine Lodge," *Heritage Canada,* September/October, p. 21.

Mount Assiniboine Lodge Web site. Available online at <www. canadianrockies. net/assiniboine>.

Renner, Sepp and Barb (1995). *Mount Assiniboine Lodge Management Tender Proposal to BC Parks,* October 31.

Unger, David G. (1994). "The USDA Forest Service Perspective on Ecosystem Management." *Symposium on Ecosystem Management and Northeastern Area Association of State Foresters Meeting,* Burlington, Vermont, July 18.

Chapter 4

Flying High:
The Airlines and the Environment—
Freedom Airlines, Inc.

Irene M. Herremans

Although this case is based on facts, some parts have been fictionalized in order to maintain the confidentiality of the persons and the company involved.

In May 1999 Freedom Airlines, Incorporated (FAI) released its first Environmental and Safety Report. Subsequently, the company has made the publication of this report an annual event. Why is FAI going through the process of writing, publishing, and releasing environmental, health, and safety reports? As Dana Winthrop from FAI's Communications Department suggests, "It was important that our stakeholders know the entire story about our environmental performance—warts and all. It was time to set the record straight." What follows is FAI's story of the process it went through to develop a major communications initiative, to carry it out, and then to learn more about its own environmental performance.

IDENTIFYING THE PROBLEM

Bob Banks, Dana Winthrop, and Ron Carch were sitting in a conference room on the eleventh floor of the FAI building on a crisp, snowy day in January. As Ron looked out the window over the city at the majestic mountains to the southwest, his mind wandered from the conversation for just a moment. He was brought back to stark reality by Dana's words: "So what is the problem?"

Both Dana and Ron worked in FAI's Communications Department. The question was directed to Bob Banks, a well-known and well-respected writer for the airline industry.

Tomi Murro arranges full boxes that have come from flights. They will undergo further waste sorting and recycling. (Photo courtesy of Finnair Catering.) Reprinted with permission.

Murro sorts glass into the large waste container. The nearby container holds aluminum. The mill in the background is for mixed waste. (Photo courtesy of Finnair Catering.) Reprinted with permission.

During the flight, plastic water bottles are crushed and placed in a trolley by flight attendants. Flight attendants play a very active role in sorting waste during flights. Once the trolley is returned to Finnair Catering, the waste is removed and placed in separate energy waste and recycling containers. (Photo courtesy of Finnair Catering.) Reprinted with permission.

DANA: If we look at the results of the Environmental Protection Agency's report, we don't seem to have an environmental performance problem. Certainly I am not saying that we are perfect, but we are doing at least as well as the other major companies in the industry. In some cases, I see us as performing better. Our problem appears to be one of communicating our performance to the public and our other stakeholders, and this is not helped by the media's portrayal of FAI as a hardheaded, arrogant company that is not willing to compromise.

RON AND DANA (together): How would you solve this communications problem, Bob?

BOB: I have had a lot of opportunity to talk with some of your people out in the field, and they seem very serious about environmental concerns . . . but I also know that very few people in the industry know about your environmental programs or that you even have an environmental policy.

WestJet fully supports recycling of waste de-icing fluid. WestJet contracts to use propylene glycol wherever possible instead of ethylene glycol for aircraft deicing in most of its routes and wherever it is logistically available. Another area of recycling is accomplished through the use of a glycol recovery vehicle (GRV), which is used to suck up the extra glycol that is sprayed on all aircraft, including WestJet's. At the Calgary International Airport, the Calgary Airport Authority has constructed a holding pond in order to best mitigate the recycling of the used de-icing fluid from the designated ramp areas. (Kevin McCauley, personal communication, November 2004.) (Photo courtesy of WestJet.) Reprinted with permission.

WestJet senior personnel are also well aware of the impact of their business on the environment and have had meetings with Canadian Aviation Services to discuss how WestJet can reduce its impact on the environment and be more in tune with the Kyoto guidelines. (Kevin McCauley, personal communication, November 2004.) (Photo courtesy of WestJet.) Reprinted with permission.

"WestJet pro-actively maintains its standard as a leader of environmental policy in the airline industry through corporate and individual responsibility. As well as adhering to all of the local, national, and international standards, WestJet takes a hands-on accountability approach where no guidelines exist to ensure that the corporation remains responsive to current environmental issues and to prevent new environmental concerns from arising. WestJet strives to use and develop technologies that are environmentally sound. It also recycles and supports the use of recycled materials where possible. Employees are also advised and encouraged to make health-conscious and environmentally sound decisions. This is ensured through proper training and the adequate funding needed to maintain a high standard of environmental responsibility." (WestJet Annual Report, 2003, p. 39.) (Photo courtesy of WestJet.) Reprinted with permission.

WestJet also structured a fleet plan to purchase twenty-six new Boeing 737-700 aircraft over the course of several years, with an additional forty-eight purchase options available until 2008. As of April 30, 2004, WestJet had retired five 200-series aircraft. The corporation expects to retire its last 737-200 by November 2008 following a process of retiring its 200-series aircraft as new next-generation aircraft enter the fleet. (Photo courtesy of WestJet used with permission.)

Your stakeholders outside the industry certainly are not aware of the work you have done on decreasing your emissions and noise levels. Let's look at your history for a minute and see why we have this situation. The public's perception of FAI environmental performance was determined by past environmental-related accidents. I think it started because of some of the chemical and fuel spills that you have had in the past from poor handling and maintenance techniques. These spills have the potential for entering the water supply and creating hazardous health effects. Although you caught the problems in time, the incidents were broadcast on television and radio and in many of the major newspapers worldwide. The public has a memory and still associates FAI with these incidents. Also, your name made the papers when you were issued notice to stop violations of the Resource Conservation and Recovery Act for your leased facility that is used to maintain and overhaul your aircraft. Even though it is expected that other airlines will be cited for hazardous waste cleanup, you were the first, so your name made the news. You have had other incidents that have kept your name in the media, such as major battles with unions and that plane crash several years ago. Some of these incidents have nothing to do with the environment, but you are getting a reputation for not being concerned about the social or environmental aspects of your operations. I was up at the university recently talking with some researchers in the School of Management. I have some very interesting information about the airline industry and individual carriers' reputations that they gathered through focus groups. Overall, the industry's environmental reputation is not that bad. People usually do not think of the airlines as having major impacts like the oil and gas industry or the forestry industry. But they did give me some quotes that pertain specifically to FAI.

- FAI has been proactive in moving forward on reduced noise regulations; [however,] FAI blew it on three or four other initiatives. (environmental nongovernment organization [ENGO] representative of ENGO)
- Well, FAI has this corporate view, I guess. Sometimes they have done really good work and in other cases they haven't. So, it depends on your criteria. (Regulator government agency)
- Their [FAI's] environmental people are very good, but they isolate themselves from the public and that is a problem. (ENGO)

RON: The public seems to be confused.

BOB: On the other hand, one strong indicator of FAI's good performance is a review completed by the EPA [Environmental Protection Agency] at FAI's request. In December 1997 FAI asked for a report card on its operations. The report card was developed from a review of the EPA's files, consultation with field offices, comments from the International Air Transport Association (IATA), and the Federal Aviation Administration (FAA) in the United States. The findings indicated FAI is at the high end of the industry's performance scale. Included in the report were those areas that require more attention, such as emissions. The process was repeated in the next year, with FAI receiving an acceptable rating.

DANA: The public doesn't know anything about this. People get what they know about environmental performance from the news and the news only prints the negative stuff.

BOB: You face some big challenges in altering or changing this reputation to one that is more positive and your reputation does not reflect the same level of high performance as shown in the measures used by the regulators. You remember the other opinions such as those in *Business Magazine* and the *The Wall Street Journal*? To summarize, even though FAI has a reputation for operating efficiently and complying with the law, you also are seen as not very flexible or proactive with public concerns.

DANA: So what do we do?

FINDING SOLUTIONS

The next afternoon this problem came to the forefront at the meeting of the Executive Committee designed to deal with FAI's reputation problem. The question that the meeting hoped to resolve was this: How could the company communicate to its stakeholders its true environmental performance? As the meeting progressed, Dana presented the idea of an environmental report. The following is some of the discussion from the meeting.

DANA: Considering some of our past mishaps, a lot of attention is paid to the negatives in FAI's environmental and safety performance record, and FAI has been labeled as "environmentally irresponsible." This fact, combined with the *perceived* lack of attention that FAI gives to its external audiences, FAI has received a poor environmental reputation even though it performs very well in some areas.

EXECUTIVE BOARD MEMBER: But if our performance is good, why do we need to worry about the public's perception?

DANA: Do you remember Dow's situation in the 1980s? Seems like we are replaying that company's situation. Maybe we can learn from them. I know that Dow is a chemical company and we are in a totally different industry, but there are some similarities in our histories. Dow was chasing inspectors from the EPA off its property because management felt the company's environmental performance was adequate. Also, its executives spent long hours in congressional hearings explaining the company's position. Even though the company felt its environmental performance was good, eventually it decided to take a proactive, cooperative approach. Now Dow is known as a very socially and environmentally responsible company. The Dow name comes up frequently as an example of good environmental performance in many of the environmental publications. Given the current perception of FAI's performance, we will continue to run into problems if we don't take a different approach. But we need to go further than just educate the public about our performance. If we look at the media's comments, we have a performance problem in a couple of areas: the public believes that we don't perform well environmentally and that we are insensitive to local concerns because we are one of the largest airlines in the world. Many of the media's comments emphasized the local concerns.

DANA: I *know* we cannot afford another public relations disaster.

CEO: Why? Does reputation really matter when it comes to the bottom line? Do consumers think about our environmental performance when it comes to buying a ticket or do they just go for low cost?

DANA: Well, you're talking about something that is hard to prove, but I am sure there have been some studies done on the benefits of a good reputation.

CEO: Assuming, for the moment, that there is some economic benefit in having a good reputation, what do you suggest we do to change FAI's reputation?

DANA: One of the first things we are considering is the publication of an environmental report, but we need to resolve at least one major concern. I recently read a study by Angus Reid. We know that credibility is an issue for information coming from any business, and it may be even a greater issue for us given our reputation. We know that we don't have a particularly good reputation, and according to the study, any information coming from the business is rated as the least credible. So, will anyone believe us when we talk about the good things we are doing for the environment?

CEO: So there is a downside.

DANA: No, I would say that we have nothing to lose in publishing an environmental report. Coming from a communications viewpoint, I don't think there is a downside. We need to determine how to write the report so it will actually be read and it will be believable.

CEO: Well, it looks like you have your work cut out for you if this project is going to be a success. I look forward to hearing about your action plan at our next executive meeting.

As the members of the Executive Committee left the room, Dana thought to herself: *I know the CEO is right. It is not going to be easy to overcome this credibility concern.* Dana looked at her watch. It was time to go home, but she would not be much of a conversationalist with her family until she resolved this issue in her own mind. She walked back to her office where she could think more clearly about her action plan. Even more important, if an environmental report is published, how could she convince the Executive Committee that the benefit exceeded the cost of this project?

Chapter 5

The Greening of the Fairmont Palliser

Robin E. Reid

This case study is a snapshot in time of the challenges associated with the development and implementation of Phase One of the Canadian Pacific Hotels & Resorts (CP) Green Partnership Program. In 1990 Canadian Pacific Hotels & Resorts undertook the development of a green program for all of their hotel properties across Canada. To explore the challenges associated with implementing the CP Green Partnership Program this case draws on specific examples from the Fairmont Palliser Hotel located in Calgary, Alberta, Canada (see Figure 5.1).

Since the time of this writing, an acquisition of Fairmont Hotels and Resorts by Canadian Pacific Hotels has resulted in a name change for all of the Canadian Properties in the CP hotel chain. The focus of this case is on Phase One of the Green Partnership Program which occurred prior to the acquisition and subsequent name change. During the discussion of the initial implementation of Phase One of the Green Partnership Program the Fairmont Palliser will be referred to as the Palliser Hotel.

INTERNATIONAL GREEN INITIATIVES

Over the past century, human impacts on the natural environment have become more noticeable. Growth in human population, wasteful use of resources, increasing consumer demands, and global economies have contributed to the destruction of the natural environment to such an extent that our long-term viability as a human species may be threatened. We depend on nature for the basic necessities in life. At the most fundamental level, clean water, uncontaminated air, and soil and energy resources are the basic requirements for human life on this planet. In the past, these resources were thought to be plentiful and resilient to our impacts. Our knowledge of our ecological footprint on this blue planet was limited and has resulted in actions that have degraded and depleted nature's capital at an astounding rate. Today, continued squandering and degradation of these resources has been

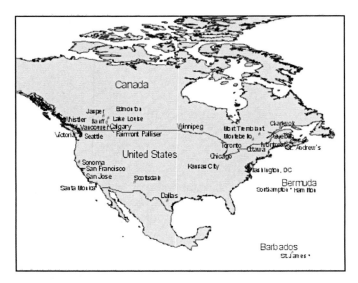

FIGURE 5.1. Fairmont Hotels and Resorts. Cities indicate locations of Fairmont Hotels. (Map prepared by Hanako Saito.)

Fairmont Chateau, Lake Louise, Alberta. (Photo courtesy of Robert Bott and Fairmont Palliser.) Reprinted with permission.

Fairmont Palliser, exterior view. (Photo courtesy of Robert Bott and Fairmont Palliser.) Reprinted with permission.

Fairmont/Palliser lobby. (Photo courtesy of Robert Bott and Fairmont Palliser.) Reprinted with permission.

Fairmont Banff Springs Hotel, Banff, Alberta. (Photo courtesy of Robert Bott and Fairmont Palliser.) Reprinted with permission.

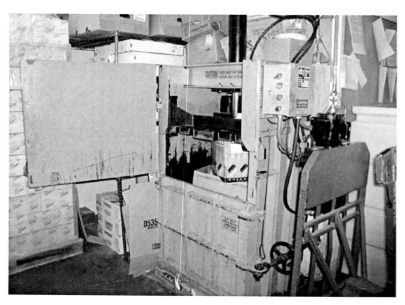

Fairmont Palliser box-crushing machine for recycling boxes. (Photo courtesy of Robert Bott and Fairmont Palliser.) Reprinted with permission.

Fairmont Palliser composts is kitchen waste. (Photo courtesy of Robert Bott and Fairmont Palliser.) Reprinted with permission.

Fairmont Palliser provides good recycling directions to employees. (Photo courtesy of Robert Bott and Fairmont Palliser.) Reprinted with permission.

questioned at a global level. At the 1992 Earth Summit in Rio de Janeiro, nations around the world gathered to discuss the issue of sustainable development in the context of global climate change. Many countries signed a nonbinding agreement, called the Rio Declaration, to reduce emissions to 1990 levels by the year 2000 for most industrial nations. After many meetings and conventions subsequent to Rio, nations are debating their commitment to the Kyoto Protocol, which mandates thirty-eight industrialized nations to lower their emissions of greenhouse gases by an average of 5 percent by 2008-2012 to reduce the threat of global warming.

One of the challenges of introducing environmental initiatives is the requirement of changing our perspectives and actions toward how we use resources. If environmental initiatives are seen as a threat to economic growth or limiting economic benefits, then the likelihood of their success is questioned at a global, regional, and local level. However, as more companies as well as individuals recognize the economic benefits of conserving energy, water, and resources, the momentum toward introducing environmental programs is gaining support. On an international level, a number of initiatives raise awareness and introduce environmental practices in the hotel industry. For example, the International Hotels Environmental Initiative (IHEI) is actively working to raise awareness of the necessity of the hotel industry to perform well environmentally. The World Travel and Tourism Council provides its Green Globe certification, which is recognized internationally as an environmental standard for tourism organizations.

One hotel chain, a leader in accepting the idea that the hotel industry needs to be attentive to its environmental impact, is Fairmont Hotels and Resorts. Even though the hotel chain, under the name of CP Hotels, developed its Green Partnership Program before the IHEI was formed, it has benefited from the sharing of ideas and the services offered from the community of organizations supportive of the industry's efforts.

FAIRMONT/CP HOTELS & RESORTS

Fairmont Hotels & Resorts is headquartered in Toronto, Canada, with U.S. headquarters in San Francisco. The company's Web site declares that Fairmont is the largest luxury hotel management company in North America, with hotels and resorts throughout Canada, the United States, Mexico, Bermuda, and Barbados.

Pierre Blum, supervisor of Electronic Marketing at Fairmont Hotels & Resorts, suggests that the CP Hotels environmental initiatives will soon be incorporated in all of its hotels and resorts worldwide.

First of all, I want to assure you that the progressive environmental vision championed in the hospitality industry by Canadian Pacific Hotels has not changed now that we have merged to become Fairmont Hotels & Resorts. Quite the contrary—we are now exporting our "Made in Canada" environmental initiatives to our new hotels and resorts in the United States, Mexico, Bermuda and Barbados. To their credit, the staff at these properties have been very excited in making these initiatives their own. And with the future growth that is planned for Fairmont, our environmental programs will spread even further. (personal communication)

CP Hotels & Resorts was Canada's premier luxury hotel chain and has been offering service to travelers since 1886 when it catered to guests in its first railway dining station in the Canadian Rockies. Many international visitors will recognize the CP Hotel name from its castles in the mountains, such as the Banff Springs Hotel and Lake Louise. However, CP Hotels can be found across Canada as well as the United States under the Fairmont name. Other hotel banners owned by the company are Delta, Princess, and Legacy. Its portfolio includes city center hotels, heritage resorts, and tropical destinations, where it offers premier, luxury service to its guests.

HISTORY OF PHASE ONE OF THE CP GREEN PROGRAM

In response to public pressures, customer desires, and worldwide trends for stronger efforts to preserve the environment, CP Hotels & Resorts was one of the first businesses in the hospitality industry to introduce a Green Partnership Policy. The objective of the policy was "to become a world leader and pace setter in establishing responsible environmental practices for the hotel industry" (Troyer, 1992, p. 1). Although the Green Partnership Policy was one of the first models, other hotel chains and organizations have introduced and implemented their own environmental policies, and CP Hotels & Resorts has learned from other hotels' initiatives as well as its own. For example, part of the *CP Hotels Green Partnership Guide* was used to develop sections in the IHEI environmental operations manual (Troyer, 1992).

The *CP Hotels Green Partnership Guide* (1992) was written by the late Warren Troyer and was designated to be fully implemented, company wide, by the end of 1992. The plan utilized information provided by Ontario Hydro, various government branches, and other companies. In addition to these outside sources, 10,000 employees of Canadian Pacific Hotels & Resorts were also asked for their opinions about introducing a Green Partnership

Program. CP Hotels & Resorts received overwhelming support from its staff and their suggestions provided the basis of the original Phase One action plan.

When the document reached its final form, twelve steps were introduced to address sixteen goals. Each of the twenty-six properties of CP Hotels at that time received a copy of the *Green Partnership Guide* to be used as a format for implementing Phase One of the Green Partnership Program. The policy was not mandatory and it was left to the discretion of the general manager at each property to determine if and to what extent the Green Partnership Policy would be implemented.

Most of the aspects of the guide were easily achievable because they were based on short-term goals that did not require a great deal of planning. Short-term goals seemed to be a good place to start to achieve small successes, as CP Hotels, or very few other hotels for that matter, had little or no experience in reducing environmental impacts. If CP could be successful in achieving short-term goals, then it would be ready to start tackling longer-term, more difficult projects.

For example, introducing recycling bins into guest rooms is an easily achievable, short-term goal. However, not all the goals in the plan were short-term. Other aspects were based on midterm and long-term goals that required time, money, and accountability. An example of a midterm goal is to reuse and recycle motor oil and printer ribbons. These goals can be implemented only as the oil or ribbons are needed. Some of the goals that were initiated as short-term ended up having an implementation period of a midterm goal.

Achieving external and internal long-term goals often requires long-term commitment on the part of the hotel. For example, relationships between suppliers and the hotels may take time to cultivate. Consequently, relationships with suppliers could be described as long-term external goals. Guest training may also require a long-term commitment on the part of the hotel. Long-term internal challenges include rethinking operations, retraining employees and management, the creation of a new environmentally aware culture, and the availability of funds to achieve short-, mid-, and long-term goals.

The CP Approach

The success of the Green Partnership Program was ultimately determined by the approach taken toward achieving goals at the operational level. The policy of Phase One was approached from three different levels; these include the corporate level, the employee volunteer committee level, and the operational level. At the corporate level, policies and goals were set and the employee volunteer committees were assigned to implement the policies and achieve the goals. The true decision power resided, and still resides, within the operational level, where funds can be made available and internal policies can be changed to meet the demands of the other two levels. At the corporate level, involvement was strictly on the public relations level, in that corporate wanted to be seen as caring for the environment. Corporate did not create a special budget or develop a mandate for management to achieve environmental goals. Corporate directed management of individual properties to create an environmental committee to work toward achieving the environmental goals outlined in the Green Program.

The employee volunteer committee level was responsible for caring for the environment. All of the hotels had volunteer committees; some had representatives from management. The volunteer committees made recommendations to management at the operational level on how things should be done. Some of the committees relied on the efforts of young employees whose long-term goals lie outside the hotel industry. Consequently, high turnover in staff might have impacted the success of some environmental goals at the operational level. The success in achieving the goals of Phase One was also affected by the level of communication between environment committees at each hotel. If an environmental program was successful at one hotel, other properties might benefit from learning how the program was implemented so that mistakes or delays could be avoided at the others.

As mentioned, the corporate level saw itself as the policy setter and chose to allow the financial and operational aspects associated with the environmental initiatives to be left up to the individual properties. No financial resources were available from corporate. At this point in time, hotels did not have to officially include environmental operational costs in their annual budgets as the emphasis was on obtaining short-term goals. Sometimes the number of environmental goals each property was able to achieve was determined by geographic location. For example, the hotels located in cities were better able to handle cost-efficient waste and recycling programs than hotels in more remote areas such as national parks.

Interestingly, there was a difference between corporate's and individual hotels' interpretations of the Green Partnership Program. Corporate saw the Green Partnership Program as something all properties must do regardless of how much it will cost the individual properties (all the money must come from individual properties, not corporate). Since corporate had made the commitment to guests and employees to "green" its operations, corporate expected the Green Partnership Program to be approached as an achievable project. The Palliser Hotel (as well as other CP properties in Alberta at the time) felt the goals were important if they were cost beneficial and if a volunteer committee could coordinate them.

Regional Coordinator

Realizing the challenges faced by the hotels in developing their environmental programs, CP management in Alberta hired Jacques Bouchard as a regional environmental coordinator. The primary goal of the coordinator was to help management to achieve the environmental goals set by corporate and the individual hotels' environmental committees. His tasks were as follows:

• Design and perform environmental audits for the properties.
• Design and manage environmental report cards for each property.
• Review and assist in contract management for waste disposal, energy management, water management, and renovation/expansion projects.
• Research and determine the feasibility of all environmental initiatives suggested by management and by the environmental committees.
• Analyze and determine the viability of the recyclable material markets.

Some of the benefits of having an environmental coordinator included

• bringing accountability to environmental programs before and during their implementation;
• making management accountable for their decisions (especially if projects are refused);
• internally conducting environmental audits (internal audits are less expensive and completely site specific); and
• providing the environmental committees with background information so they could make realistic and implementable recommendations.

The environmental coordinator could affect the extent to which any decisions were taken seriously. Any suggestions regarding environmental programs now had a specific name attached to them. In the past, the responsibilities of getting things done fell totally on the volunteer committees. Responsibilities were now shared with the specific departments involved with the programs or projects.

Palliser's Interpretation and Implementation

One of the first locations in the CP chain to embrace the program was the Palliser Hotel located in downtown Calgary. The environmental mission statement of the Palliser Hotel was as follows:

> The Palliser will consistently reduce, reuse, recycle and rethink in or-
> der to provide an environmentally friendly hotel for our guests and
> employees. We will always strive to look for new Green Initiatives
> and continue to teach those around us. (personal communication with
> Jacques Bouchard, 1997)

The Palliser's interpretation of the Green Partnership Program led to two main areas of concentration: (1) diversion in the waste stream, and (2) water and energy efficiency. The regular waste stream refers to all chemicals and all materials that could end up in a landfill site. The stream is further divided into three categories: wet, dry, and hazardous waste. In the hotel business wet waste usually refers only to food waste in the regular (nonhazardous) waste stream. Dry waste refers to the rest of the regular waste produced by other departments and consists of recyclables, refundables, and mainte-nance of industrial waste. Regular waste and industrial waste (excluding hazardous waste) are generally controlled by municipal bylaws and by the provincial Environmental Protection and Enhancement Act (EPEA, Sep-tember 1, 1993). Hazardous waste consists of all unwanted and used chemi-cal products that require specific disposal procedures such as paints, aero-sols, and leftover cleaning products. Disposal of hazardous waste is strictly controlled by provincial and federal regulations such as the Transportation of Dangerous Goods (TDG) regulations. Workplace Hazardous Material Information System (WHMIS) applies to chemicals used in the workplace.

The second area of concentration at the Palliser was water and energy ef-ficiency. According to the *Green Partnership Guide* (Troyer, 1992), the kitchen and the laundry are the two areas in any hotel that have the greatest impact on the environment and the hotel budget. Both the kitchen and the laundry create the most pollution and waste the most energy. The kitchen in particular uses 20 to 30 percent of a hotel's total energy; approximately 60 percent of the energy consumed in the kitchens is not used for cooking purposes. For example, running faucet taps in vegetable washing areas is unnecessary. The *Green Partnership Guide* suggests cleaning and peeling vegetables in a partly filled sink, not in a continuous stream of running wa-ter (Troyer, 1992). Ideally, the departments with the highest concentration of water and energy usage should be the most active in finding alternative practices or products.

Cooperation between departments is important in the greening of hotel operations. For example, saving energy and water is accomplished with the collaboration of housekeeping and maintenance. Maintenance is responsible for repairs and upkeep but needs the attendants to report problems, such as leaks and faulty equipment, so that the hotel runs at peak performance.

To conserve energy, the maintenance department at the Palliser Hotel installed special light filters (tinting film) on the windows facing the daytime sun. Although the light filters were installed, room attendants still needed to close the drapes to make sure the rooms did not get any extra heat and force the air conditioners to run unnecessarily. The Palliser has also replaced all incandescent light fixtures with more efficient fluorescent lights. The Hotel Macdonald in Edmonton has taken energy conservation one step further by installing heat-censored fluorescent lights in high-traffic areas such as corridors throughout the hotel.

Ultimately, simply turning off all lights and equipment when not in use will create the greatest savings. There are, however, exceptions to the standard. Televisions and lights are left on in business-class rooms when guests are expected. Disturbingly, it would appear that appearance and image take priority over true energy conservation efforts for some situations. Furthermore, leaving the television on is part of a standard mandate in place as part of a welcoming practice for business guests. This mandate is enforced at the corporate level and is in effect at the operational level. Consequently, there is little an environmental committee can do in addressing this mandate at an operational level. Although this mandate may seem minor, it does bring into question the seriousness of CP Hotels' commitment to the Green Program.

The Purchasing Department also plays an important role in establishing green purchasing practices and vendor relations. For the Alberta region, the purchasing department at the Palliser Hotel is directly involved in

- sourcing and testing new products and services that are friendlier to the environment;
- reviewing existing products and services to see if they can better meet CP's environmental goals and policies;
- working with suppliers and manufactures in adopting environmentally friendly polices and practices that are consistent with CP's vision;
- negotiating contracts on a regional basis to increase the viability of some environmental programs; and
- reviewing the levels of environmental awareness of the suppliers while tendering for new contracts.

Employee Participation

To be effective, the staff and guests must be introduced and educated about the goals. In terms of making employees aware of the importance of the environmental policy, the hotel utilized a number of tools to encourage participation. For example, the environmental program and expected performance were made an important part of employee orientation. In Alberta, job appraisals for each hotel employee were being expanded to include evaluations of environmental performance. As well, the Palliser scheduled monthly environmental meetings and representatives from each department, including management, were expected to attend.

During Phase One of the Green Partnership Program the employees of the green committees were volunteering their time. The success of the CP Hotels & Resorts Green Partnership Program was a result of the employees hard work and dedication to caring for the environment. This energy went a long way in achieving the initial goals of the program. However, during the development of Phase Two, it became evident that the employees needed an extra boost to keep the momentum going. In 1998, under the new title of Fairmont Hotels and Resorts, an environmental incentive program was introduced to the employees. The incentive program provided "Green Teams" with rewards for the completion of environmental initiatives. The program, titled "Seeing the Forest AND the Trees" created friendly competition between the individual Green Teams throughout the hotel chain. As teams created and implemented environmental initiatives they were rewarded with tree stickers displayed on a sticker board. At the end of the year the Green Team with the most trees (largest "forest") won an all-expense-paid trip to the Caribbean for all ten members of the team. They also received the title of Fairmont Hotels and Resorts "Environmental Hotel of the Year."

Guest Education

The hotel also took steps to educate patrons about the hotel's approach to reduce and conserve valuable resources. An insert explaining waste and energy programs was developed for guest-orientation binders in hotel rooms. This insert explained how the guests themselves could help in the conservation effort.

Phase Two of the *Green Partnership Guide* (Fairmont Hotels & Resorts, 2001) suggests communicating to guests when a property is using organic produce. The rationale is that the term *organic* is a buzzword that creates interest in the menu.

Waste Management Programs

An efficient waste management program includes more than the usual philosophy of reduce, reuse, and recycle. At the Palliser, the waste management program includes reduce, return, donate, refund, reuse, compost, and recycle.

Reduce

Efforts to reduce waste involved all departments at the Palliser as well as the hotel's suppliers. Employees and management were constantly looking for ways to reduce the amount of potential waste coming into the hotel. The idea was if it does not come into the hotel in the first place, you will not have to dispose of it later. The purchasing department played a key role in reducing waste by finding new suppliers that used less packaging. The hotel did conduct an experiment to reduce plastics by attempting to eliminate the use of garbage bags. However, other problems occurred. The kitchen was dependent upon collection services to pick up the garbage. During this trial period the smell of the garbage was greater than when it was contained in garbage bags. The garbage also leaked onto the property creating additional cleanup. Consequently, the hotel went back to using garbage bags.

Return

Return policies are supplemental to reduce policies. If packaging cannot be reduced significantly, the next best step was to see if the packaging could be returned to the suppliers to be used again. This policy worked well with the salmon supplier. The salmon were sent to the Palliser in polystyrene boxes, which used to be thrown out with the regular waste. However, CP Hotels was successful in creating a regional purchasing policy that convinced the salmon supplier to take the boxes back for reuse. This return program not only helped to reduce the hotel's waste, it also helped to reduce the costs associated with the product.

In Calgary, the city in which the hotel is located, the municipality could not dispose of plastics. In an effort to divert plastic containers from the landfill sites, the Palliser sent containers, such as orange juice, back to suppliers. The company that supplied orange juice to the hotel was awarded the contract only if it was willing to take back the plastic juice containers. The hotel took the first step toward proper disposal of plastic orange juice containers. However, there is still the question life cycle management and what the orange juice supplier is doing with the plastic containers. If the suppliers are affected by health and safety regulations, they may not be able to reuse the containers for beverages. Consequently, the containers may still end up in a landfill site.

Donate

CP Hotels in general, and the Palliser in particular, are actively pursuing agreements with agencies such as the United Way to donate amenities such as soap, shampoo and conditioners, and toilet paper to local homeless shelters. For example, the Fairmont Royal York in Toronto sends "more than 20,000 pounds of soaps and 4,000 pounds of shampoos, conditioners and lotions to agencies and missions every year" (Canadian Pacific Hotel & Resorts Partnership Guide, 2001, p. 42). At the Fairmont Empress in Victoria soap is donated to the local maritime museum for scrimshaw carving classes. From a social perspective, this charitable act is commendable, as it will certainly benefit local agencies. It only makes sense to donate all articles that are still usable but that are no longer in use. However, the same question is raised as with the orange juice containers. Are the used plastic containers still ending up in the landfill site if suppliers of amenities do not take them back? In other words, the hotel might have simply passed the responsibility of diverting plastics from the waste stream onto the charitable agencies receiving the donations.

Refund

Making sure that hotels collect and return all refundable goods is important as it helps reduce the waste stream and money is returned to the purchaser. By not returning the refundables, the hotel is essentially paying twice for disposal. Bottles and glass containers are obvious goods to be recycled. "A 475-room hotel generates approximately 10,000 liquor and wine bottles a month, none of which should ever go in a landfill (Canadian Pacific Hotel & Resorts Green Partnership Guide, 2001, p. 45). Other items such as aluminum cans, plastics, newspapers, fine and mixed paper, and mixed glass can also have considerable market value.

Reuse

In conjunction with redistributing used amenities to charities the hotel asks suppliers of bathroom amenities to take back used plastic shampoo containers and refill them. If suppliers were in a position to comply, both the charitable organizations and the hotel would be able to participate in good environmental citizenship. However, as discussed previously, there are health and safety standards that can affect any organization's efforts to divert plastics from the waste stream. Reusing can take on many forms. In the kitchen, plastic containers are constantly reused for storage of food. Also, the housekeeping department used old linens to make reusable laundry bags for the staff.

Compost

From a waste management perspective, food waste averages 42 to 47 percent of the waste stream of a hotel. Consequently, the composting program is the most important environmental program at the hotel. It contributes directly in diverting an average of 45 percent of the total waste stream of the hotel. By comparison, a composting program at the municipal level that achieves 20 to 25 percent diversion of the waste stream is considered successful. At the Palliser composting is done by an outside contractor. Kitchen waste to be composted is put into colored garbage bags, distinct from the rest of the hotel waste, and later sorted and composted.

Recycle

Finally, the last step in waste management is recycling. The Palliser switched waste management companies because the previous company was not participating in the separation of garbage and recycling efforts. The waste management company now employed by the hotel is actively involved in diverting garbage from the landfill site through the separation and appropriate disposal of glass, tin, cardboard, and paper. At the Palliser, the kitchen recycles all tin cans. Housekeeping recycles all remaining soaps and amenity containers, and maintenance recycles all scrap metal.

When the blue recycling boxes were first introduced in the guest rooms they were placed in the bathroom under the sinks. However, the guests were not using the blue boxes because they were not located in an area that reminds guests to recycle. Over time, the hotel recognized the need to place the blue boxes in the guest rooms in locations where they could be seen and utilized more frequently.

Rethinking

Rethinking is an ongoing process of any program that attempts to make environmental changes. For example, the Palliser introduced a whole line of environmentally friendly cleaning products as an alternative to cleaning products that contain toxic chemicals. Ecolab, a cleaning supply company, developed the line of environmental cleaning supplies for the hotel chain. According to a past representative of the Green Committee, "you could actually drink these cleaning supplies." The hotel has eliminated other environmentally damaging substances such as phosphates in dishwashing and washing detergents.

Eliminating environmentally damaging products and finding alternative products and services requires research. An environmental committee does not usually have the time to research alternatives. As the regional environmental coordinator, Jacques Bouchard is in a position to contact companies and investigate various alternatives for the hotels. On a regional basis, the environmental damage of polystyrene containers was addressed by the regional vice president for CP Hotels. Through the direct involvement of the regional vice president, polystyrene containers are no longer used by hotel operations such as room service. Although the Palliser has made the transition back to dishes used as serving containers, there is still the demand for take-away service. Presently, there are no alternatives on the market that work as well as polystyrene for insulating hot and cold beverages. Consequently, the elimination of polystyrene containers appears to be a long-term goal that is dependent upon further research into the development of alternative containers.

At the postconsumer level, waste levels are more difficult to calculate. For example, it is difficult to determine how much food a customer will leave on his or her plate after a meal. Serving smaller portions is not always an option. If the Palliser served smaller portions, the guests may conclude that the value for the money was no longer acceptable. The Palliser does not want to be perceived as being cheap by serving portions that are too small. One way to approach the issue of serving size is to give the customer the choice of ordering a half portion at a lower price. This approach may address the perceived problem of value for the money when initiating postconsumer waste programs.

Elimination of All Excess Packaging

The elimination of all excess packaging is a program that has been reassessed as a long-term goal. The company's Green Partnership Policy states that the elimination of single-serving packages is an immediate goal. However, the hotel has been unable to meet this goal in the short-term due to health and safety issues. In particular, the elimination of individual creamers requires careful consideration to ensure that the cream does not go bad prematurely when stored in larger containers. This is a challenge not only to the Palliser but also to other food and beverage outlets and services. Presently, there are no alternative cream containers in the marketplace. Time is required to investigate alternative methods of serving cream; the CP's goal to eliminate individual creamers is being re-assessed as a long-term goal.

The Palliser has been successful in finding an alternative to using single-serving packages of sugar. The hotel has been working with a supplier to develop china sugar shakers to match the CP's dishes. As an alternative, china shakers not only meet an environmental goal of the Green Policy, the shakers also contribute to the perception of added value for the guests. For example, when room service is called the guest will be presented with china dishes instead of disposable containers.

Organic Foods

One of the sixteen goals in Phase One of the Green Partnership Program was to buy organically grown foods. However, geographical locations and market demands can influence the efforts of each hotel to realize this goal. For example, according to the CP Green Partnership Program, Quebec consumers were more concerned about buying organic foods than any other provinces in Canada. In response to this demand, the Quebec provincial government estimated that 30 percent of all provincial farmers would supply organic foods (Troyer, 1992). Based on this, CP Hotels in Quebec was in a position to stock greater amounts of organic foods. In Alberta, however, demand is less for organic foods. Consequently, there are not many organic farmers. Alberta is known for beef products, and organic beef producers are a minority. Furthermore, organically grown foods tend to be associated with vegetarians who are still a small percentage of the population. However, efforts are being made by the hotel to work with organic farmers to supply a greater amount of organic foods.

Green Meetings

Increasingly, green meeting planners are looking for environmentally friendly settings to hold conferences and meetings. In response to green meeting demands, hotels and planners have developed categories and criteria for evaluating hotels' services and operations. Specifically, Green Suites International has developed a green meeting planners' "Preservations" rating system. The system has six categories (general, recycling, energy conservation, water conservation, effluents and emissions, and guest rooms) and a set of criteria to evaluate a hotel's environmental programs. From a marketing perspective, hotels such as the Palliser that have been proactive in establishing green programs are in a position to capture the attention of green meeting planners.

Green Tour Operators

Partnership between hotels and tour operators is becoming more of a focus at the Palliser. According to a representative of the Sales Department, efforts are being made by CP Hotels to identify "green" or "eco" tour operators that offer environmentally friendly tourism experiences. One of the barriers to this initiative is that there are no internationally or nationally recognized standards for environmental performance in the tourism industry. Consequently, identifying tour operators on the basis of environmental criteria is not an easy task. However, as more pressure is placed on the tourism industry to develop environmental performance standards, there is more potential for green hotels to link up with green tour operators.

CONCLUSION TO PHASE ONE

Purchasing policies and waste, water, and energy conservation programs have been discussed in terms of short-, mid-, and long-term goals. Many of these goals can be measured in the report-card format used to describe the progress of CP Hotels. According to Jacques Bouchard (personal communication, 1997), a report-card format is used as an audit procedure to monitor progress. Specifically, the report card includes an audit of three levels of progress:

Level 1—Environmental initiatives that do not cost much to implement
Level 2—More serious environmental initiatives, looking specifically at cost savings
Level 3—Areas of hotel operations that have been committed to environmental performance

THE BEGINNING OF PHASE TWO

Ideally, all three levels of Phase One of the *Green Partnership Guide* (Troyer, 1992) should be realized before Phase Two has been initiated. However, there are external influences, such as municipal waste management policies, that could be considered barriers to accomplishing all aspects of Phase One. If external barriers take time to overcome, it is not unreasonable for a hotel to move ahead to Phase Two and continue to strive toward creating an environmentally friendly hotel setting. Phase Two contains a section on Environmentally Responsible Golf Course Management. The management strategies are based on the Audubon Cooperative Sanctuary System for Golf Courses (ACSS). According to the Fairmont Hotels & Resorts *Green Partnership Guide* 2001, the ultimate goal is for all golf courses to "be members of the Audubon Cooperative Sanctuary System or, at least, strive for certification" (p. 119).

In Phase Two of the *Green Partnership Guide* (Fairmont Hotels & Resorts, 2001) the benefits of a waste audit are discussed. The purpose of a waste audit is to track the production, quantity, and composition of a hotel's waste over a given period of time (twenty-four hours is recommended). The goal of a waste audit is to identify the sources of waste, the degree to which the waste stream is contaminated, and possibilities for reusing and reducing the amount of materials going into the waste stream. (See Fairmont Hotels & Resorts *Green Partnership Guide,* 2001 for more information on the characteristics of a basic waste audit, available from its Web site.)

REFERENCES

Canadian Pacific Hotel & Resorts (2001). *Green Partnership Guide.* Author.
Environmental Protection and Enhancement Act (EPEA) September 1, 1993. http://www3.gov.ab.ca/env/protenf/approvals/factsheets/enhanact.html.
Fairmont Hotels & Resorts (2001). *The Green Partnership Guide: A Practical Guide to Greening Your Hotel* (2nd Ed). Canada: Friesens.
Troyer, W. (1992). *Canadian Pacific Hotels & Resorts Green Partnership Guide.* Canada: Best.

AND THE WINNER IS... FAIRMONT HOTELS

Part III:
Sustainable Nature-Based
and Adventure Tourism Activities

Sustainable tourism, alternative tourism, ethical tourism, green tourism, special-interest tourism, appropriate tourism, responsible tourism, conservation-supporting tourism, environmentally aware tourism, sustainably run tourism, ecotourism, adventure tourism—confused yet?

All these terms have been used in discussions about tourism activities. If we take a closer look at these descriptors, we recognize some similarities. First, these terms imply that all tourism should be sustainable; thereby suggesting that it is both responsible and ethical. Second, in terms of the environmental aspect of tourism, "sustainable" means that tourism conserves the resource base and its activities are nondegrading. Third, in terms of the social aspects of tourism, activities also respect the culture and heritage of the local communities.

A tourist can choose to participate in an activity that involves nature; thus, we have nature-based tourism, which is sometimes incorrectly referred to as "ecotourism." The assumption is that both nature-based tourism and ecotourism are also sustainable. However, these terms have been abused and used in circumstances in which the experience is not sustainable but still involves an encounter with nature. Finally, that involvement with nature might involve an adventure in the sense that it provides an exciting, challenging, and sometimes adrenalin-enhancing experience, hopefully, in a sustainable fashion.

The International Ecotourism Society defines ecotourism as "responsible travel to natural areas that conserves the environment and improves the well-being of the local people." Using that definition, ecotourism should have the following characteristics:

- Minimal environmental impact by all parties
- Environmental education

- Long-term benefits to the communities affected by the tourism
- Conservation and management of the ecosystem affected by the tourism

How can a tourist identify ecotourism operations in the true definition of the term? Several organizations offer codes of ethics or guidelines for ecotourism operations. Others, although few in number, do provide some form of ecotourism certification. Probably the most advanced system of certifying environmentally responsible tourism is the Nature and Ecotourism Accreditation Program (NEAP) of Australia. The International Ecotourism Society provides an extensive set of guidelines for nature tour operations but does not provide a means of determining if operators adhere to the guidelines as does NEAP.

The cases in this section, depending on the choice for use, can provide discussions for identifying ecotourism or adventure tourism activities that are also sustainable. Some also involve an adventure tourism experience, although what is an "adventure" is best defined by the tourist. Activities highlighted in the cases are mountain biking, whale watching, heli-skiing, alpine resort skiing, and scuba diving. If a clarification of the term *sustainability* is needed before addressing the particular issues presented in these cases, then the Waterton Lakes National Park case will be a good preliminary exercise.

The Pacific Northwest whale watching case highlights the advantages and disadvantages of the growth of this activity. It emphasizes the problems that exist in governing an area that consists of a diverse number of stakeholders on both sides of the Canadian/United States border.

The issues addressed in these cases are diverse. Part 1 of the two-part Treadsoftly cases couples the development of an environmental plan with the business plan of a start-up venture.

Part 2 addresses how to ensure that the plan is implemented—that the company actually "walks the talk." The Canadian Mountain Holidays heli-skiing case addresses the risks associated with adventure sports and how tourists must not only be aware of the risks but take partial responsibility for reducing the risks associated with certain adventure sports. The ski resorts case provides an awareness of what various resorts around the world are doing to reduce their environmental impacts. It also introduces a U.S.-based organization, called the Ski Area Citizens' Coalition, that has been active in rating ski resorts on their environmental performance. Vacations by the Sea introduces the plight and devastation of the coral reefs of the world and the level of pollution that exists in our waters.

Chapter 6

The State of the Pacific Northwest Whale Watching Industry, 1999

Neil Symington

INTRODUCTION

The increasing popularity of adventure and nature tourism throughout the world has caused tourism operators to continually push further and further into the outdoors in order to satisfy this huge demand. Because of its enormous expanse of mountains and coastline, as well as its abundant wildlife, the Pacific Northwest has become an important destination for tourism. From hiking the West Coast Trail and kayaking in Desolation Sound, to numerous coastal activities available on the San Juan and Gulf Islands and their surrounding waters, visitors are coming from around the world to take in this area's beauty (see Figure 6.1).

One industry that has followed this trend and grown exponentially over the past decade is the whale watching industry. As reported in Whale Watching 2000, for the International Fund for Animal Welfare, the whale watching industry in 1998 was worth $1 billion (USD), attracting more than 9 million participants a year in eighty-seven countries and territories (Hoyt, 2000). In that same year, worldwide whale watching tourism expenditures were estimated at $1,049 million USD. The Whale Watching 2000 report defines whale watching as "tours by boat, air or from land, formal or informal, with at least some commercial aspect, to see, swim with, and/or listen to any of the some 83 species of whales, dolphins, and porpoises" (p. 5).

Whale watching activities are becoming available in new countries every year. Since 1994, twenty-two new countries have started whale watching tours. Now tourists can sight whales in a variety of locations, both old and new. Such varied countries as Namibia, Taiwan, and the Soloman Islands are new to the industry; however, three areas (the United States, Canada, and the Canary Islands in Spain) each have attracted over 1 million whale watchers a year. Both Australia and South Africa are fast approaching the 1 million watchers' mark. The World Tourism Organization (WTO) expects

FIGURE 6.1. Whale watching areas, San Juan Islands, United States, and Gulf Islands, Canada. (Map prepared by Hanako Saito.)

The orca surfaces. (Photo courtesy of Neil Symington and Leah Adair.) Reprinted with permission.

A tour group sights a whale. (Photo courtesy of Neil Symington and Leah Adair.) Reprinted with permission.

Their size is impressive at close range. (Photo courtesy of Neil Symington and Leah Adair.) Reprinted with permission.

growth in the whale watching sector to increase 3 to 4 percent annually in the early years of 2000s, faster than world tourism as a whole. According to the IFAW (2005) whale watching operations now exist in more than ninety countries and as one of the fastest-growing sectors of the tourism industry is worth more than $1 billion in revenues to coastal communities.

Popular destinations in the United States for watching whales are New England, the Eastern United States, and the Gulf of Mexico areas, the Pacific Northwest area (including Alaska), California, and Hawaii. Canadian destinations include Newfoundland, the Maritimes, Quebec, the Arctic (Manitoba), and British Columbia.

THE PACIFIC COAST

With an abundance of resident and migratory whales, British Columbia has witnessed the birth of three major centers for whale watching: Tofino, Robson Bight, and Victoria. Tofino, on the West Coast of Vancouver Island, regularly receives visits from resident and migratory grey whales. The Robson Bight whale watching industry centers from Telegraph Cove on the northeast Coast of Vancouver Island and concentrates primarily on the northern resident killer whale population for its tours. The final industry location is in Victoria, British Columbia, on Vancouver Island and the San Juan Islands of Washington state. Haro Strait, which divides Canada and the United States, has several attractions that bring tourists from all over the world. The Whale Museum in Friday Harbor, Washington, offers multiple activities to better understand whales and their habitants. Although humpback, grey, and minke whales, as well as various other cetaceans and bird species use these waters, the primary focus of operators is on the southern resident killer whale population due to its predictability and popularity.

Whale watching is popular along the entire Pacific Coast. In the United States, Alaska, Oregon, California, and Washington have strong whale watching industries. As well, Mexico, and many of the countries of South America, as far south as Chile, have growing industries that offer many activities for education as well as enjoyment.

WHALE WATCHING
IN THE PACIFIC NORTHWEST

The whale watching industry in the Pacific Northwest commenced in the late 1980s and has grown into an integral part of the tourism industry in

British Columbia and Washington State. Although there are many socio-economic benefits from the whale watching industry, including recreational, scientific, educational, heritage, aesthetic, spiritual, psychological, and financial, some operations are not run in a sustainable manner. The ecological costs sometimes exceed the social and financial benefits of these operations. Some of the ecological costs incurred include pollution from boat fuels, noise and exhaust from whale watching boats, and the cumulative impacts of all human activities on the whales. Some say that all factors must be considered when assessing the impact of the whale watching industry and its growth. When commercial whale watching of killer whales began in Johnstone Strait in 1980 and in Greater Victoria in 1987, it was a peaceful and private enterprise. However, in recent years ecotourism and the increasing interest in viewing whales in a wild and free environment has produced a brash industry. Whale watching companies attempt to develop certain competitive advantages or characteristics in order to provide better customer satisfaction.

Spotting

One of the most important factors in the industry is a company's ability to find whales and provide this information to the boat pilots in order to provide the customer with a positive nature-watching experience. Most companies either have their own spotters or are part of a whale watching network and pay for spotting services. Companies race to find the whales at the beginning of the day and to keep their location secret from the competition as long as possible.

> Spotters on the hills over Victoria have reported whales on the U.S. side of Haro Strait, swimming below the cliffs on San Juan Island. Word has swept through the whale-watching network—a guaranteed sighting—and boatloads of tourists are racing out from the British Columbia ports of Victoria, Sooke, and Sidney, and from Bellingham, Friday Harbor, and other Washington ports. (Obee, 1998, p. 6)

Different methods of spotting include using scout boats and even aircraft. The most common method is using a shore-based spotter located at an elevated land-based position equipped with high-powered binoculars and various communication devices (e.g., cell phones, pagers, and radios).

Type of Boat

The type of boat a whale watching company operates depends largely upon where it is based and the regulations it must abide by. For the most part, Canadian companies operate smaller, ridged-hulled inflatable boats equipped with outboard engines that carry twelve passengers, while the Americans operate larger, solid-hulled boats capable of carrying twenty to 100 passengers. Even when business is slow, the Canadians can operate cost-effectively due to the smaller passenger payload and add-on trips and/or boats when demand increases.

The inflatables are also closer to the water, which allows better whale viewing, and have greater speed and thus greater range for the limited three-hour trip. This allows the Canadians an operating area as far west as the entrance to the Pacific Ocean, as far north as the Fraser River, and as far east as the Washington state mainland. The Americans, limited in boat size by regulations, operate primarily in the San Juan Islands/Haro Strait or Puget Sound area.

Marketing

Attracting customers has become increasingly competitive as the number of operators entering the market has increased. It is very difficult for companies to distinguish themselves one another in terms of quality, and the costs of marketing are very high to the small operators. Companies in Victoria have tried several tactics to gain a competitive edge: location, advertising, alliances, and price.

Location

All whale watching companies have attempted to gain exposure and visibility, and many companies have sought high-priced waterfront locations in the Victoria Inner Harbour. One Victoria-based operation, Ocean Explorations, has also leased storefront space just off Government Street, Victoria's biggest tourist draw, in order to gain a bigger presence in the downtown core.

Advertising

Many operators are trying to attract customers through advertising. They market their services around Victoria on billboards, in tourist entry points such as the airport and ferries, in tourist and other publications, and more recently on the Internet.

Alliances

Many operators have also created alliances with hotels and tour agencies in order to attract more customers. Whale watching operators have partnered with hotels such as the Ocean Pointe Resort and Spa, the Oak Bay Beach Hotel & Marine Resort, and the famous Fairmont Empress.

Price

In 1999, the competition got so fierce that the operators began competing on price, lowering the average price from $75 down to $50 per tour (Canadian). Some companies went out of business or were sold due to the cut-throat nature of the industry.

Whale Watcher Operators Association Northwest (WWOAN)

The Whale Watcher Operators Association Northwest (WWOAN) was established in 1996 to address the changes taking place in the industry and provide standards for its members. In 1997 a separate Canadian chapter was established in Victoria to deal exclusively with Canadian issues and to liaison with American counterparts on industry-wide issues.

The WWOAN strives to accomplish the following:

1. Establish and maintain professional standards for marine wildlife tour operators
2. Encourage the education of operators and the public with respect to marine wildlife
3. Communicate, in a single unified voice, with government agencies and public bodies
4. Assist the research community with their research work on marine wildlife

WWOAN's area of operation essentially encompasses the entire summer range of the southern resident killer whale population: Georgia Strait in the north, Puget Sound to the east and south, Juan de Fuca Strait, and the southwest tip of Vancouver Island. Although WWOAN members watch other whales and wildlife, the southern resident killer whales are the most predictable and frequent visitors to the area.

WWOAN members can be found in the following locations (http://www. nwwhalewatchers.org/members.html):

Canada

1. Victoria, British Columbia—separate Canadian WWOAN chapter were established to address exclusively Canadian issues and concerns
2. Sidney, British Columbia
3. Sooke, British Columbia

United States

1. San Juan Islands, Washington—the majority of the American operators organize out of Friday Harbor on San Juan Island itself
2. Bellingham, Washington
3. Anacortes, Washington

ISSUES

Decline in Number of Whales

Over the past years there has been a decline in the southern resident killer population. The population in 1998 was eighty-three, down from ninety-eight in 1995, according to the Center for Whale Research (2005) in Friday Harbor (Whale Museum, 1999c) (http.//www.whaleresearch.com/). Researchers cannot make definite conclusions as to direct cause and effect relationships between certain environmental factors but assume that these factors contribute to the decline in the population. These factors are seen as adding increased stresses to the whales' health that may cause them to succumb more easily to natural phenomena, such as diseases, due to a lowered immune system (Graham Ellis, telephone interview, November 12, 1999). The cumulative effects from these factors are likely leading to the decline in the southern resident population. Several factors have been cited by the Whale Museum in Friday Harbor including declining fish populations, toxic exposure, surface impacts, and underwater noise.

Declining Fish Populations

All killer whales are opportunistic feeders, but the southern resident population feeds almost exclusively on fish. Some studies show that up to 90 percent of their diet is salmon, with Chinook salmon being their preferred food source.

Over the last 50 years hundreds of wild runs of salmon have become extinct due to habitat loss and over-fishing of wild stocks, including the winter runs of Chinook and Coho. Although the surviving stocks have probably been sufficient to sustain the resident pods, many of the runs that have been lost were undoubtedly traditional resources favored by the Southern Residents. This may be affecting the whales' food supply in the winter months and may require them to change their patterns of movement in order to search for their food. (Whale Museum, 1999b)

Toxic Exposure

Manmade toxic substances accumulate in higher concentrations as they move up the food chain. Because killer whales are one of the top predators in the ocean and are at the top of several different food chains in the environment, they tend to be more affected by cumulative exposure to pollutants than other sea creatures.

Examinations of stranded killer whales have shown some extremely high levels of lead, mercury, and polychlorinated hydrocarbons (PCBs). Abandoned marine toxic waste dumps and present levels of industrial and human refuse pollution of the inland waters probably presents the most serious threat to the continued existence of this Orca population. (Whale Museum, 1999b)

Surface Impacts

The waters around the Victoria/San Juan Islands area are extremely congested due to recreational and commercial fishing, heavy commercial deep sea vessel traffic transiting to and from Vancouver and Seattle, as well as an ever-increasing whale watching industry, and a large contingent of recreational boaters. During an average summer weekend it is rare to be the only boat traveling with the whales through this area.

The surfacing and breathing space of marine birds and mammals is a critical aspect of their habitat which they must consciously deal with on a moment-to-moment basis throughout their lifetimes. With all the boating activity in the vicinity, there are three ways in which surface impacts are most likely to affect marine animals: a) collision, b) collision avoidance, and c) exhaust emissions in breathing pockets. (Whale Museum, 1999b)

Underwater Noise

Similar to surface impacts, a primary source of acoustic pollution for this population of orcas would also be derived from the cumulative underwater noise of whale watching and pleasure-boating vessel traffic. For cetaceans, the underwater sound environment is perhaps the most critical component of their sensory and behavioral lives. (Whale Museum, 1999b)

Because whales navigate and hunt using echolocation, underwater noise can hinder these activities as well as any efforts to communicate with vocalizations to other members of the pod.

Committee on the Status of Endangered Wildlife in Canada

"On April 22, 1999, the Committee on the Status of Endangered Wildlife in Canada (COSEWIC) listed the southern resident community of J, K and L pods as 'threatened.' COSEWIC also listed all killer whales in Canadian waters as 'vulnerable'" (Whale Museum, 1999b).

Whale researcher Dr. Robin Baird's (1999) report titled *Status of Killer Whales in Canada* was the primary reason for the listing. The report sighted the previous factors for the decline in the southern resident population and the need for protection.

The implications for this listing could be far-reaching, especially if the United States follows suit and lists the resident orcas as threatened under the Endangered Species Act. When a population is listed in this way, special management measures that go beyond existing regulations or guidelines are often taken to ensure the species' protection. (Whale Museum, 1999b)

Public Perception

In the past years there has been increased media attention, mostly negative, against the whale watching industry. This negative media coverage was mostly the work of a few outspoken locals who believe that boats are harassing the wildlife. More recently, this sentiment has begun to grow in momentum and as a result the number of WWOAN stakeholders has increased over time (see Appendix 1). Perceived harassment hot spots include Race Rocks off Metchosin, British Columbia, the Gulf Islands, British Columbia, San Juan Island, Washington, and Puget Sound, Washington.

> As the business has grown over the past decade, so have public complaints, said [marine mammal coordinator for Fisheries and Oceans Canada, Ed] Lochbaum. Many people have voiced concern that three local [resident] killer whale pods, which draw the most tourists, are being harassed and bothered by the flotilla of boats offering sightseeing cruises during the peak summer season. ("Ecotourism's Question," 1999, p. E11)

Increased boat traffic around whales, both commercial and private, has been perceived by the public as potentially harmful to the health of the whales. Viewed by people onshore as harmful to whales, the industry has a hard time shaking this perception. In one instance (July 5, 1996), there were 107 boats (both commercial and private) off the coast of San Juan Island watching approximately twenty-one whales (Obee, 1998). Complaints from opponents to water-based whale watching have gained the attention of the Canadian and American governments at all levels and there is the risk that changes to whale watching practices will be implemented without input from WWOAN.

Thus far, the industry has felt the pressure of San Juan Island residents to have whale watching boats stay one-quarter mile from its shores, allowing visitors from its land-based whale watching park to have a clearer view. Pearson International College, as the new custodian of the Race Rocks area, may ban whale watchers from the area. Race Rocks is an abandoned lighthouse and nature refuge, fifteen miles south of Victoria, that is used by sea lions and seals as a haul out. This attracts transient killer whales and therefore whale watchers.

> Few people have witnessed the damage as closely as Carol and Mike Slater, caretakers at Race Rocks Ecological Reserve. Since 1989, they have tended the light [house] here in Juan de Fuca Strait, and kept an eye on the animals. (Obee, 1998, p. 11)

This perception is becoming more common among community members (see Appendix 2).

Regulations for the Industry

In Canada, the Department of Fisheries and Oceans (DFO) is responsible for the management and protection of all marine mammals, including killer whales. In the United States, the National Marine Fisheries Service is the responsible agency. "In both countries, regulations specifically prohibit disturbances of whales. Infractions are subject to fines and or imprisonment" (Ford et al., 1994, p. 57). Unfortunately, both American and Canadian marine wildlife regulations are rarely enforced, primarily due to resource-related issues.

The whale watching industry conceived standard guidelines that established acceptable boat behavior around whales which all whale watchers, both commercial and private citizens, are now encouraged to abide by. These guidelines are stricter and more detailed than existing government regulations on either side of the border.

In the American San Juan Islands an organization called Soundwatch observes the behavior of boats around the whales and tries to educate the public, as do some of the WWOAN boats in all waters, about their impact on the whales. WWOAN provides donations that allow Soundwatch to operate, and Soundwatch, in return, issues individual companies monthly report cards on their boats' performance around the whales (Whale Museum, 1999a). On the Canadian side, the government has been issuing marine mammal educative pamphlets to recreational boaters but has no enforcement presence to ensure compliance.

Safety

Incidents with unsafe boating practices involving WWOAN operators have received little media coverage to date even though there have been incidents in the recent past. One incident involved a wake-jumping incident involving a new Victoria operator that resulted in serious client injury. The second incident involved the near sinking of a Victoria-based whale watching boat in the vicinity of San Juan Island due to poor hull design and lack of operator maintenance. The owner of the boat (his second incident) is now out of business.

These incidents were not as drastic as the accident that shook the Tofino whale watching industry in March 1998. Two people were killed, including the boat pilot, and a third was seriously injured (Griffin, 1998). Before the accident, WWAON had commenced drafting industry guidelines for boat safety (as vessel operators with twelve or less passengers do not require any formal qualification in Canada). In an article from the *Canadian Press,* it was noted that despite explosive growth during the past four years the British Columbia whale watching industry essentially operates without regulation. Anyone possessing a boat that accommodates twelve or fewer passengers can be considered a tour operator. This lack of regulation has been the catalyst for the establishment of a voluntary code of standards by Victoria-based whale watching operators. The code contains guidelines pertaining to boat specifications, the type of equipment on board, and proper training for a skipper ("Ecotourism's Question," 1998).

THE FUTURE

A meeting was held in April of 1999 involving DFO and WWOAN (and other stakeholders) in an attempt to form a whale watching council to determine acceptable regulations for all parties.

A federal mammal coordinator is working to form a whale watching advisory council comprising researchers, environmentalists, members of industry, and the general public. The council would offer advice on new federal regulations for 2001. These new regulations, drafted with the assistance of an East Coast whale expert at Newfoundland's Memorial University, aim for a greater protection of whales without being detrimental to business. In order to assist the courts, the regulations provide detailed descriptions of the behavior of whales, and could include the licensing of whale watching operators.

APPENDIX 1:
STAKEHOLDERS OF WHALE WATCHING
OPERATORS NORTHWEST

	Primary	**Secondary**
Internal	Association members/operators	Other employees
	Boat Pilots	• Naturalists
	Soundwatch	• Office staff
	Marine mammal monitoring	
External	Canadian government	Other tourism industries
	Federal	Hospitality
	Ministry of Fisheries and Oceans	Royal BC Museum
	Fisheries	Vancouver Aquarium
	Coast Guard Boating Safety	Fishing communities
	Transport Canada Marine Safety	
	RCMP	

Primary	Secondary
Provincial	
Ministry of Small Business and Tourism (Ministry of Competition, Scientific and Enterprise)	
Municipal	
Tourism Victoria & Vancouver	
U.S. government	
Federal	
National Marine Fisheries Service U.S. Coast Guard	
State	
Washington State Office of Travel & Economic Development	
Washington State Tourism	
Regional	
Olympic Peninsula Travel Association	
Nonmember whale watching operators	
General public	
Media	
Research groups	
Center for Whale Research (United States)	
The Whale Museum (United States)	
University of Victoria	
Marine Advisory Council, Victoria	
Customers	
Referrals	
Tour companies	

APPENDIX 2: PUBLIC PERCEPTION

These two letters to the editor of the Victoria *Times Colonist* are representative of the feedback that the public provided about the predicament of whales. They show two very different views on an incident involving orcas.

On July 29 I witnessed three whale-watching vessels trap a small orca between their boats and Island View Beach for their clients' viewing pleasure. It was directly in front of the beach, in an area that is extremely shallow. The whale had no idea where to go, was given virtually no space to move within and came close to being beached. As I watched this scene unfold, I could not help but feel sorry for the whale as it was trapped and harassed at close distance and then chased along the coast by members of the "self-regulating" whale-watching industry. A thrill for the whale watchers, perhaps, but a scary situation for the whale.

How long is the federal government going to wait before ensuring that some essential standards—such as distance and a basic sense of respect—are adhered to when it comes to whale-watching activities?

Re: The Aug. 13 letter, "Protect Orcas,"

The writer presents a very personal interpretation of the event witnessed. ("On July 19 I witnessed three whale-watching vessels trap a small orca between their boats and Island View Beach for their clients viewing pleasure . . . the whale had no idea where to go . . . and came close to being beached . . . was trapped and harassed at close distance and then chased along the coast by members of the 'self-regulating' whale watching industry.") What the writer witnessed was one of three transient killer whales foraging for harbor seals close to shore with whale-watching boats looking on. The particular whale observed was T6, part of the T3 pod, hunting in a routine fashion. At no time was this whale "trapped" or uncertain of where to go or "close to being beached." In fact, transient killer whales often forage in very shallow water, occasionally beaching themselves in pursuit of prey. They are not easily harassed or chased as they can submerge for eight to 12 minutes and go in any direction at any time. With respect to the writer's swipe at the "self-regulating" whale-watching industry, many people, myself included, are working hard to ensure that essential standards are adhered to. It is not a perfect situation and some operators occasionally get too close, but most industry participants are conscientious in their approach to the whales and excellent stewards of the marine environment. Many have a deep and abiding respect for the wildlife they observe.

REFERENCES

Anderson, Charlie (1999). Whale Watching Put on Watch: A Conference Will Look at the Industry's Problems, Including Animal Welfare. *The Province (Vancouver)*. February 14. Final Edition, p. A31.

Baird, Robin W. (1999). *Status of Killer Whales in Canada*. Contract report to the Committee on the Status of Endangered Wildlife in Canada. Ottawa. April. Available online at <http://is.dal.ca/~whitelab/rwb/kwstatus.htm>.

Center for Whale Research (n.d.). Available online at <www.whaleresearch.com>.

Ecotourism's Question: Who Watches Whale Watchers? (1999). *The Edmonton Journal,* April 15, Final Edition, p. E11.

Ford, John K.B., Graeme M. Ellis, and Kenneth C. Balcomb (1994). *Killer Whales: The Natural History and Genealogy of* Orcinus orca *in British Columbia and Washington State.* Vancouver: University of British Columbia Press.

Griffin, Kevin (1998). Two Killed When Whale-Watching Boat Capsizes: The Deaths Near Tofino May Be the First in the Multi-Million-Dollar Industry. *The Vancouver Sun,* March 23, Final Edition, p. A1.

Hoyt, Erich (2000). *Whale Watching 2000: Worldwide Tourism Numbers, Expenditures, and Expanding Socioeconomic Benefits.* Crowborough, UK: International Fund for Animal Welfare.

International Fund for Animal Welfare (2005). *IWC Notes Growth of Whale Watching Industry Worldwide.* Available online at www.ifaw.org.au.

Obee, Bruce (1998). Eco-Tourism Boom: How Much Can Wildlife Take? *Beautiful British Columbia Magazine,* (1), p. 6.

Pynn, Larry (1999). Whale-Watching: Is Protection Taking a Backseat to Profits? *Vancouver Sun.* August 7. Final Edition, p. B1.

Times Colonist (Victoria). 1998. Protect Orcas (letter to the editor). August 16, Final Edition, p. 14.

Times Colonist (Victoria). 1998. Whale OK (letter to the editor). August 24, final Edition, p. A9.

Whale Museum (1999a). Available online at <www.whalemuseum.org/downloads/soundwatch/programdescrip.pdf>.

Whale Museum (1999b). Available online at <www.whalemuseum.org/issues.html.>.

Whale Museum (1999c). Available online at <www.whalemuseum.org/museum/press/archives/declining.htm>.

Whale Watch Operators Association Northwest (WWOAN) (2005). Available online at <www.nwwhalewatchers.org/members.html>.

Whale-Watching Operators Create Operating Code (1998). *Canadian Press Newswire.* July 21.

Chapter 7

Treadsoftly An Environmental Education Company Inc.—The Environment and the Business of Backcountry Tours, Part 1: Understanding Stakeholder Issues

Cameron Welsh

THE IDEA

One day during lunch, Cameron and Grant (two MBA students) were discussing their mutual interests in bicycles when Cameron started to reminisce about his summer mountain bike trips to little known backcountry lodges and spectacular alpine meadows in Southern Alberta as well as other parts of the world, such as Indonesia. Grant, butting in, exclaimed that he had spent the summer cycling around Europe. "It would be great to make your avocation your vocation instead of returning to the big business scene after graduation," Grant sighed. "Yeah," said Cameron. "I would choose to take people on trips in the southwest corner of Alberta. It is a beautiful place. Have you ever been there?"

Cameron and Grant had to hurry back to class, but the idea of a mountain biking operation kept popping up in Cameron's mind. He even discussed the idea with several friends and acquaintances concerned about the future of the Crowsnest Pass and received positive responses about this idea from almost everyone. Another friend, Mike, who writes about recreational interests in Southern Alberta, suggested that such a company could become a very successful venture. This was the same message Cameron got from his discussions with some local businesses, residents, and Alberta Economic Development and Tourism. He also attracted the attention of several potential business allies such as two local bed and breakfasts and the general manager of the local interpretative center.

With all this positive response, Cameron started sketching together a management team and drafting the company's goals. *To be successful,* Cameron thought, *the company needs to be environmentally and socially*

Treadsoftly, welcome sign. (Photo courtesy of Robert Bott and Irene M. Herremans.) Reprinted with permission.

View from Crowsnest Mountain. (Photo courtesy of Robert Bott and Irene M. Herremans.) Reprinted with permission.

responsible, involved in responsible backcountry travel, have respect for the environment, lead to long-term sustainability of the local community, respect history, educate about the ecology of the "Crown of the Continent" ecosystem.

From these thoughts Cameron developed the company's mission statement: "To offer environmentally and socially responsible travel that respects the resources of the environment, educates its participants, and contributes to the long-term sustainability of the local community."

Cameron started to wonder what would be a good name for a company with such an elegant mission statement. The name, in a few words, had to capture the entire mission statement but still tell his stakeholders for what the company stood. Finally, he had it! Treadsoftly—that would be the company name. Certainly, that name would remind him of the mission to which he aspired.

Cameron's next step would be to develop a business plan for Treadsoftly, a company that would market and conduct backcountry tours. These tours should include the potential to learn about the history and ecology of the region and to participate in a variety of exciting backcountry activities. Cameron wanted Treadsoftly, unlike its nearest competitor, to base its operations in the local community and use local bed and breakfast operations, restaurants, and other facilities as integral parts of its tour packages.

The best place to provide bicycle tours seemed to be in an area north of a proposed protected area, the Waterton-Castle Wildland Recreation Area (see Figure 7.1). Although the area of operation was currently free from environmental restrictions, Cameron was afraid that it might soon see the effects of the environmental initiatives that were taking place in the region.

FIGURE 7.1. Crowsnest Pass, Alberta, Canada. (Map prepared by Hanako Saito.)

These initiatives included the effort to protect lands from industrial development and the increasing use by a variety of user groups, such as off-highway vehicle users, hunters, fishers, hikers, and industry. If these initiatives materialized, Cameron's bicycling tours might also be excluded.

Cameron started thinking about his management team. He started writing down the strengths of each member and thought about what they might do together to overcome the potential barriers:

1. The lead entrepreneur, Cameron, and his brother, Todd, have roots in the area and their family is well respected in the community, going back four generations.
2. Cameron has recently completed an MBA and has an extensive knowledge of the environment (BSc in biology) and environmental issues, cycling, the cycling industry, and backcountry activities.
3. Todd has a great deal of knowledge of the history of the area, experience in interpretative guiding, and close contacts with members of the community. Todd has spent the past four years as the head guide and researcher for the Ecomuseum Trust in the Crowsnest Pass. The trust operates historical tours in the region and has a mandate to "preserve and interpret the cultural and historical resources of the area."
4. The third member of the team is Cameron's wife, Cheryl. She brings seven years of managerial experience in the service/hospitality industry to the team, as well as a knowledge of cycling and backcountry activities.

See the appendix for the full corporate structure.

If community support for Treadsoftly could be combined with the strength of its entrepreneurial team, Cameron thought it had the potential to become a strong competitor in its industry. However, it needed to overcome the potential drawbacks. Even though Cameron received considerable support for his business idea, further investigations uncovered some potential problems.

BACKGROUND INVESTIGATIONS

Local Economic and Environmental Concerns

As Cameron investigated the prospects for Treadsoftly, he found there were concerns about the sustainability of the local economy and issues related to the effects of economic development on the local ecosystem. Currently, the economy of the area is based primarily on resource extraction industries, such as coal mining, oil and gas, logging, and agriculture (ranching and some crops). This region of Alberta has been looking to expand its economic base especially with industries that result in sustainable economic development for the region such as tourism. Also of note are the following facts:

1. The government of Alberta's realization that tourism will play an important role in Alberta's future economic development
2. The strong attraction this region of Alberta has to visitors looking for something different from the province's main tourist attractions: the cities of Edmonton and Calgary, and Banff and Jasper National Parks

Cameron also found that many residents were concerned that although economic development is needed, the types of development currently under consideration, such as more oil and gas, logging, and the proposal for a large resort area, would have negative effects on the environment. Locals, especially environmentalists, were concerned that the wrong kinds of development could have devastating effects on prime wildlife habitats, watersheds and fish habitats, sensitive ecological areas, and in general disrupt the "Crown of the Continent" ecosystem of Southern Alberta and Northern Montana.

In conversations with local naturalists and environmental groups, Cameron discovered some of the specific environmental concerns:

1. The protection of wildlife habitats for species such as grizzly bears, wolves, elk, deer, moose, wolverines, the wandering shrew, the red-tailed chipmunk, cutthroat and bull trout, and the endangered fisher
2. The protection of some of the top trout streams in Alberta from overfishing and effluents
3. The protection of sensitive alpine lake shorelines, alpine meadows, and the rare plant and animal species that exist within them
4. The increasing use of off-road vehicles
5. The potential for increased hunting
6. The effects that economic development will have on the aesthetic quality and value of the neighboring land
7. The concern about the government invoking environmental access restrictions on nonindustry users in an area that has been free of these types of restrictions in the past

Local Views

Although Cameron could identify with the concerns of the locals, he continued to follow his vision to uncover any environmental barriers to entry. In the process, he came across a 1991 article by Eric Bailey in which concerned local citizens were asked about their views on management of the land in the "Crown of the Continent." Their concerns included compromised wilderness areas and the introduction of ATVs on foot trails.

Cameron pursued these people in his investigation and found that their views had not changed much, and they remained concerned for the sustainability of the region's environment and its economic base.

The Westcastle Development

In a meeting with officials in the town of Pincher Creek, a neighboring community, Cameron got the facts on Vacations Alberta's development proposal for a $72 million resort in the Westcastle Valley just to the north of Waterton Lakes National Park (the Canadian part of the Waterton-Glacier International Peace Park that extends into Montana). Vacations Alberta's plans call for the expansion of the current Westcastle Ski Area to a neighboring ridge, the addition of accommodation facilities, and the development of two eighteen-hole golf courses. The total plan would result in a ski area that would accommodate 3,200 skiers per day and consist of two hotels, eight chateaus (1,198 apartment units), twelve villas (forty-eight townhouses), twelve chalets (forty-eight fourplexs), seventy-two spots for recreational vehicles, twenty-four staff housing units, and the necessary maintenance buildings and access roads. This resort has been planned for the past eighteen years and although it is on hold at present, the idea never seems to die. The Natural Resources Conservation Board (NRCB) approved the plans for the resort in 1994. The NRCB is a quasi-judicial board in the province of Alberta that has responsibility for approving non-energy-related industrial development in the province's wilderness areas. Recent problems and political decisions put the Westcastle project on hold.

The NRCB Ruling

The Westcastle Resort was approved by the NRCB pending the provincial government's willingness to set aside land for a new wildland recreation area and the developer's willingness to alter some of its development plans. The conditions of approval include the following:

1. The creation of the Waterton-Castle Wildland Recreation Area north of Waterton Lakes National Park by the provincial government. The proposed wildland recreation area would be 800 square kilometers in size and under the current ruling the area would consist of 0.6 percent resort area, 7 percent recreational zone, and 92.4 percent wildland zone. A commission of local representatives would manage this new protected area.
2. The accommodation facilities and the golf courses are confined to the west side of the Westcastle River to allow for wildlife movement along existing wildlife movement corridors.
3. The golf courses are developed at least 400 meters downstream from the important wetlands area (massive beaver ponds) lying immediately north of the ski hill.
4. Vacations Alberta proves that there is enough water before proceeding with the development.

The NRCB's ruling has three goals beyond environmental protection including job creation in the area, an enhanced quality of life, and increased opportunities for recreation in Southern Alberta. These goals are stated in the context of the board's perception of a good potential for year-round tourism in the region if it is based on an environmentally sustainable management strategy. However, in its report on the Westcastle development, the NRCB has given little indication as to what this environmentally sustainable management strategy is.

Land and Forest Service

In addition to the Westcastle Development were a number of initiatives from the Land and Forest Service of Alberta Environmental Protection and Alberta Environmental Protection itself. The first initiative was the introduction of the Castle Access Management Plan that was developed with the backcountry users and special interest groups to control access by motorized vehicles to the lands within the Crowsnest Forest District (Land and Forest Service, personal communication, 1994-1995). Although not directly affecting the access for Treadsoftly, it could have affected its operations, depending on the plan's defined area for off-highway vehicle (OHV) traffic, once the plan was put in place in 1996. In addition, Special Places 2000, an initiative by the provincial government to designate protected tracts of land within the province of Alberta, was of some concern. The ENGOs (Environmental Nongovernment Organizations) applied pressure on the government to designate the Castle region as a Special Place, if the

Westcastle development did not occur. The program of Special Places is poorly defined.

Mountain Biking Concerns

From his years of experience in the cycling industry and from reading the literature on mountain biking, Cameron found that the mountain bike provides access to the backcountry for those who did not travel into the backcountry before. Mountain bikes have increased the speed and the distances that groups can travel and changed the way that many bike tour companies operate. Tour companies can offer backcountry tours to a more diverse group of clientele as these bikes and their hybrids are a comfortable way to access the backcountry.

Because the mountain bike is still a relatively new vehicle in which to access the backcountry, many established backcountry users, such as hikers and equestrians, question its impact on the environment. Some scientific evidence suggests that mountain bikes are less impacting than horses and equal to walking if ridden in a sensitive manner, but this evidence is not conclusive.

Other conflicts arise from the perceptions of mountain bikers by other backcountry users. Mountain bike riders often appear to be dressed for some sort of combat; and the bike, although human powered, is still a machine. Other users also perceive a threat to their safety on crowded and multiuse trails due to factors such as speed and the quietness of the bike. As machines, mountain bikes are capable of greater speeds than most other modes of transportation in the backcountry and can cover greater distances in shorter time periods in the backcountry.

While reading a Sierra Club newsletter, Cameron also discovered a startling development—an agreement about mountain bikes signed between the Sierra Club and the U.S. International Mountain Bicycling Association (IMBA). The agreement between IMBA and the Sierra Club states: "Mountain biking is a legitimate form of recreation and transportation on trails, including singletrack, when and where it is practiced in a environmentally sound and socially responsible manner" (Sierra Club Issues New Guidelines, 1998). This is a somewhat shocking development as the Sierra Club has continuously worked to ban mountain bikes from trails since their invention in 1974. What this will actual mean remains an open question.

In further discussions with the rangers in Glacier National Park in Montana, Cameron discovered that the United States Forest Service has made a decision to promote mountain biking on lands within its jurisdiction, something that has been discouraged on most U.S. Forest Service lands in the past.

Cameron feels that these new agreements and new findings will help reduce some of the environmental access concerns. He also feels that the greater need is to develop a community of responsible backcountry users who respect both the environment and other users.

CONCLUSION

Cameron remains active in planning for the future of his company and pondering how he can make sure it satisfies the diverse needs of all the stakeholders. In this process Cameron continues to look for management tools he can use to ensure the future of his company.

APPENDIX: CORPORATE STRUCTURE

1. Cameron: president (off-season planning and administration, and marketing); mountain biking and hiking guide, bike mechanic
2. David: chairman; host, part-time guide, vehicle maintenance
3. Eva: treasurer and secretary; host, bookkeeper, part-time guide
4. Todd: VP interpretative programming; mountain biking and hiking guide
5. Cheryl: mountain biking and hiking guide; in-season administration once the company becomes established
6. Seasonal employees: office duties (e.g., phone); equipment maintenance (e.g., bikes); guiding

BIBLIOGRAPHY

Bailey, E. (1991). Whose Crown Is This? *Environmental Views,* Summer, 13-17.

Eagles, P.J. (1992). The Travel Motivations of Canadian Ecotourists. *Journal of Travel Research,* (31/2) Fall, 3-7.

Galloway, D.J. (1994). Control Models in Perspective. *Internal Auditor,* December, 46-52.

Herremans, I. M. and Welsh, C. (1999). A Model for Regulatory Reform in Canada: From "Command-and-Control" to "Assured Compliance." *Journal of Corporate Environmental Strategy,* 6(2), 152-162.

Reichheld, F.R. (1994). Loyalty and the Renaissance of Marketing. *Marketing Management,* (2/4) 10-21.

Shocker, A.D. and Sethi, S.P. (1974). An Approach to Incorporating Social Performance in Developing Corporate Action Strategies. In Sethi, S. P (Ed.) *The*

Unstable Ground: Corporate Social Policy in a Dynamic Society (pp. 67-80). Los Angeles: Melville Publishing Co.

"Sierra Club Issues New Guidelines on Mountain Biking." (1998). *IMBA Trail News,* 11(1). Also available online at www.imba.com/news/trail_news/11_1/ itn_11_1_sierra_club.

Tourism Canada (1994). *Survey of Adventure Travel Operators in Canada 1993—Preliminary Report.* Tourism Canada.

Welsh, C.N. (1994). *Environmentally Responsible Tourism: An Environmental Audit Framework for Backcountry Bicycle Touring* (First Edition). Working Paper, Faculty of Management, University of Calgary. (and references cited therein).

Welsh, C.N., (1995). *Environmentally Responsible Tourism: An Environmental Audit Framework for Backcountry Bicycle Touring* (Revised Edition). Working Paper, Treadsoftly An Environmental Education Company Inc. (and references cited therein).

Welsh, C. and Herremans, I.M. (1998). Treadsoftly: Adopting Environmental Management in the Startup Phase. *The Journal of Organizational Change Management,* Special Issue on Environmental Entrepreneurship, 11(2), 145-156.

Chapter 8

Treadsoftly An Environmental Education Company Inc.—The Environment and the Business of Backcountry Tours, Part 2: Creating Environmental Controls

Cameron Welsh
Robin E. Reid

Treadsoftly is a family-owned and operated business with five family members currently involved. It is located in the growing tourist area of southwest Alberta in western Canada. Through strong alliances with other tourism organizations, the company now offers a variety of service products:

- Guided outdoor recreational activities including mountain biking, hiking, ridge walking, rock scrambles, trail running, cross-country skiing, and fly fishing
- Cultural and environmental education programs for school-aged children
- Corporate incentive trips
- Corporate and professional development programs

Treadsoftly's original plans were to offer mountain biking and hiking tours, exclusively. However, the product offerings of the company have evolved to capture other market opportunities and to capitalize more fully on the diverse experience and capabilities of its management team. The common link among all of Treadsoftly's programs is creating education- and environmentally friendly experiences in the outdoors for its guests. All product offerings are consistent with the owners' core values.

Time for a break. (Photo courtesy of Robert Bott and Irene M. Herremans.) Reprinted with permission.

Getting ready for a ride. (Photo courtesy of Robert Bott and Irene M. Herremans.) Reprinted with permission.

BEGINNINGS OF ENVIRONMENTAL MANAGEMENT

Prior to opening, Cameron, Treadsoftly's founder (now president), prioritized stakeholder concerns and identified those whom he considered to be the key stakeholders. In this process Cameron identified the land use managers in Alberta's Land and Forest Department, especially those in the Crowsnest Forest District. After numerous discussions with several of Alberta's public lands managers, Cameron knew he needed to develop a vision that could not only satisfy the wants of the land managers but could also satisfy Treadsoftly's corporate values, the concerns of all stakeholders, and Cameron's personal values.

As Cameron was pedaling his bicycle through Fish Creek Park one evening, he found he was continually distracted by thoughts of how to create a plan that would allow him to access the public lands. He stopped pedaling and sat down on the grass so he could think more clearly. If the land managers only knew him better, he was sure they would recognize his strong sense of environmental stewardship and respect for the area in which he wanted to operate.

ADOPTING VALUES AND ETHICS

Cameron began to review what he thought the company concept should be. Treadsoftly is to be a family-run business, and its members are the third and fourth generations of a family that settled during the area's formative years near the turn of the century. One of the goals of the company is to influence others to adopt environmental ethics that will allow the next generations (at least four or more) of the family to enjoy the beauty and biodiversity of the region just as the first four generations of the family did. Then Cameron flashed back to a meeting with the Castle Region's Special Places Committee where Dave, his dad, discussed his vision for the area:

> We set aside a physical space or area as a special place, but really for that space to become special it has to become "special" in the hearts and minds of people. When that happens we begin to treat it in a special way. I'll illustrate that with a story. In the late fall of 1953 my dad and uncle and I came out from Hillcrest in the early hours of the morning, up the Carbondale, crossed it at the Twin Bridges and climbed the hills on the west side of Crawford Valley to hunt elk. At that time the whole of the forest reserve south of the Carbondale was a game preserve and had been for many years. When you combined that with the fact that the fires of the thirties had resulted in a perfect combination

of graze, browse and shelter there were many, many elk, which could be legally hunted outside the forest reserve. From those high hills we watched the sun turn the snow dusted peaks along the South Castle first purple then pink. The beauty of the scene and the fact that it was inaccessible made us forget about the hunt for a good length of time. It was a magical moment. We didn't take home an elk that day, but I know that each of us took home something far more valuable. It was on that day that the Castle became a special place for me

Cameron decided that Dave's vision had to be central to Treadsoftly's management plan, as Dave was chairman of the board for Treadsoftly.

More thoughts flashed trough Cameron's mind. The issue of what is a special place and how to protect the environmental resources of the area are very prominent concerns of the members of the communities. The major concern is that the Crowsnest area might become the next Banff. The Banff-Canmore corridor to the north had seen a large influx of visitors and landowners in the past decade; consequently, there have been significant impacts on the surrounding ecosystem. Therefore, the federal government established a task force to study the environmental impacts occurring in the park. To minimize the potential threats, the park adopted the majority of the task force's 500 recommendations. The people of the Crowsnest Pass area do not want to see the same thing happen to them. Certainly, Cameron said, nearly out loud, "I don't want to see that happen. It would ruin my business."

Then he remembered that in recent years the Crowsnest Pass area had become concerned with the potential growth of backcountry recreation. How do the land managers control these activities along with the industrial activities of oil and gas production, logging, and free-range cattle grazing?

Cameron knew if he could just get access to the public lands that the land managers would not be disappointed with Treadsoftly's performance. Treadsoftly's management had already determined that the key to success was to create a company that could accomplish two things:

1. address the concerns of the community and stakeholders, and
2. at the same time reflect the strong commitment that the members of Treadsoftly had toward protecting their special place.

He just needed to convince the land managers that the company would be responsible. Cameron looked out at the horizon as the last rays of the sun were sliding away. It was getting late and he knew he would be able to think more clearly with a good night's sleep.

THE COMPANY

Cameron reviewed Treadsoftly's mission statement. He recalled that the concerns of the stakeholders along with his personal commitment led to its development. Treadsoftly's mission statement reads as follows:

> Environmentally and socially responsible travel that respects its natural and cultural resources, educates its participants during a firsthand nature experience, modifies their behaviour with respect to actions toward their environment and contributes to the long-term sustainability of the host communities. (Treadsoftly, 1997)

Implicit in this mission statement is that Treadsoftly's success will be the result not only of an environmental and social commitment but an economic commitment as well. If the company is not economically successful, it cannot contribute to the long-term sustainability of the communities.

THE APPROACH

Threat or Opportunity

The process of identifying threats and opportunities had been a drawn-out process. During the process, Cameron identified the main initial threat: The area in which his tours were to take place was under consideration as a protected area. To develop his understanding of what this meant, Cameron asked himself the following questions:

1. What does a protected area mean?
2. How would the area's designation as a protected area change the current policies concerning commercial recreation and land use?
3. Protected areas are designated and regulated by members of the local community. How will the communities' perception of Treadsoftly affect its ability to carry on business?

Instead of allowing these questions to distract the progress of building the company, Cameron looked for a solution that would allow Treadsoftly to proceed and prosper in this environment, be it protected or unprotected. Cameron remembered that other industries, such as oil and gas, forestry, and some commercial recreation, were operating in areas where their operations could be potentially hazardous to the environment. Cameron reviewed these companies again. As he ran down the list, he suddenly stopped. He knew he had the solution to his access problem! Many of the companies in these industries have adopted extensive and comprehensive control systems. The development of a system of environmental controls can be used both to demonstrate a company's commitment to the environment and to measure and report back to the community and key stakeholders.

In reviewing stakeholder concerns, government/commercial recreation, and land-use policies, Cameron identified what could be viewed as threats using a SWOT analysis (strengths, weaknesses, opportunities, and threats). He decided that instead of perceiving them as threats he would turn threats into opportunities with the right controls and systems.

THE STRATEGIC PLAN

Given Cameron's viewpoint the next important questions he had were the following:

1. What is the right control system and what does it have to accomplish?
2. How is the control system executed?

To answer these questions, Cameron identified the key components necessary for the success of Treadsoftly's strategy.

- Identify the potential threats and the strategic approach that will create opportunities from these threats
- Recognize and develop both informal and formal controls
- Lay the groundwork for the use of environmental performance audits
- Identify policy, preliminary measures of performance, and future development of measures
- Communicate with stakeholders

How did Treadsoftly go about the task of putting controls and strategies in place? Cameron learned from industries (such as forestry, mining, and petroleum) that are viewed as having significant environmental risk and impact. These industries are usually comprised of large multinationals (oil and gas) with significant risk from customer boycotts, environmentalist campaigns, etc. These industries are also not viewed as being environmentally benign like tourism. The common factor among the companies in these industries is an Environmental Management System (EMS). So Cameron began by planning an EMS for his business.

EMS

The Environmental Management System (EMS) balances formal control systems (such as policies, codes, and procedures) with informal control systems (beliefs and ethics). The management of Treadsoftly recognized that controls needed to be structured to reflect the company's core commitments. Also, the control system should be part of an ongoing process of self-assessment. Consequently, the monitoring and control measures are selected on the basis of helping the company reach its objectives and to re-set its objectives if appropriate. The management of Treadsoftly recognized the value in developing good control systems at the time of starting a new venture rather than later in its development. The question is which control systems will provide reasonable assurance of achieving the desired outcome set out by the management of Treadsoftly?

Informal and Formal Control Systems

Cameron knew he now needed to identify and select both informal and formal controls. Cameron recognized some important points about controls before proceeding with the development of Treadsoftly's control system:

- Formal controls are guidelines, policies, codes, and procedures but policies can be informal also
- Informal controls include beliefs and ethics
- Informal and formal controls may be interactive or overlap

This latter point was important when it came to one of Treadsoftly's core commitments: "to minimize environmental impact by all parties." To support this commitment, Treadsoftly developed a formal policy to obtain trail use agreement with disposition holders. Although the policy was formal, the coordination of Treadsoftly's activities with other industry activities was accomplished with informal conversations with representatives of companies in the other industries.

Before Cameron developed the core commitment for Treadsoftly, he communicated with local stakeholders to identify local economic and environmental concerns. He recognized that if community issues were identified up front he would be in a better position of aligning Treadsoftly's policies and action plans with the values of the community. Cameron then identified the appropriate control systems by concentrating on balancing stakeholder concerns with developing an ethical code that reflects the core commitments of the company. Policies were then created, followed by action plans, and then methods of measuring whether the company was achieving its intended goals and objectives. By identifying and addressing local values and concerns and aligning these concerns with the values of the company in the planning stage, Treadsoftly experienced very few difficulties in moving through necessary approval processes with land managers and municipalities.

In developing a formal control system, action plans and measurements must be aligned with specific policy statements to be effective. At first, the policies created by Treadsoftly were to be acknowledged with "yes" or "no" answers, as there was not enough detail to develop specific measurements. However, at the end of the first season of operating, Cameron was in a better position to identify how much and what kind of detail are useful measurements of policy.

Treadsoftly's ethical code provides the core commitment and provides direction in the development of policies, procedures, and measurements of progress. The ethical code is based on the following characteristics:

- minimizing environmental impacts by all parties;
- environmental and cultural education;
- creating long-term benefits for the communities affected by tourism; and
- the preservation, conservation, and management of the ecosystem affected by tourism.

The ethical codes provide the background for both informal and formal controls (see Table 8.1).

SUMMARY

Obtaining the end result is contingent upon the approach taken. When Cameron presented his vision and environmental management to the land manager for the Crowsnest Forest District the plan was accepted with a great deal of enthusiasm. The comment from the land manger makes this clear when he said "he wished all operators did their homework like Treadsoftly as it would make his job much easier."

REFERENCE

Treadsoftly: An Environmental Education Company Inc. (1997). Mission Statement. Lundbreck, Canada: Treadsoftly.

TABLE 8.1. Implementation plan: Treadsoftly's mission.

Mission	Objective	Control (Guidelines and Policies)	Examples of Action Plans (Procedures)	Measurement: (input (I) vs. output (O))
Environmentally responsible travel (respects natural resources)	Minimize visitor impacts on the environment	(I) Remain in constant communication with land managers for updates on restrictions (I) Be aware and follow any restrictions on areas (F) Use preexcursion session to judge both technical and physical proficiency of the group members and alter itinerary to match the groups' ability. Provide instruction on riding techniques and bicycle maintenance	(F) Visit or call land manager's office before each excursion (I) Remain flexible in itineraries so that changes can be made when areas are experiencing unacceptable impacts (F) Brief visitors on proper and acceptable behavior and any backcountry regulations in pretrip package and reminders before start of trip	(I) Number of times land manager's office checked before each excursion (I) Number of riders per trail per season (O) Number of infractions and number of infractions resulting in visible environmental degradation
Socially responsible travel (respects cultural resources)	Prepare travelers for encounters with local cultures	(F) Provide quality orientation and interpretation	(I) Pretrip package and Web site contains information on the historical development of the area (F) Provide historical and cultural information during each rest stop	No. of clients indicating "yes" to the questions on the customer satisfaction survey: "Did you read the historical development information contained in the pre-trip package?" "Did your guide provide historical/cultural information on your trip?" "Did you enjoy hearing this information?"

TABLE 8.1. *(continued)*

Mission	Objective	Control (Guidelines and Policies)	Examples of Action Plans (Procedures)	Measurement: (input (I) vs. output (O)
Educates its participants during a firsthand nature experience	Ensure client expectations are realistic.	(I) Pretrip package material discusses likelihood of seeing wildlife and appropriate behavior when sighting wildlife. (F) Discuss appropriate behavior before each excursion and during wildlife sightings.	(F) Monitor behavior during wildlife sightings	No. of wildlife sightings, type of animal, client behavior
Modifies their behavior with respect to actions toward the environment	Encourage preservation, conservation, and management of the ecosystem affected by tourism.	(I) Facilitate visitor contributions to local conservation initiatives during and after the trip.	(F) Provide literature about the conservation groups in the area in a follow-up letter about next year's excursions (Friends of Crowsnest Pass)	Dollar amount of contributions coming from Treadsoftly
Contributes to long-term sustainability of the host communities	Develop a relationship with the local community and adopt local values if compatible with company values	(F) Use locally owned businesses and supplies including transport, accommodations, and restaurants and trip food.	(F) Cross-promotions with other facilities and tour operations	Percentage and dollar amount of costs incurred from vendors within the surrounding area. Economic multiplier of Treadsoftly's operations.

Note: Not all guidelines, policies, procedures, and measures that Treadsoftly is using are included. These are simply given as examples.

I = informal, F = formal.

Chapter 9

Canadian Mountain Holidays: Risk Assessment and Management

Fergus T. Maclaren

Although this case is based on facts, some parts and names of individuals have been fictionalized in order to convey certain theoretical concepts in a setting that is more conducive for instructional purposes.

WHISTLER: Maximum Heli-Skiing Ltd., which operates out of Whistler, British Columbia, had three of its guests killed by an avalanche on Vanguard Mountain on February 17, 1996. Prior to landing on the slope, it had been tested for stability, the skiers had been checked for ability and all skiers and their guide wore emergency radio beacons, which would help rescuers locate them in case of an accident. The operator had also dropped several helicopter loads of clients this year into the area without incident. Yet the police investigation of the tragedy concluded that "it is understood (in the heli-skiing industry) that people know they are pushing adventure to the etreme . . . and no amount of preparation, equipment, and expense can eliminate all risk."

David Chance is an Interior B.C. reporter for the *Vancouver Sun.* He read the press note and was intrigued. After the recent deaths of three European skiers at Tyax Mount Resort near Whistler, a flurry of public opinion had been stirred up regarding heli-skiing safety issues. His editor wanted to look at how the industry was setting its standards for environmental risk assessment while providing high-end skiing for an exclusive clientele. The first and biggest operator, Canadian Mountain Holidays, had agreed to be a subject for this report (see Figure 9.1).

David's background research into risk assessment had uncovered the following information from the Foundation for American Communications (1996):

It is a scientific process of evaluating the adverse effects caused by a substance, activity, lifestyle, or natural phenomenon. The uncertainty inherent in environmental risk assessment means that risk assessors cannot precisely describe the risk. Rather, they should state the range of probabilities, which they found. Although economic, social, and legal factors should not figure in risk assessment, risk assessment is not completely devoid of what might be termed policy decisions.

Three factors should be considered in risk assessment in the back-country.

- *Risk perception:* The perceived degree of risk in undertaking an activity, use of a product or service (e.g., climbing, heli-skiing, or mountain biking).
- *Trust:* The degree of confidence that is placed in the operator, service provider, or manufacturer of a good or service; they have ensured that risk has been considered and minimized (e.g., organizational level of experience, safety procedures, and instruction for both guests and staff).
- *Liability:* The degree to which an operator or service provider and the person(s) affected or involved are liable for the use of its good or service, given the risk minimization controls in place (e.g., waivers, degrees of defined and accepted risk, application of control mechanisms).

With regard to the heli-skiing industry, it is said that there is no thrill in skiing that compares with the sensation of floating through virgin, powder puffs of feathery snow flying over both shoulders as you gently cruise through acres of unmarked snow. Heli-skiing remains, for many, the ultimate ski adventure. It is also one of the most expensive forms of winter recreation, with an average cost of $5,000 to $9,000 per week (Canadian Mountain Holiday, 2005).

Perhaps the biggest perceived drawback to heli-skiing is the number of down days due to inclement weather. However, this is not so; on average, only one half-day per week is lost due to poor weather. Many operators guarantee 60,000 to 100,000 vertical feet of skiing for clients on a weeklong package. However, safety margins can be reduced when storms move in (CMH staff, personal communication).

Given the millions of vertical feet skied each winter by heli-skiers, it is in fact remarkable that there have not been more avalanche deaths. Guides play close attention to snow and wind conditions, frequently stopping during the day to gather information and assess risk. Clients are well-drilled in

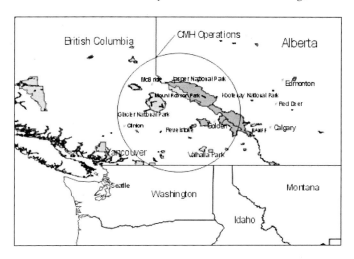

FIGURE 9.1. Canadian Mountain Holidays operations. (Map prepared by Hanako Saito.)

The guide leading the other skiers. (Photo courtesy of Canadian Mountain Holidays.) Reprinted with permission.

Skiing through powder. (Photo courtesy of Canadian Mountain Holidays.) Reprinted with permission.

Checking snow profiles for avalanche conditions. (Photo courtesy of Canadian Mountain Holidays.) Reprinted with permission.

Helicopter and skiers in the Selkirk Mountains. (Photo courtesy of Canadian Mountain Holidays.) Reprinted with permission.

Helicopter getting ready to pick up skiers. (Photo courtesy of Canadian Mountain Holidays.) Reprinted with permission.

safety precautions and rescue techniques should any unfortunate circumstances arise. Of course, no outdoor wilderness activity is ever perfectly safe, and unfortunate accidents can occur. Ironically, many skiers who have lost friends in avalanche accidents return to the mountains to ski another day.

Canadian Mountain Holidays (CMH) was established in the British Columbia Rockies during the winter of 1965, where its first eighteen guests were towed by skidoo into an abandoned lumber camp at the foot of the Bugaboo Glacier. A two-passenger helicopter was used to lift the inaugural group of heli-skiers into the powder-packed bowls. The organization has since built lodges especially for heli-skiing in the remote mountain areas of the Bugaboos, Cariboos, Monashees, and Selkirks in southern and central British Columbia, where the skiing actually takes place. Today, CMH operates twelve areas, sixteen helicopters, accessing about 16,000 square kilometers, and handles between 6,600 and 6,800 clients a season.

David was assigned to visit the Cariboo Lodge at Valemount, near Jasper, close to the B.C./Alberta border. Although he would not be considered an expert skier, he intended to stay for a few days to experience what this promised "thrill" was like and to interview guests and CMH staff on their approach to risks in the deep snowpack at high altitudes.

His contact was Juergen Schmidt, manager of the lodge. That first evening, they sat down together and had a brief interview.

DAVID: Can you tell me a bit about your heli-skiing operation at Valemount?

JUERGEN: Well, David, here in British Columbia, heli-skiing is done in two very different ways: as a day trip or part of a weeklong package. The fourteen heli-skiing operators across the province have their own permit areas, which are licensed by the Crown [government]. These permit areas are strictly adhered to so that operators do not intrude on each other's terrain. Of course, avalanche safety [or danger] is the greatest concern for operators and clients alike.

DAVID: Yes, I read about the Tyax incident last week.

JUERGEN: Well, bookings have been very strong for weeklong trips this winter, and partly because there haven't been any really major accidents in the past three years or so.

DAVID: But this adverse publicity could possibly affect your business?

JUERGEN: Somewhat. This industry is often about perception. If the number of fatal accidents increases, then our client numbers may go down because our professional reputation, and the industry's as a whole, may be tarnished by the negative publicity. There will always be those people who pursue risks like those people who do ice climbing or bungee jumping, but we cater to guests who enjoy the skiing and, for the most part, are risk-adverse.

DAVID: Any other reasons for CMH to manage risk?

JUERGEN: We are first and foremost concerned about the safety of our clients and staff. We also recognize that if we do not take the necessary precautions in terms of staff training, guest education, and equipment maintenance, that there is the potential of being sued by clients for wrongful death or injury for ruinous amounts of money.

DAVID: How does CMH approach the aspects of risk assessment in the training of staff and preparation of guests?

JUERGEN: One approach toward risk is to minimize it by avoiding completely any perceived hazardous activity. CMH's intent instead is to optimize the risk, making the most effective use of control policies and procedures. Each season our personnel, from the area managers to the guides and the house staff, are trained to look after both the guests' safety and enjoyment. We recognize that there is a shared risk. CMH strongly emphasizes the fact that there are risks beyond our control that guests must share with us. Heli-skiing depends to a large degree on weather and snow conditions, elements over which we have no control and that are impossible to predict. Therefore, heli-skiing is not always perfect and guests should prepare themselves for it. The fitter one is, the more that person will enjoy heli-skiing. It is mountain skiing in a totally uncontrolled environment. There are no guarantees as to what guests will encounter during their stay with us. It could be the best skiing of their lives, but it also could be poor and very demanding. In spite of all of our efforts, there are inherent risks and hazards that we cannot control. Since 1965 these hazards have resulted in thirty-one fatalities.

DAVID: Thank you for your frank responses. I'm going for a ski tomorrow. Is there anyone you recommend that I talk to?

JUERGEN: You should also talk to the guides at the crew meeting tomorrow morning, and maybe a few of the guests to get their opinions.

David decided to look around the lodge to identify prospective interviewees among the guests. Juergen had mentioned that Dr. Ian Martin, a prominent Calgary psychologist, and Joan Evans, a CPA from Denver, had been regular guests over the years and might be able to give some perspective on why they ski with CMH.

DAVID: I'm doing a story on risk in the heli-skiing industry. Juergen tells me that you've been CMH "regulars" for the past ten years, and I'd like to get your opinions concerning risk and safety issues when you go heli-skiing.

IAN: Well, CMH provides a handbook to guests before they arrive at a lodge to orient them to the risks and safety issues inherent within the sport. This is reinforced in briefings with guides and emergency procedures such as tracking with Pieps, which are search beacons for skiers buried in avalanches.

JOAN: I've always felt pretty confident in terms of how we are looked after and the precautions that are taken on the choppers and the slope.

DAVID: What are the concerns about the risks inherent in heli-skiing?

IAN: From a professional perspective, I look at it in terms of *risk homeostasis theory*. This theory maintains that in any activity people accept a certain level of subjectively estimated risk to their health, safety, and the other things that they value in exchange for the benefits they hope to receive from that activity—fast cars, exciting jobs, eating and drinking, recreational drug use, romance, adventure sports or whatever. In any ongoing activity, people continuously check the amount of risk that they feel they are exposed to. They compare this with the amount of risk they are willing to accept, and try to eliminate any difference between the two. Thus, if the level of subjectively experienced risk is lower than acceptable, people tend to engage in actions that increase their exposure to risk. If, however, the level of subjectively experienced risk is higher than acceptable, they make an attempt to exercise greater caution. Consequently, they will choose their next action so that its subjectively expected amount of risk matches the level of risk accepted. During the next action, perceived and accepted risks are again compared and the subsequent adjustment action is chosen in order to minimize the difference, and so on.

JOAN: In accounting, we are a little less psychographic and look at the facts instead. Three aspects of risk that we deal with are risk identification, risk measurement, and risk prioritization. We must first determine what risks are inherent in a certain type of business. There are several approaches that we use depending on the situation: exposure analysis; environmental analysis; or threat scenarios. Then, it is necessary to measure each of these risks in some way. Risk can be measured quantitatively through the use of probabilities and numbers, but it can also be measured qualitatively through some rating system such as high, medium, or low. Finally, based on the risk identification process and the risk measurement process, we have to prioritize the risks in order to determine how and in what order we will address them. The difficulty with heli-skiing is that there are so many different parameters in assessing risk.

Guests' attitudes represent only a part of the risk equation. Heli-skiing operators must account for unpredictable factors that include weather monitoring, assessing snow hazards, overall equipment maintenance, and the training of guides and helicopter pilots.

IAN: That may be so, but when you put your money down to ski here, you are recognizing that you are participating in a sport that can have a high degree of risk.

JOAN: I concur that you will want to feel that you are secure, but you should also be aware of the fact that there are factors beyond your own skiing ability that cannot be controlled and may affect your own personal safety.

DAVID: Do either of you follow this pattern?

JOAN: A good friend of mine died in a freak accident. All the avalanche and weather precautions had been taken prior to the day's skiing. Unfortunately, he hit a half-buried tree in a glade, lost consciousness, and suffocated under a foot of snow. As a consequence of this unfortunate experience, I am fairly cautious about where I ski.

IAN: On occasion, I have gone off the marked trail to follow terrain that is blanketed with powder. I'm pretty careful and have not been in any serious situations though. It is the chance to experience the freedom on powder that makes you just break loose.

The next morning before takeoff, David met with Kyle Porter, a senior guide with CMH.

DAVID: Kyle, can you tell me a bit about your background?

KYLE: The focus of our work is the safety and enjoyment of our guests. CMH guides are active mountaineers who have passed a series of comprehensive international examinations to qualify as members of the IFMGA, the International Federation of Mountain Guide Associations. As an ongoing basis we take refresher courses in avalanche hazard evaluation and stabilization, weather analysis, and emergency medical techniques.

DAVID: How do you face risks?

KYLE: Mountain guides think about safety in a situational context. Consideration of safety for each situation necessitates a sequence of cognitive processes: the perception of danger attendant to the situation, the assessment of hazard in light of uncertainties, and the management of risk by free choice. Perception of danger refers to the anticipated level of danger in any given situation that may influence further consequential safety measures. The anticipated safety margin is dependent on the margin of security that is determined and the anticipated margin of survival that would arise with a mishap (see Exhibit 9.1).

KYLE: For example, if the probability for an avalanche is twenty percent on open slopes in warm weather, then the probability of not having an avalanche is eighty percent. This percentage is referred to as your margin of security. If we ski on treed terrain or in cold weather the margin of security might increase to ninety percent. The margin of security is multiplied by the probability of survival if an avalanche does occur. The margin of survival can be increased with the use of good avalanche equipment and skiers that are trained in avalanche rescue. If the margin of survival is thirty percent, then the anticipated margin of safety is either twenty-four percent or twenty-seven percent.

DAVID: What sort of risk issues do you face as a guide?

KYLE: There are constantly changing elements of risk that we have to deal with, such as operating rotary-wing aircraft in a difficult environment, clients' expectations, and constantly changing weather and snow conditions in the high alpine.

DAVID: Can you address some of these issues?

KYLE: In terms of our helicopters, the pilots are capable and very experienced in mountain flying. Full-time engineers based in each area provide ongoing maintenance. Weather conditions, however, can either ground or limit flights. We also have to carefully educate guests on how they should properly debark from the helicopters, given the slight tilt of the main rotor, which can suddenly dip in shifting snow conditions. Continuous communication between all areas of the operation allows for rapid access to outside facilities, if necessary. In the helicopter we carry resuscitation/rescue equipment and the guides carry a pack of equipment, which enables them to handle accidents, "on the spot." In most cases, the

---

EXHIBIT 9.1. Margin of safety.

Anticipated Margin of Safety = Margin of Security × Anticipated Margin of Survival

When the snow becomes very soft in the spring due to increasingly warmer temperatures, the anticipated margin of safety (AMS) is gauged by the margin of security in terms of snowpack stability (in case of avalanche) and weather conditions, multiplied by those elements such as treed and/or level terrain that holds the snowpack better than open slopes. If the AMS is too hazardous, then CMH will simply not allow guests to ski.

helicopter is able to land close to the injured person and evacuate quickly. If evacuation is necessary, the cost is the guests' responsibility and we recommend that guests carry insurance for any ambulance-type service. Clients' expectations are also an important consideration, considering the promise of one hundred thousand vertical feet of skiing in virgin powder and the amount of money they spend to ski with CMH. Although the safety and enjoyment of our guests are paramount, clients expect both, but these considerations can also pull in different directions. The advent of specially designed "fat boy" skis, which are shorter and much wider than traditional downhill skis, have been promoted as the most significant development in helicopter skiing since the helicopter. The skis' broad surfaces make them float on, rather than dive through, deep snow. Before the fat skis, we advertised that strong intermediate skiers could come heli-skiing and have a good time. In reality, only about a few catch on immediately, while others gradually get the hang of it through the week. Now, it's more like seventy-five percent, since the fat skis facilitate the transfer of skills from groomed-slope downhill skiing to powder skiing. Unfortunately, new developments in ski technology also mean that skiers become overconfident in terms of their own abilities, which can sometimes result in less control in hazardous situations. It also means that aggressive skiers will use them to go off marked trails into areas that are "steeper and deeper."

DAVID: And what about snow conditions?

KYLE: Probably the most important aspect of our work is assessing changing weather and snow conditions. We are constantly trying to expand our understanding of the complexities of snow and avalanches. A continuing effort is made to monitor weather and snow conditions and to evaluate snow stability. This information is shared among all our areas on a daily basis. Occasionally, stabilization with explosives is done from the helicopter. Changing weather and snow conditions also create snow instability which leads to avalanche hazard. This refers to the exposure of people or property to the probability of avalanches starting, which is also affected by changing terrain. Uncertainties in the probability of avalanches starting are further compounded with the uncertainties in the extent of people's exposure to them. We use a rating scale for these kinds of hazard assessments (see Exhibit 9.2).

KYLE: This can be understood better if we use an example of risk associated with driving a car. One variable used to determine car insurance premiums is your degree of risk. Statistically, we can determine the probability of a person getting into an accident. If we multiply the probability by the magnitude or consequences of the accident (how much damage will be

EXHIBIT 9.2. Risk rating scale.

Risk = Consequences × (Exposure × Probability)
or
Risk = Consequences × Hazard

When flying helicopters from CMH lodges, the risks can be predicated on the hazard of bad weather and the potential consequence of crashing. Risk management in terms of pilot experience and the helicopter's flight capability would determine unsuitable flying conditions. The risk would be lessened if you fail to fly in bad weather or do not expose yourself to other hazardous conditions.

done), then we can quantify the risk. To the extent that the person does not expose himself or herself to hazardous driving situations [such as driving to work, driving at night, driving on icy streets], the probability of getting into an accident is lessened and therefore the hazard is lessened.

DAVID: How do you manage these risks?

KYLE: We try to align our own expectations of safety and enjoyment with those of our clients. Then, rather than applying a maximum/minimum analysis to risk, we seek an optimum solution. As risks are determined, control corresponds with the extent of perception, and guests and guides then take appropriate steps in terms of avoidance, mitigation, or the conscious acceptance of the choices made. In exercising our free choice in any given situation, commensurate with their levels of training, experience, and instinct, guides are continuously determining margins of security through a sequence of situations. Allowance must be made for human error on the parts of both guests and the guide; and given the threshold of acceptable risk over a background of residual risk, provision must be made for an accident.

DAVID: Any final comments?

KYLE: I should add that the risk is all of ours—it belongs to each individual and each corporation involved on the run that day, not just the individual guide who led them on the trip that day. A guide will never know the actual margin of safety, only the anticipated one, and he or she will never truly know how safe a day's program actually was.

As David walked to the helicopter that would take him up for the first run of the day, he felt reassured by the professional manner exhibited by CMH staff loading gear and assisting guests. Yet Kyle's last comments had made him a little uneasy.

BIBLIOGRAPHY

Bailey, Reade. (1993). Breaking Rank. *Ski.* January, 57(5).

Bruns, Walter. (1996). Snow Science and Safety for the Mountain Guide. Presented at the *International Snow Science Workshop.*

Canadian Mountain Holiday. (2005). www.canadianmountainholilday.com.

Carlson, Lee. (1995). The Fresh Revolution. *Skiing.* December, 48(4).

Center for Environmental Journalism (CEJ). (1994). Risk Assessment: Useful or Overused? Available online at <http://campuspress.colorado.edu/CEJ/Brfings/Risk.html>. Panel presentation at the University of Colorado at Boulder April 27.

Foundation for American Communications (FACS). (1996). *Reporting on Risk: A Journalist's Handbook on Environmental Risk Assessment.* Available online at <http://www.facsnet.org/report_tools/guides_primers/risk/main.html>.

Hi-tech Sports Hazard to Alps: Roads, Rails Hard on the Environment. (1995). *The Vancouver Province,* March 28, p. A36.

Howard, Ross. (1996). Three European Skiers Die During Ultimate Adventure. *The Globe and Mail,* December 18, p. A10.

Korobanik, John. (1995). Heli-Ski Is the Ultimate Thrill; Fat Skis Make it Fun and Easier. *The Edmonton Journal,* December 21, p. C6.

McNamee, David. (1996). *Assessing Risk.* Altamonte Springs, FL: The Institute of Internal Auditors.

Pearl, Judea. (1988). *Probabilistic Reasoning in Intelligent Systems: Networks of Plausible Inference.* San Francisco: Morgan Kaufmann Publishers, Inc.

Ski the High Country: Endless Powder and Awesome Scenery Make Heli-Skiing an Exhilarating Experience. (1995). *The Vancouver Sun.* January 27, p. B6.

Threndyle, Steven. (1994). Your Own Time: Powder to the People. *The Globe and Mail,* November 25, p. 93.

von Neudegg, Marty. (1996). *Who's Risk Is It?* Presented at the Banff Festival of Mountain Films. November, Banff, Alberta.

Wilde, G.J.S. (1994). *Target Risk.* Toronto: PDE Publications.

Chapter 10

Ski Resorts: Enjoyment versus Environmental Responsibility— Does There Have to Be a Choice?

Simon Hudson

"You know, it gets harder and harder to choose where to snowboard," said Rob. "To top it off, we're supposed to consider the environment too before going anywhere!"

"What do you mean?" said Jason and Steve in unison.

The lads had gotten together to decide where to go for their annual snowboarding trip. Steve was checking out resort Web sites for special lift pass deals. Jason was looking through a big pile of *Ski* magazines to find out about new lifts and trails in the resorts. Rob was reading an article from *Ski Area Management.*

Rob continued: "It says here that there is a new scorecard report produced by a coalition of conservation groups that grades ski areas on environmental criteria, and they are urging us to choose the resorts with the best grades."

"What do you think?" he asked his friends.

INTRODUCTION

Of the number of skiers, there are approximately 70 million downhillers worldwide, but these numbers have been stagnant since the late 1980s (Hudson, 2000). Consolidation has led to fewer ski resorts, and in a highly competitive marketplace, these resorts have to satisfy an increasingly

Quotes from Hudson, S. (2002) "Environmental Management in the Rockies: The Dilemma of Balancing National Park Values while Making Provision for Their Enjoyment," previously published in *Journal of Case Research,* 22(2): 1-14.

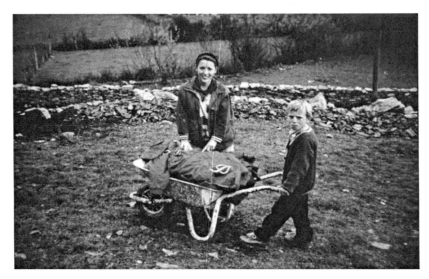

Aspen snowmass uniforms in Kosovo. (Photo courtesy of Aspen Skiing Company.) Reprinted with permission.

Snowboarding. (Photo courtesy of Aspen Skiing Company.) Reprinted with permission.

A snowboarder works his way down the snowy mountain. (Photo courtesy of Aspen Skiing Company.) Reprinted with permission.

Composting at Aspen. (Photo courtesy of Aspen Skiing Company.) Reprinted with permission.

Aspen Snowmass - Hotel Jerome in Aspen. (Courtesy of Aspen Skiing Company.) Reprinted with permission.

demanding and fragmented market, while facing major challenges to further product development. One such challenge is the growing opposition to development based on environmental issues. Skiing is now cast in the same light as timber and mining and is being called the next extractive industry, rather than a socially beneficial form of recreation. The dilemma of balancing the protection of the national forests or national parks while making provision for their enjoyment is a long-standing one, which has become progressively more difficult with the continued increase in recreation and tourist demand. Commercial skiing evolved when attitudes were quite different to those that apply today. Primary importance is attached to heritage and preservation.

"That is pretty heavy stuff," said Steve. "Tell me more."

REACTIONS TO THE ENVIRONMENTAL
IMPACTS OF SKIING

Conflicts between environmentalists and ski resort developers can be found in ski areas around the world. In the Alps, the mountains are among Europe's most threatened wilderness, with the rapid growth of skiing central to the crisis. Destruction has been caused by deforestation and altering the use of traditional alpine land for construction of dams, skiing facilities, and hotels, and by the dumping of waste which has polluted nearby lakes. It is not just a matter of physical destruction and the disappearance of rare habitats. Problems have been created by building ski lifts and cable cars, new roads to allow coaches (buses) up the mountains, avalanche fences, car pollution, and litter. The landscapes of the western Alps in France, Switzerland, and Austria are under serious threat from tourism, especially from the development of higher-elevation resorts (Hudson, 1996).

In North America, opposition to ski resort expansion and development has centered on environmental issues. Well-financed environmentalists are now battling ski resorts of all sizes. With a few exceptions, virtually every form of construction or expansion that is proposed for ski areas is being challenged. Even replacement lifts and improvements to on-mountain lodges are drawing intense opposition (Castle, 1999a). In Colorado, the Canadian lynx population currently have land needs that are reportedly dwarfing those of Vail, Steamboat, and other ski areas (Best, 1999). The U.S. Forest Service, whose land accommodates 134 ski areas and 60 percent of skiers, wants a higher priority to physical and biological resources than to human uses of the forest lands.

In Canada, Lake Louise and three other ski areas in Alberta are pursuing legal action against Parks Canada and the Heritage Minister over a new policy that would cut back ski area operations, cap daily skier capacity, and restrict future expansions in Banff and Jasper National Parks (see Figure 10.1). In the spring of 2000, legislation was introduced in Parliament outlining new rules for restrictive development in Banff and other national parks—and more changes are pending (Dolphin, 2000). The ski areas immediately hired attorneys and a high-profile former newspaper editor, Crosbie Cotton, spokesperson for the National Ski Areas Association, who says that "the federal government has come down with arbitrary, autocratic rulings that threaten the long-term future of skiing in Alberta . . . and they could cause the industry here to die the death of 1,000 cuts" (Cotton, 2000, personal communication).

In Japan, the construction and enlargement of ski resorts has caused serious environmental problems (Tsuyazaki, 1994), but environmentalists have little power. Like Europe and North America in the 1960s and 1970s, the

FIGURE 10.1. Ski resorts in Canada and the United States. (Map prepared by Hanako Saito.)

construction of new ski resorts in Japan today is for tourism rather than for the recreation of residents, and therefore the primary motivations are economic. Environmental deterioration includes landscape fragmentation, soil erosion, and noise and air pollution. Environmental considerations are often ignored during ski resort construction, and any legal regulation to restrict ski resort construction is not effective (Tsuyazaki, 1994).

In Australia, the community benefits accruing from skiing have not been without environmental degradation and impacts will be difficult and costly to repair and maintain (Good and Grenier, 1994). Severe soil erosion has occurred in many construction sites, as well as damage to hiking trails, adjacent vegetation, and groundwater. Also, aquatic ecosystems have suffered from sedimentation and pollution; water quality has deteriorated; and weed and feral animal populations have increased in villages. The environmental impacts have the potential to exceed the capacity of management to adequately control the causes and to rectify the environmental damage.

"Wow!" said Jason. "I didn't realize these problems existed. I would have thought that skiing and snowboarding were environmentally friendly. Surely they can't be as bad as other industries?"

"Well," said Steve, "that's what the ski operators are claiming. The next part of this article puts forward the arguments from the opposite camps. Listen to this . . ."

KEY STAKEHOLDERS

The key stakeholders in most conflicts have been depicted in Figure 10.2 and consist of the following groups:

1. ski operators/businesses;
2. residents/employees;
3. environmental groups;
4. government/regulatory agencies; and
5. skiers.

Point of View: Ski Operators/Businesses

Notable among the arguments countering the position of environmentalists include: ski areas around the world represent a tiny percentage of land, and the ski industry has traditionally maintained that its effects are far less

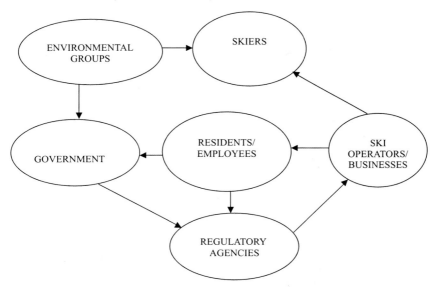

FIGURE 10.2. Key stakeholders in the conflicts. Note that arrows indicate direction of influence.

damaging than economic alternatives such as logging, mining, and agriculture. Ski operators argue that skiing, as with most forms of tourism, is essentially a low-impact activity. Other alternatives to tourism for the purpose of income creation, such as the manufacturing industry, often have more impacts on the environment than tourism. In the United States, compared with logging, mining, and grazing, skiing constitutes a minute percentage of national forest lands—less than one-tenth of 1 percent, or 190,000 acres out of 191 million acres—but accommodates recreation for millions of people (Castle, 1999a).

Also, skiing focuses on a concentrated, high-density recreational use, leaving millions of acres available for dispersed uses such as hiking, camping, cross-country skiing, and mountain biking. These other activities can cause a much wider impact and create more serious management challenges for public resource agencies. In Banff National Park, the ski areas are contained within long-established, unalterable boundaries that comprise a little less than 0.5 percent of Banff and Jasper's combined area (Koch, 2000). Furthermore, in most mountain communities, summer tourism usually draws much higher visitation than winter tourism. The impact of these summer visitors extends throughout the whole altitudinal range of the mountains.

Ski operators also point to the lack of science on which many arguments are based. In a survey of environmental attitudes in the United States, researchers discovered that the environmental knowledge on which both ski operators and environmentalists base their opinions is "not encouragingly high" (Fry, 1995, p. 70). The eighty-page study concluded that inflammatory arguments over development in the mountains would not disappear until ski resort residents, environmental protectionists, and area operators better understand the environmental and economic facts. Greg McKnight, director of Banff/Lake Louise Tourism Bureau, believes that the environmentalists are too extreme, making "outrageous claims that they then back down on" (McKnight, 2000, personal interview) Crosbie Cotton of the National Ski Areas Association also questions the validity of the data that environmentalists use, believing that the "quality of science is highly emotional" (Cotton, 2000, personal interview).

Point of View: Employees/Residents

Although some have aligned themselves with environmental groups, the majority of employees and residents understandably object to calls from environmentalists to close down ski areas. The development of skiing has provided a variety of benefits, including foreign exchange earnings, income, employment, and economic diversification. For many ski resorts, tourism represents the only realistic development option. In the Alps, tourism has saved whole facets of alpine culture and economy since the nineteenth century (Prince Aga Khan, 1994). Skiing can make a significant contribution to the socioeconomic development of host societies and surrounding regions. For example, in the Rocky Mountains, environmentalists are attempting to remove skiing from the national parks, yet the Alberta ski industry constitutes a significant component of the province's tourism industry, and in the winter months skiing forms the backbone of the industry. Some locals in Banff say that environmentalists who want to restrict tourism fail to take into account that the town survives solely from the revenue brought in by visitors (Morrison, 2000). Brad Pierce, former head of Association for Mountain Parks Protection & Enjoyment (AMPPE), a body representing 150 businesses in Banff and Jasper, claims that the environmentalists are "a philosophically zealous movement who want to put an end to most recreations . . . they don't want a solution to this conflict" (Pierce, 2000, personal interview).

Recreation and leisure sports in the Australian Alps have contributed much to the general welfare of many Australians through the very large investment in facilities. Good and Grenier (1994, p. 26) say that

> it is impossible to measure the total financial benefits accruing to society from the integration of recreation and leisure sports, environmental awareness, and community health and well-being, but it is accepted as being in the order of hundreds of millions of dollars annually.

Socher (1992) points to the positive impacts of skiing in the Austrian Alps that have enabled the financing of cultural buildings and services (theaters, conventions, musical events) and the touristic infrastructure (ski lifts, pools, mountain huts, etc.) that can be used by the local population. In Calgary, Canada, Ritchie and Smith (1991) have highlighted the long-term benefits to the local population from hosting the Winter Olympic Games in 1988.

Host communities are often portrayed as passive victims of acculturation and the affluence and lifestyle of tourists. In an in-depth anthropological study of the village of St. Anton in Austria, McGibbon (2000) found that members of the community have responded creatively to the challenges and opportunities brought by tourism, actively pioneering and promoting ski tourism and generating new social forms. McGibbon describes how in the past most residents of St. Anton were extremely poor mountain farmers who had to labor intensively to wrest a living from the hostile, mountainous terrain. Children as young as six years old had to travel to Germany in the summer to find work on farms. It was against this backdrop of rural poverty and outward migration that ski tourism began to develop in the region. Now, skiing is also an important individual, social, and communal activity in the village, and it can play a major role in the formation of local identity.

> "There are some really different points of view on the environmental impact of skiing," remarked Jason. "What do the other groups say? Does anyone agree?"

Point of View: The Environmental Groups

Membership in environmental organizations is growing. Currently, there are 2.2 million members in the National Trust and 250,000 in Friends of the Earth. Surveys show that the majority of the public are sympathetic to environmental initiatives, expecially in the tourism sector (Hudson, 2004). The media are largely pro-green and tourism has been getting increasingly critical coverage. In Europe, Mountain Wilderness, Alp Action, the World Wildlife Fund (WWF), and the Pro Natura Valais (LVPN), are just a few of the many organizations that have dedicated themselves to raising the awareness of environmental problems and the prevention of further damage. Ski resort developers are finding it increasingly difficult to expand due to opposition from these groups.

In the United States, ever since the Sierra Club halted the Disney Company's development of Mineral King in 1969, environmental groups opposed to ski area expansions have run into an array of regulations (The National Environment Policy Act, Clean Air and Water Act, Endangered Species Act, etc.) designed to slow, redirect, or block the ambitions of mountain developers. The prime targets for environmental groups in the United States are the big four: Vail Resorts, Intrawest, the American Skiing Company, and Booth Creek Holdings. Using the Internet as their rallying point, the groups have formed alliances in the United States. Just recently, a coalition of grassroots conservation groups released a report that grades commercial ski areas throughout the West on a host of environmental criteria (see the appendix). The groups, known collectively as the Ski Area Citizens' Coalition, say the report is designed to give environmentally conscious people the information they need to plan a responsible skiing or snowboarding vacation. The coalition urges skiers and snowboarders to go to resorts with positive environmental grades. They are critical of the National Ski Areas Association's (NSAA) environmental charter (referred to later) because it does not include any meaningful environmental protection and skirts the real damage that ski areas cause: destruction of wildlife habitat; secondary impacts from private land development; and depletion of water supplies for snowmaking.

In Canada, several groups have been fighting ski resort development in the national parks. One of the most powerful groups, the Bow Valley Naturalists (BVN), is a nonprofit, volunteer-organized, environmental group whose focus is in the Banff National Park and the Bow Valley. The president, Mike McIvor, is a dedicated conservationist and has been working to preserve and protect the Bow Valley area for more than thirty years. He believes that downhill skiing "is not an appropriate use of the National Park," but he is worried about Parks Canada "bending to the desires of the ski operators" (McIvor, 2000, personal communication). He says that somehow the ski operators need to be convinced that survival without growth is a possibility.

Like the Bow Valley Naturalists, the Alberta Wilderness Association (AWA) belives that downhill ski areas, because of their dependence on facilities and on the manipulation of natural landscapes and processes, are inappropriate within national parks. Ben Gadd (1998, pp. 1-5) from AWA, believes skiing to be

> the crack cocaine of recreational economies: dirty, damaging, and addictive as hell. Like trail-motorcycling, like snowmobiling, like road building, logging, mining, and a host of other wilderness-wrecking activities that started small and got out of control before they were stopped, mechanized skiing should have ended in the national parks long ago.

Point of View: The Government/Regulatory Agencies

In Canada, the ski areas in the national parks believe that their war is essentially political. The Liberal party members in Ottawa are responding to pressure from a significant (in their view) voting constituency, and the vague environmental sentiments of the general public. Former Heritage Minister Sheila Copps, the minister in charge of Canada's national parks, makes decisions regarding Banff's ski areas. "Our national parks are a national treasure and among the best loved symbols of Canadian identity" (Parks Canada, 2000).

Parks Canada (the agency responsible for management of Banff National Park) insists that it has no intention of shutting down the ski hills. Charlie Zinkan, executive director of Mountain Parks for Parks Canada, states that the National Parks Act makes a clear commitment to the continuation of skiing in the parks (Zinkan, 2000, personal communication). "There won't be any more, but those that are here, are here to stay." Zinkan states that the ski areas have to be managed according to long-range plans, but these documents are at best "old, out of date, and inefficient . . . they don't reflect the changes in technology and changes in environmental legislation." He is now waiting for new long-range plans that have to be finalized with ski area operators within two years.

Zinkan denies that Parks Canada is "in the pockets" of environmentalists. "The suggestion that our priority of ecological integrity means shutting down parks to people is ridiculous" he says. Bill Fisher, the park's superintendent, suggests that assertions that special interest groups have a growing influence on Parks Canada policy are unfounded: "Banff National Park is not captive to one group and I want to make that clear" (Remington, 2000, p. A9).

In the United States, implementation of the National Forest Management Act of 1976, which called for formulation of management plans for each national forest, has resulted in widespread citizen involvement in the agency's planning and policymaking process. In addition, more specialized jurisdictions and agencies are becoming involved in the approval of ski-area development. The U.S. Forest Service has seen its "lead-agency" authority over winter recreation on public lands challenged, and sometimes compromised, by: the Environmental Protection Agency (EPA), which is now stretching its mission to include land-use issues unrelated to pollution; the Army Corps of Engineers, which is challenging threats to wetlands; and the U.S. Fish and Wildlife Service, which can trump any expansion that might impact rare or endangered plant and animal species. Thus far, coordination among the various regulatory federal agencies over ski-area permit applications has been nearly nonexistent (Castle, 1999a). Many state and local governments have extensive environmental programs that often overlap with federal regulations. This can be confusing and frustrating. In addition, the recent emphasis on cumulative effects has greatly complicated the analyses of development impacts on Forest Service lands. The lack of clarity over what "cumulative impacts" means has resulted in use of inconsistent requirements for different ski area projects.

Point of View: Skiers

The past two decades have witnessed a dramatic increase in environmental consciousness worldwide. Leisure travelers are increasingly motivated by the quality of destination landscapes, in terms of environmental health and the diversity and integrity of natural and cultural resources. The limited research on skiers and their environmental commitment has produced contradictory results. A Roper survey discovered that skiers, more than many other groups of tourists, were especially worried about the environmental results of development and growth (NSAA, 1994). Also, *Ski Magazine* conducted numerous independent surveys over the past decade showing skiers are more concerned about the environment than all other sports enthusiasts (Castle, 1999a). Skiers overall do not believe ski areas help the environment. However, Fry (1995) found that skiers don't have strong views about the environment, and more experienced skiers actually favor expansions. At a meeting of the Environmental Protection Agency (EPA) in Denver (November 1999), delegates agreed that it was unlikely consumers would make mountain resort vacation decisions based on how environmentally friendly the resort was (Harbaugh, 1999).

In a recent study of skiers in Banff, Hudson and Ritchie (2001) found a general lack of knowledge among skiers about environmental issues pertaining to skiing. The majority believe skiing and snowboarding to be environmentally friendly but say ski terrain should be limited because it disturbs wildlife habitat and migratory paths. Nearly half of the skiers agreed that skiing numbers in the national parks should be capped to protect the environment, but Canadians would be willing to pay significantly less money for lift tickets than Americans or British skiers to visit a green ski resort. In a recent Austrian survey, the majority of skiers (59 percent) were prepared to pay an environmental tax if it would mean that something constructive would be done for the environment in their chosen holiday resort (Weiss et al., 1998). Although the skiers in the Austrian study showed a high degree of environmental awareness, they were not prepared to restrict their skiing to protect the countryside and did not agree with limited sale of lift tickets.

"Well, this is all very interesting," commented Rob. "It's all very well suggesting that skiers and boarders may or may not prefer a more environmentally friendly resort. But how do we know if one resort is better than the other?"

"I think if you read the rest of the article you may well have a better idea," suggested Steve.

THE GREENING OF SKI RESORTS

For the most part, the ski industry recognizes the potential for environmental impact its activities may create (Todd and Williams, 1996). In June 2000, about 160 American ski areas, including the United States' twenty biggest, signed the Sustainable Slopes Charter. The charter was developed with input from a variety of ski industry leaders; environmental groups;

federal, state, county and local agencies; outdoor recreation groups; ski industry suppliers; and other stakeholders. The charter is a voluntary set of guiding principles and tools that assist ski resorts to effectively integrate environmental protection concepts into all aspects of design, maintenance, and operation of ski resorts. It highlights dozens of rules for ski areas in the management of their resorts and construction of new facilities. The charter calls for the following:

- use of high-density development to cut back on sprawl;
- reductions in water consumed by snowmaking; and
- savings in the energy required for lodges, vehicles, and ski lifts.

Although ski resorts acknowledge that mistakes were made twenty, thirty, and forty years ago, there is both a new management style and a new commitment to coexist with the environment (Castle, 1999b). The following examples from different countries show how some resorts have tried to tackle the environmental problems linked to mass tourism by demonstrating a commitment to environmental stewardship.

The United States

The Aspen Skiing Company has taken a lead in showing ski destinations how to be environmentally correct. It was the first to appoint an Environmental Affairs Director and its green campaign has won numerous awards, the most recent being the 2000 Travel Industry Association of America (TIA) Environmental Odyssey Award. Initiatives include the installation of a wind-powered surface lift; a state-of-the-art computer system that monitors and adjusts energy consumption among lifts and snowmaking pumps; and the ski industry's first environmental Web site and intracompany environmental newsletter. The Aspen Skiing Company states that it produced .038 tons of carbon dioxide per skier at a cost of $2.67 per skier for the 1999-2000 season. Recently, Aspen went into the deconstruction business by recycling nearly 90 percent of the building materials that came from demolishing the Snowmass Lodge and Club, a hotel that is being converted into environmentally friendly, high-occupancy timeshare units. Aspen's new consciousness is reflected in virtually every one of its departments. Employees donate $1 a week to an environmental fund, which is matched by contributions from the company and from the Aspen Foundation. Thus far, $220,000 has been divided up among wetlands development, environmental education in schools, water protection projects, and trail restorations.

In California, Sierra-At-Tahoe has won awards for its overall environmental excellence. The resort has demonstrated a determined and enthusiastic commitment to virtually all areas of environmental enhancement— from conservation to precycling, recycling, education, wildlife protection, community outreach, environmental partnering, special events, and area design. Established in 1993 to foster environmental awareness among both guests and employees, the program demonstrates continuing creative and innovative efforts in addition to challenging its neighbors to strive for environmental excellence.

At Sundance Resort in Utah, evidence of actor Robert Redford's commitment to the environment is everywhere (Trinker, 1999). In fact, according to a new report produced by the Ski Areas Citizens' Coalition of conservation groups that grades ski areas on environmental criteria, Sundance is the most environmentally friendly ski area in the western United States (Hansen, 2000). The report grades ski resorts' performance against criteria such as expansion into undisturbed land and environmental efficiency. Sundance has always resisted the temptation to grow bigger, and in the early 1990s Redford removed over 200 parking spaces in the main parking lot at Sundance Moutain's base, landscaped the area, planted additional trees, and built wooden fencing to soften the entrance to the resort. To encourage carpooling, the fourth person in every car now skis free; recycling bins are in every room; and guests can request fewer linen changes to save on water consumption. Sundance also uses its snowmaking equipment strategically to minimize impact on water and wildlife.

Also in Utah, Snowbird Resort's environmental initiatives include the creation of on-mountain interpretive signage, the publication of a field guide to trees and wildlife for area guests, establishment of a monthly ecology lecture series, and development of a Ski-Cology children's program. The programs are designed not so much to attract more customers but to inspire and educate employees and the community.

Lastly, in the United States, Heavenly Ski Resort in Lake Tahoe has made significant investments in environmental improvements. As part of its mitigation for new lifts and trails, Heavenly has created freshwater marshes along alpine streams, obliterated old logging roads, reseeded exposed runs, built rock supports to stabilize slopes, and identified important wildlife foraging areas so that they could be avoided in future construction.

Europe

In Europe, no single ski resort stands out from the others in terms of its commitment toward the environment. However, evidence shows a new trend in environmental stewardship. In Klosters, Switzerland, following consultation with all interested parties (the lift companies, forest service, ski guides, hunters, etc.), environmentally sensitive areas have been set aside to protect flora and fauna. Areas are clearly marked and a brochure highlights the location of the areas, informing skiers of the harmful effects of skiing in the forest. In order to regulate traffic, Lech, Austria, now limits the number of ski-lift passes available to day-trippers to 14,000. Signs on the motorway approaches from Germany indicate when the resort is full and advise drivers to try alternative resorts.

Canada

Intrawest has always taken responsibility seriously when planning on-mountain development. Environmental stewardship is an important part of the process. Arthur De Jong, Whistler/Blackcomb's mountain planning and environmental manager, ensures that for all projects, the environment is impacted in the least possible way. "Working with and understanding the environmental groups has always been a priority for us," he says (De Jong, 2000, personal communication). He has created something called the Habitat Improvement Team, a corps of managers and employees who help local conservation groups restore habitat for fish, wildlife, and plant species in Whistler valley. Whistler is also spending $1.5 million over a five-year period for watershed restoration on its lands in a program called Operation Green-Up. De Jong believes that "the environment is the cornerstone of making Whistler the best resort in the world . . . if we choose to lead conservation then we can control our own destiny, but if we choose to follow, others will determine it for us" (De Jong, 2000, personal communication).

Whistler has become the first community in North America to adopt The Natural Step sustainability framework as a formal, integral part of its municipal policy and plans for achieving sustainability. Leaders from all sectors of the Whistler community are collaborating in a natural, step-based program of sustainable development. "We all understand that an economically and socially sustainable resort community depends on the sustainability of its surrounding ecology," says Jim Godfrey, the Municipal Manager at Whistler (Godfrey, 2000, personal communication).

THE DECISION

The three snowboarders who are choosing their winter destination have many unanswered questions. Are environmentalists unreasonable in their demands, or should skiing be prohibited in protected areas? Are ski operators doing enough to mitigate the environmental effects of their operations? Should more weight be given to the arguments of local residents and tourism employees? Should skiers and snowboarders be expected to make vacation decisions based on environmental considerations?

"This is so confusing! How do we know the right thing to do? Maybe we should just stay home!" remarked Steve.

"No! That is not a good solution. Let's sit down and see if we can figure this out," answered Rob and Jason.

APPENDIX: 2003-2004 SKI AREA ENVIRONMENTAL SCORECARD

Ski Area Citizen's Coalition System of Scoring

Resorts are graded on the following criteria, each worth a quantity of points commensurate with its importance in protecting the environment. The criteria are as follows:

Criteria	Points
1. Maintaining ski terrain within the existing footprint	30
2. Preserving undisturbed lands from development	28
a. Maintaining development and/or parking lot construction within currently disturbed lands	
b. Avoiding road constructions on undisturbed land	
3. Protection or maintaining threatened or endangered species and their habitat	22
4. Preserving environmentally sensitive areas	30
a. Protecting/preserving wetlands	
b. Protecting/preserving mature, late successional or old growth trees	
c. Protecting/preserving unique geological formations	
d. Protecting/preserving unroaded or roadless areas	
5. Conserving water and energy by avoiding new snowmaking	20
6. Preserving water quality	12
7. Not opposing/supporting environmentally sound policy positions	10
8. Promoting and implementing recycling, water and energy conservation	37
a. Utilizing wind and solar energy	
b. Purchasing recycled office and food service products	

Criteria	Points
c. Recycling non-customer use products	
d. Using non-disposable or compostable products for food service	
e. Using recycled or refined motor oil	
f. Employing water conservation and use minimization measures	
g. Recycling customer use products	
h. Employing energy efficient retrofits	
9. Minimizing raffic, emissions, and pollution	25
a. Addressing climate change through an official policy statement	
b. Promoting/sponsoring commuter buses and shuttles from off-mountain sites to ski area	
c. Providing incentives for car pooling and use of mass transit	
d. Using biodiesel fuel in snowcats and other diesel equipment	
Total	214

Source: www.skiareacitizens.com.

Grading Scale

$$\text{Numerical Score} = \frac{\text{Total points attained} \times 100 \text{ percent}}{\text{Total points}}$$

Letter Grade

A = 70-100%
B = 64-69.9%
C = 50-63.9%
D = 40-49.9%
F = Less than 40%

2005/2006 Most Environmentally Friendly Ski Resorts

Resort name	Grade	State
1. Aspen Mountain Ski Resort	A	Colorado
2. Buttermilk Mountain Ski Resort	A	Colorado
3. Sundance Resort	A	Utah
4. Alpine Meadows	A	California
5. Mount Bachelor Ski Area	A	Oregon
6. Sierra-at-Tahoe Ski Resort	A	California
7. Bogus Basin Mountain Resort	A	Idaho
8. Aspen Highlands Ski Resort	A	Colorado

Resort name	Grade	State
9. Wolf Creek Ski Area	A	Colorado
10. Taos Ski Valley	A	New Mexico
11. Eldora Mountain Resort	A	Colorado

Source: www.skiareacitizens.com

2005/2006 Least Environmentally Friendly Ski Resorts

Resort name	Grade	State
1. Breckenridge Ski Resort	F	Colorado
2. Crested Butte Mountain Resort	F	Colorado
3. Copper Mountain Ski Resort	F	Colorado
4. Crystal Mountain, Inc.	F	Washington
5. White Pass Ski Area	F	Washington
6. Big Sky Resort	F	Montana
7. Silver Mountain Ski Resort	F	Idaho
8. Snowbasin Ski Resort	F	Utah

Source: www.skiareacitizens.com

REFERENCES

Best, A. (1999). The Lynx: Coming to a Ski Area Near You? *Ski Area Management,* 38(6): 51,77.

Castle, K. (1999a). The Battle Lines Are Drawn: What It Means for Other Ski Areas. *Ski,* 64(3): 118-120.

Castle, K. (1999b). Mitigation Over Litigation. *Ski,* 64(4): 134-142.

Dolphin, R. (2000). Banff: Mountain Paradise or Political Hot Potato? *Calgary Herald,* March 26, pp. A6-A10.

Fry, J. (1995). Exactly What Are Their Environmental Attitudes? *Ski Area Management,* 34(6): 45-70.

Gadd, B. (1998). Why Ski Areas Should be Removed from Canadian National Parks. Paper submitted to the Parks Canada OCA Review Panel Draft Ski Guidelines Round Table, December 18, pp. 1-5.

Good, R. and Grenier, P. (1994). Some Environmental Impacts of Recreation in the Australian Alps. *Australian Parks & Recreation,* 30(4): 20-22.

Hansen, B. (2000). Ski Areas Graded on Environmental Practices. *Environment News Service.* <http://ens.lycos.com/ens/nov2000>.

Harbaugh, J. (1999). EPA Sustainable Industry Initiative—Mountain Resort Sector Meeting in Denver. <http://www.saminfo.com/feature23.htm>.

Hudson, S. (1996). The Greening of Ski Resorts: A Necessity for Sustainable Tourism, or a Marketing Opportunity for Skiing Communities? *Journal of Vacation Marketing,* 2(2): 176-185.

Hudson, S. (2000). *Snow Business.* London: Continuum Publishing Group.

Hudson, S. (2004). *Marketing for Tourism Hospitality. A Canadian Perspective.* Toronto: Nelson Thomson Learning.

Hudson, S. and Ritchie, J.R.B. (2001). Cross-Cultural Tourist Behavior: An Analysis of Tourist Attitudes Toward the Environment. *Journal of Travel and Tourism Marketing,* 10(2/3): 1-22.

Koch, G. (2000). The Battle Continues. *Ski,* 29(2): 23.

McGibbon, J. (2000). Tourism Pioneers and Racing Heroes: The Influence of Ski Tourism and Consumer Culture on Local Life in the Tirolean Alps. In Robinson, M., Long, P., Sharpley, R., and Swarbrooke, J. (Eds.), *Expressions of Culture, Identity and Meaning in Tourism* (pp. 151-166). Sunderland, UK: Business Education Publishers Limited.

Morrison, S. (2000). Where Hikers, Wealthy Tourists Rub Shoulders. *National Post Financial Times,* June 26, p. E8

National Ski Areas Association (NSAA) (1994). Enhance Ski Areas' Environmental Image. *Ski Area Management,* 33(1): 4.

Parks Canada (2000). Minister Copps Announces Decisions to Ensure National Parks Will Remain a Legacy for all Canadians. News Release. <http://parkscanada.pch.gc.ca>, October 30.

Prince Sadruddin Aga Khan. (1994). Tourism and a European Strategy for the Alpine Environment. In Cater, E. and Lowman, G. (Eds.), *Ecotourism: A Sustainable Option* (pp. 103-110). New York: John Wiley & Sons.

Remington, R. (2000). Parks Study Slams Preservation Push. *National Post,* December 4, p. A9.

Ritchie, J.R.B. and Smith, B.H. (1991). The Impact of a Mega-Event on Host Region Awareness: A Longitudinal Study. *Journal of Travel Research,* 30(1): 3-10.

Socher, K. (1992). The Influence of Tourism on the Quality of Life in the Evaluation of the Inhabitants of the Alps. *Revue de Tourisme,* 47(2): 17-21.

Todd, S.E. and Williams, P.W. (1996). From White to Green: A Proposed Environmental Management System for Ski Areas. *Journal of Sustainable Tourism,* 4(3): 147-173.

Trinker, G. (1999). The Resort that Redford Built. *Ski,* 64(5): 94-96.

Tsuyuzaki, S. (1994). Environmental Deterioration Resulting from Ski-Resort Construction in Japan. *Environmental Conservation,* 21(2): 121-125.

Weiss, O., Norden, G., Hilscher, P., and Vanreusal, B. (1998). Ski Tourism and Environmental Problems. *International Review for the Sociology of Sport,* 33(4): 367-379.

Assiniboine Lodge in winter. (See Chapter 3.)

Dusk on Mount Assiniboine. (See Chapter 3.)

Tomi Murro, a platform processor, leans on two of the recycling trolleys. Murro's job is to receive serving and waste trolleys that come from their worldwide flights and sort the waste they contain. (Photo courtesy of Finnair Catering.) Reprinted with permission.

"In the fall of 2003 WestJet began installing blended Winglet technology on its fleet of 737-700 aircraft. Winglets are extensions to the tip of the wings that are angled upwards at 90 degrees to the wing. The effect . . . is to increase lift and decrease drag, thereby increasing fuel efficiency and allowing the aircraft to carry more weight and fly longer distances. The provision of Winglets permits the use of reduced thrust at takeoff, which can reduce engine maintenance costs and extend engine life because less jet fuel is burned. This reduction in fuel burn further reduces emissions. By improving the aerodynamic performance and handling characteristics of the 737-700, Winglets are expected to reduce fuel burn an average of 4%. The corporation expects to experience a corresponding and immediate reduction in fuel costs on these aircraft." (WestJet Annual Report, 2003, p. 23.) (Photo courtesy of WestJet.) Reprinted with permission.

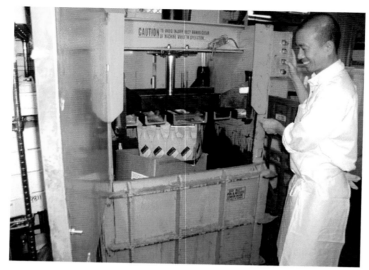

Fairmont/Palliser assigning responsibility to Julian Lee, chief steward, who is operating a box-crushing machine. (Photo courtesy of Robert Bott and Fairmont/Palliser.) Reprinted with permission.

Fairmont/Palliser recycles mixed paper, bathroom supplies, and batteries. (Photo courtesy of Robert Bott and Fairmont/Palliser.) Reprinted with permission.

A view from the tour boat. (Photo courtesy of Neil Symington and Leah Adair.) Reprinted with permission.

Watching whales not far from land. (Photo courtesy of Neil Symington and Leah Adair.) Reprinted with permission.

Cameron Welsh, TreadSoftly's company founder on Lost Creek trail. (Photo courtesy of Robert Bott and Irene M. Herremans.) Reprinted with permission.

Riding high. Bike riders participating in a TreadSoftly outdoor adventure. (Photo courtesy of Robert Bott and Irene M. Herremans.) Reprinted with permission.

Three skiers enjoying the Monashee Mountains. (Photo courtesy of Canadian Mountain Holidays.) Reprinted with permission.

The well-trained and experienced guides. (Photo courtesy of Canadian Mountain Holidays.) Reprinted with permission.

Gondola. (Photo courtesy of Aspen Skiing Company.) Reprinted with permission.

An experienced skier. (Photo courtesy of Aspen Skiing Company.) Reprinted with permission.

Underwater treasures. (Photo courtesy of Irene M. Herremans and Dixon Thompson.) Reprinted with permission.

Divers waiting their turn to board the tour boat. (Photo courtesy of Irene M. Herremans and Dixon Thompson.) Reprinted with permission.

El Capitan in Yosemite Valley. (Photo courtesy of Irene M. Herremans.)

Sequoia groves in Yosemite National Park. (Photo courtesy of Irene M. Herremans.)

Helicopters waiting to provide overflights of the Grand Canyon. (Photo courtesy of Irene M. Herremans.)

Beautiful views of the Grand Canyon. (Photo courtesy of Irene M. Herremans.)

Lake Minnewanka, located in the Cascade Mountains, provides a tranquil view. (Photo courtesy of Marcus Eyre and Irene M. Herremans.)

Banff Avenue, which runs through the town of Banff, Alberta, Canada, in early summer. The view north toward the Cascade Mountains is in the background. (Photo courtesy of Marcus Eyre and Irene M. Herremans.)

Wildflowers growing in Waterton Lakes National Park. (Photo courtesy of Paul Gray.) Reprinted with permission.

Three hikers enjoy the surroundings in Waterton Lakes National Park. (Photo courtesy of Paul Gray.) Reprinted with permission.

A tour group enjoys a rafting trip in Costa Rica. (Photo courtesy of Joaquín García.) Reprinted with permission.

A Costa Rican dancing group performs a traditional dance. (Photo courtesy of Costa Rican Specialties.) Reprinted with permission.

A sunset in Zimbabwe. (Photo courtesy of Patti Dolan.) Reprinted with permission.

A local worker engages in maize grinding, step 1, in Zimbabwe. (Photo courtesy of Patti Dolan.) Reprinted with permission.

Maize grinding, step 2. (Photo courtesy of Patti Dolan.) Reprinted with permission.

Chico Mendes' workshop. (Photo courtesy of Marcos M. Borges.)

Cajari house. (Photo courtesy of Marcos M. Borges.)

Chapter 11

Vacations by the Sea:
Troubled Waters

Agnieszka M. Wojcieszek
Irene M. Herremans

It was going to be another gorgeous day in sunny Florida. On this particular morning Dorian and Joanna were just getting ready to leave their bungalow for the beach. The couple had won a weeklong, all-expense-paid trip to the Florida Keys through a local radio station contest. They had taken diving lessons years ago and very much enjoyed the sport but had not participated in diving for several years because of family commitments. The radio station made all the arrangements with a dive shop called Nautilus, located in the Keys. Dorian and Joanna simply had to have their gear fitted, and they were ready for a day of diving. The store salesperson, Peter, mentioned that Nautilus offered daily boat dives as well as shore dives. A couple of spots were avilable on today's boat dive, so the couple decided to sign up. Peter also mentioned that a brief training and orientation session would be given before the boat would take off at 9 a.m. and that both snorklers and divers would be visiting the dive site.

As it was not quite 9 a.m. yet, Dorian decided to look over some of the latest dive gear that was displayed in the store. As Joanna waited for Dorian, she flipped through a tourist pamphlet that had been left on their dresser by one of the resort staff. The Florida Keys had become quite the hotspot for vacationers over the years.

> Over 3 million tourists visit South Florida and the Florida Keys each year. The Florida Keys coral ecosystem is the third largest coral reef tract in the world—over 200 miles long, covering over 2,800 square nautical miles—including over 5,500 marine species and the world's largest sea grass bed. It is the only barrier reef in North America. The Florida Keys' coral reefs are the number one dive destination in the world, attracting over 1.5 million divers and snorkelers annually.

Scuba divers. (Photo courtesy of Irene M. Herremans and Dixon Thompson.) Reprinted with permission.

Fish among the brain coral. (Photo courtesy of Irene M. Herremans and Dixon Thompson.) Reprinted with permission.

A variety of corals including elkhorn, finger, and leaf corals. (Photo courtesy of Irene M. Herremans and Dixon Thompson.) Reprinted with permission.

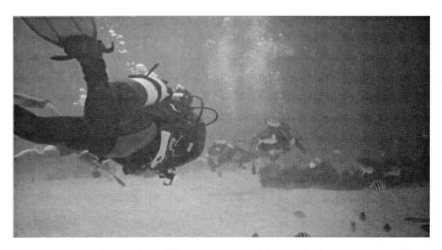

Diver checking air and time. (Photo courtesy of Irene M. Herremans and Dixon Thompson.) Reprinted with permission.

These coral reefs are a vital part of Florida's tourism industry, generating some U.S. $1.6 billion from recreation uses annually.

A few minutes later, Dorian appeared and suggested that they head for the dock. The couple was looking forward to spending the day in the water.

At 9 a.m. the group gathered on the dock, ready to go. The dive master began an orientation for the day and finished with this advice:

"Now as responsible individuals we should do all that we can to ensure that we leave the environment as it was before we got here. This means that we don't touch the coral, we don't walk across the reef flat, we don't take any of the coral for souvenirs, and we don't harass the marine life."

One curious diver put up his hand and asked the following question: "What would happen if we touch the coral?"

The dive master replied:

"Well, unfortunately, there have not been a lot of studies done on the impact of humans' touching on coral. But the few that have been done show evidence that the coral's growth might be stunted or that the coral might even die. The disadvantage of touching to the diver is that the coral is sometimes sharp and causes scratches that can result in infections if not cared for properly."

During the orientation, Joanna was not paying much attention to the dive guide as she was busy reviewing the itinerary for the next few days of her vacation. The Florida Keys was the perfect destination: plenty of beach access and great shopping, what more could one ask for?

Finally, the boat was ready to take off. After about a half-hour boat trip, everyone was at the dive site. As the captain of the boat stabilized the boat on a permanent mooring, the dive master gave the snorklers and divers some ideas of what types of marine life they would see and what time to be back to the boat. The dive guides helped everyone get their equipment ready. After a gear check, Joanna and Dorian were ready to jump into the water. In the water, the couple signaled that each was ready to go and they slowly disappeared under the surface of the water. Just before reaching the bottom, they adjusted their buoyancy so that they were swimming about one foot from the reef.

Both were overwhelmed with the abundance of marine life. The coral reefs were breathtaking. They were surrounded by colors: blues, reds, oranges, yellows, blacks, and purples. Every kind of fish imaginable was seen: jacks, goatfish, snappers, butterfly fish, angel fish, and parrot fish. They had to look closely because of the camouflage, but they also caught a glimpse of the occasional ray, lying almost motionless on the bottom and partly buried in the sand. Although the Florida Keys is known for its elkhorn corals, Dorian and Joanna found numerous different sizes and shapes of corals, including brain corals, tube corals, and fungus corals.

The reefs looked so peaceful, so gentle; sea fans of many colors waved back and forth with the current. Joanna and Dorian began their swim just above the coral reef where they could watch all the marine life go about their daily activities. Joanna's eyes caught a glimpse of a particularly unusual piece of elkhorn coral. She thought to herself that it would look great in her bathroom alongside her bathtub. As Joanna reached out to grab the coral, Dorian caught her hand and signaled not to touch the coral. Joanna looked confused and did not completely understand what Dorian was suggesting as it was impossible for them to talk underwater. However, it was getting near the end of the dive, and after checking their dive instruments, the couple decided that they should head back to the boat.

As they neared the boat, they noticed that there were several other divers and snorklers getting ready to get back in. There seemed to be somewhat of a traffic jam in this area. As divers were waiting their turns, it was necessary to adjust their buoyancy frequently in order to maintain a neural position in the water. Several less-experienced divers would become slightly negatively buoyant, meaning they would lose their position in the water and head toward the bottom of the ocean until they adjusted their buoyancy again. This activity was resulting in some stirring of dirt on the coral below and the occasional nick of the coral by the divers' fins. Finally, everyone was back in the boat, enjoying cookies and beverages.

The morning passed by quickly. Shortly after noon, the divers were back on the docks. Dorian and Joanna were just leaving when one of the dive guides caught up with them. He asked how their dive had gone, and if they might want to come back again. The couple definitely planned to return in the future. Joanna asked if the dive shop gets a lot of repeat business. The instructor said that some people do return, but the local dive shops see more and more new tourists each year. He added that while new tourists are great for business they have some negative effects on the conditions of the reefs. This dive shop requires that people who use its services have been previously certified in open-water diving; however, divers are certified in various places and have different levels of knowledge and diving experience. As a result, some of the divers lack the skills and awareness to dive and snorkel responsibly. In the overview, dive guides attempt to raise environmental awareness but there is only so much they can do. Snorkelers who are not careful may kick sand on top of coral heads and walk across the reef flat, while divers with poor buoyancy skills may collide with the reef or touch the delicate corals. Many want to take back souvenirs and do not understand the harm in this activity.

Consequently, waters surrounding most of the 1,700 islands that make up the Florida Keys have been designated as a national marine sanctuary since 1990. This sanctuary, extending 220 miles, was established to stem mounting threats to the health and ecological future of the coral reef ecosystem.

The guide stopped talking as they approached the dive shop. Joanna had been taking in every word that he said, and now felt rather guilty since she had not acted in a responsible manner that morning. She now understood Dorian's underwater gesture. Concerned that there may be many others who behave the way she did, Joanna decided that she must do something about this. She asked the guide if there were any initiatives to prevent further damage to the reefs. The instructor pointed out a table in the corner of the shop. On it were various informational brochures and newsletters from organizations that had been created for the very purpose of raising awareness about the state of the reefs. Joanna picked up a copy of each, determined to make some changes.

Later on that evening, Joanna was sitting outside on the porch, enjoying the cool breeze, and reading her brochures. Dorian noticed his wife's obvious fascination with the material and put down the novel that he was reading. He couldn't help but ask what had sparked her interest. She told him about the interesting organizations and activities that she was reading about and how she felt embarrassed about wanting to take a piece of coral back to her bathroom.

Here is what she found out.

NATIONAL OCEANIC
AND ATMOSPHERIC ADMINISTRATION

The U.S. Department of Commerce's NOAA has primary responsibility for stewardship of marine resources with activities including monitoring the health of domestic coral reefs, restoring damaged or destroyed sections of coral reefs, and maintaining the health of coral reefs through management, research, and education. One of the organization's initiatives includes the development of a National Marine Sanctuaries Program. To create a sanctuary, NOAA selects a site from a Site Evaluation List (SEL). Each site on the SEL must possess qualities of special national significance based on conservation, recreational, educational, ecological, historic, research, and aesthetic values. To date, thirteen national marine sanctuaries protect some 18,000 square miles of ocean and coasts. Sanctuary managers must develop and follow a plan to prevent abuse and degradation of the sanctuary's resources, while fostering research projects, educational programs, and responsible recreational and commercial activities. National marine sanctuaries are protected areas where taking of aquatic life forms is illegal. The program applies an ecosystem approach to marine environmental protection and asks the public to adopt a new ethic of marine stewardship (see Figure 11.1).

REEFKEEPER INTERNATIONAL

A major project of ReefKeeper International is its own Coral Reef Initiative. The organization has submitted formal requests to the governors of Florida, Puerto Rico, and the U.S. Virgin Islands to develop and adopt a formal policy document for a state-sponsored Coral Reef Initiative. As an absolute minimum, the adopted declaration calls for a coordinated, three-pronged program:

1. resource management, capacity building, and public awareness;
2. research and monitoring of reef conditions; and
3. coastal zone management responsive to coral reef environmental needs.

ReefKeeper International argues that although at this time some coral reef habitats are designated as special protected areas under either federal or state programs, those designations fail to include many coral habitats, and they do not protect any coral habitats from the effects of detrimental activities on shore.

INTERNATIONAL YEAR OF THE REEF, 1997

The International Year of the Reef campaign was originally launched at the Eighth International Coral Reef Symposium in Panama (1996). The goals of the symposium included evaluating and improving the conditions of coral reefs by getting government and media involved. Specific events included Reef Check '97: the first global survey of human impacts on coral reefs. Reef Check involved over 100 marine scientists and 750 recreational divers who surveyed 300 coral reefs in thirty countries. The results from 230 of the sites reported that corals were in better shape globally than fish and shellfish. The mean percentage of living coral cover on reefs was 31 percent globally, with the Caribbean recording the lowest value at 22 percent.

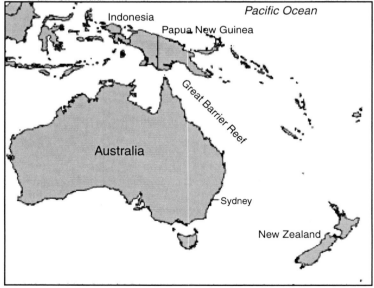

FIGURE 11.1. Vacations by the sea. At top, Florida; at bottom, Australia's Great Barrier Reef. (Maps prepared by Hanako Saito.)

The goal, derived from the results, is to achieve sustainable use of marine resources. The survey will be repeated each year to monitor the conditions of these reefs. As of 2005, "significant progress has been made in building an integrated observing system to map, monitor and assess shallow water coral reef systems" (NOAA, 2005). Though a report by the National Oceanic and Atmospheric Administration titled "The State of Coral Reef Ecosystems of the United States and Pacific Freely Associated States: 2005," cautions that environmental degradation and human factors continue to endanger coral reef ecosystems, positive gains have been made. For example, in Puerto Rico laws pertaining to fishing have been revised, and in Palau the Protected Areas Network Act came into force in 2003 providing the support for marine reserves (NOAA, 2005).

The Ninth International Coral Reef Symposium was held in October 2000 in Bali, Indonesia. The theme was bridging research and management for sustainable development. The objective of this symposium was to provide an international forum for exchanging information and ideas and transfer technologies and knowledge among researchers, managers, policymakers, and other stakeholders in coral reefs. It aimed to encourage cooperation among the coastal states in the tropical regions to meet regional needs for sustainable coral reef development and global needs for international monitoring and assessment of global climate change and human impacts on coral reef.

On an international level, the increase in coral reef awareness resulted in the World Conservation Union (IUCN) signing a contract with the World Bank/GEF (Global Environment Facility) to develop proposals for Marine Protected Areas in Tanzania, Western Samoa, and Vietnam. The IUCN Web site can be accessed at www.iucn.org.

INTERNATIONAL CORAL REEF INITIATIVE

The International Coral Reef Initiative (ICRI) is a partnership among nations and organizations seeking to implement international conventions and agreements for the benefit of coral reefs and related ecosystems. This movement was founded by eight governments—Australia, France, Japan, Jamaica, the Philippines, Sweden, the United Kingdom, and the United States in the mid 1990s. The international scientific community has been raising concerns over the serious decline of reefs. Table 11.1 indicates some of the most prevalent causes of coral reef ecosystem degradation.

Dorian thought that the organizations meant well, but he wasn't so sure that the costs of protecting the coral reefs could be justified. Joanna quickly jumped in, quoting more information that she had just read in the pamphlets.

TABLE 11.1. Causes of coral reef degradation.

Anthropogenic (human) stresses	Natural stresses
• Pressure from population increases, including migration and intensified uses	• Crown of thorns (starfish) predator outbreaks
• Depletion of fish stocks	• Tropical storm damage
• Destructive fishing methods, such as dynamite blasting and poisons (cyanide)	• Warmer ocean temperature fluctuations resulting in coral bleaching
• Untreated domestic sewage and industrial effluent	• Earthquakes
• Excessive nonpoint source pollution, e.g., from agricultural runoff and contamination of aquifers	• Wave action
• Ship-based pollution; including oil, plastics, and bilgewater	• Flooding and surface water runoff
• Mangrove harvesting or displacement for aquaculture ponds	
• Increased sedimentation as a result of deforestation and poor land use	
• Coral and coral sand mining	
• Land-based and urban construction activities including dredging, filling, and increased siltation	
• Poorly planned tourism—including inadequate wastewater treatment, unregulated construction, collection of corals and ornamental reef species, spear fishing, and more	

Coral reefs have been compared to tropical forests in their diversity and productivity. Although they occupy only 2 percent of the oceans, they contribute up to 12 percent of the world's fisheries. Coastal and marine communities depend on reefs for their social, economic, and cultural life. As a result, millions of people depend on reefs for food and livelihood. Coral reefs are among the oldest ecosystems, having existed for 500 million years. Unfortunately, the 600,000 square kilometers of coral reefs worldwide are now in decline. Ten percent of the world's reefs have been lost and another 20 to 30 percent are at risk of disappearing over the next thirty years. Rapid population growth and migration to coastal areas where coral reef ecosystems occur further exacerbate the problem. The resulting coastal congestion leads to increased competition for limited resources, coastal pollution, and problems related to coastal construction.

Joanna paused to catch her breath and noticed that Dorian was asleep. She decided to call it a night. Tomorrow she would head into town and see what other information she could pick up.

The next morning was spent relaxing on the beach and shopping at the local market. There Joanna and Dorian ran into another couple who had also been part of the dive group the previous day. They started talking and decided to have lunch together. As it turned out, Margaret and Steve were avid divers who visited the Keys every summer. Upon sharing her new concerns of the diving environment and practices, Joanna found that the other couple was also interested in these matters. They had received their training through the Professional Association of Diving Instructors (PADI). Joanna had heard of the international organization but was not aware of any of its ongoing initiatives. Margaret then told her about the Project AWARE Foundation established in 1992. The ongoing efforts include an emphasis on ensuring that PADI divers are taught to respect the fragility of the environment. They are taught to be responsible divers who are constantly aware of their bodies and equipment and how they may impact the flora and fauna around them. To keep PADI members up-to-date on important dive issues, safety, training techniques, and business information, PADI publishes an *Undersea Journal* magazine and various newsletters throughout the year. As evening approached, the couples exchanged addresses and parted ways.

Back in the room, Joanna spent some time reading before she went to sleep. She had picked up a book in the dive shop that provides information on great diving destinations and reefs all over the world. A few caught her eye: The Great Barrier Reef Marine Park in Australia and Stingray City off the coast of Grand Cayman in the western Caribbean.

The Great Barrier Reef Marine Park was established in 1975. It covers an area of 344,000 square kilometers adjacent to the northeast coast of Australia. It is managed as a multiple-use area, with major uses being commercial tourism, private recreation, and commercial fishing. The essence of the marine park is zoning and defining what people can do in each zone. The major threats to the park include pollution, overfishing, and destruction of habitat; all are derived from human activities. The enforced zoning led to three basic kinds of zones being instituted:

- General use zones (76 percent of the park)—Most nondestructive activities are allowed.
- Marine national park zones (23 percent of the park)—Allow activities similar to those permitted in national parks on land (commercial fishing is not permitted).

- Preservation and scientific research (1 percent of the park)—Only approved scientific research is allowed in these areas.

Joanna also read about Stingray City:

During the peak tourist season, it is not uncommon for 500 divers and snorkelers to visit the stingrays. Visitors are allowed to feed and stroke the rays. The stingrays know that they will be fed when visitors arrive. As soon as the boats are anchored and divers and snorkelers are in the water, rays will approach them and bump and nuzzle them for food.

Joanna thought either of these would be a great dive destination, but she also wondered how so many visitors and their activities affect the stingrays, and if there were any regulations (similar to those at the Great Barrier Reef) regarding this activity. Why did this activity occur here and nowhere else?

Joanna wanted to know more about marine activities. She was now sure that the preservation of reefs was a worthy cause in which to get involved, but she also had many questions about marine activities and their effects on the quality of water, biodiversity, and ecosystems. She looked forward to returning home so that she could phone her local dive shop and find out what instructional programs the store offered. She also wanted to find out more about the organizations and their initiatives before choosing with which ones she might want to get involved. Before she left the Keys she planned to make a list of the types of things that she could do as an individual to help out.

BIBLIOGRAPHY

Collins, T. (1998). Awareness, responsibility and education: Getting involved with PADI Project Aware. *Skin Diver Magazine.* www.skindiver.com.

Common, M. and Driml, S. (1996). Ecological economics criteria for sustainable tourism: Application to the Great Barrier Reef and Wet Tropics World Heritage Areas, Australia. *Journal of Sustainable Tourism,* 4(1), 3-15.

Florida Keys (2003). Introduction. www.sanctuaries.noaa.gov.

International Coral Reef Initiative Report to the United Nations Commission on Sustainable Development. (n.d.). (URL no longer exists.)

International Year of the Reef (1997). (Document no longer exists.)

Kelleher, G. (1997). Australian treasure. *People and the Planet,* 6(2), 17-19.

NOAA (2005). The state of coral reef ecosystem of the United States and Pacific freely associated states: 2005. www.ccma.nos.noaa.gov.

NOAA Coral Reef Initiative (1996). www.nos.noa.gov.

Protect the Living Reef—Environmental Awareness Campaign (1998). (URL no longer exists).

Reef Guardian International (2005). www.reefguardian.org.

SEI: Coral Reefs. (Document no longer exists.)

Summary of Reef Check 97: Reef check press conference (October 16, 1997). (Document no longer exists.)

The State of the Reefs—ICRI's Major Concern (1995). www.oceanservice.noaa.gov.

Viders, H. (1995). *Marine conservation for the 21st century.* Flagstaff, AZ: Best Publishing.

Welcome to the National Program. www.sanctuaries.nos.noaa.gov.

Who Is PADI? (1999). www.padi.com.

Part IV:
Wrestling with the Sustainability
of National Parks

Due to the crowding and development that has resulted in many parks, their administrative bodies are undergoing a redefinition of the parks' missions and their reasons for existing. Years ago, national parks were created with a heavy emphasis on the social aspect of sustainability (for the enjoyment of the people). However, today many national parks are finding that an imbalance between the social and ecological dimensions is resulting in a compromising of ecological integrity. Too much emphasis on creating activities in which visitors can engage has lead to a lack of attention to the environmental problems that are created by the social activities. For example, swimming pools, restaurants, shopping facilities, ski resorts, and luxury lodges have allowed visitors to forget the original reason for creating national parks: to enjoy their natural beauty. Therefore, national parks are rethinking which activities are appropriate. Many activities that were acceptable in the past when fewer visitors created a smaller ecological footprint are now disallowed.

Under revised missions for national parks, acceptable activities are those that help visitors enjoy a special engagement with nature not those that distract them from beauty, emotional appeal, and spirituality.

Some of the questions that are currently debated among the national parks' stakeholders follow:

- Should snowmobiles be allowed in Denali National Park and Yellowstone National Park?
- Is it appropriate to allow jet skis in national parks?
- What environmental damage do automobiles create in national parks?
- What types of alternative energy should be used for buses and other public transport?
- Do air tours over national parks create too much noise and disturb other visitors and wildlife?
- Should powerboats be allowed in national parks?

- How should we stop people from feeding the wildlife?
- Can alpine ski resorts located in national parks be allowed to expand their facilities without hurting wildlife habitats?
- Should ski facilities be allowed to use their gondolas and lifts for summer activities?

The cases in this section focus on national parks in both the United States and Canada that are vigorously addressing these issues. Even though many of the issues are similar in these two countries, one major difference should be recognized. Generally a residential community (a town) is located within the park boundaries of the national parks in Canada. These towns contain residents who live in the park all year, whereas in the United States only the necessary facilities needed to maintain the park are found within the park boundaries. However, what is necessary to maintain the park frequently is hotly debated.

The two cases in the United States question which activities should be allowed in Grand Canyon and Yosemite National Parks, while the two cases in Canada (Banff and Waterton Lake National Parks) wrestle with interpreting and implementing sustainability on a strategic level.

Using private vehicle transportation in Yosemite and providing air tours over the Grand Canyon can easily be adapted to local concerns. Expanding the discussion into nonrecreational activities, such as why we use personal automobiles rather than public transportation, helps to gain insight into our recreational habits and values. As more national park users engage in different activities, user conflicts are bound to arise. The Waterton Lakes case can create an excellent discussion about the definition of sustainability in the context of the social, economic, and ecological dimensions. Then, it raises the question of how the political dimension supports or hinders sustainability and questions whether the model we use is really a model of sustainability. The Banff-Bow Valley Case illustrates a process to bring together very diverse special interests in order to save the park from ecological disaster.

The cases can be used separately or together. Although they have quite different emphases, the methods presented in either the Waterton or Banff-Bow Valley cases can also be applied to either the Yosemite or Grand Canyon cases or vice versa. All of the cases can be adapted to a local concern.

Chapter 12

Yosemite National Park:
Parks Without Private Vehicles

Irene M. Herremans
Robin E. Reid

Although this case is based on facts, for the sake of brevity, some of the dialogue has been adapted to summarize and convey certain theoretical concepts in a setting that is more conducive for instructional purposes.

INTRODUCTION

Edward Abbey, a popular novelist and defender of wilderness and public lands, was a strong critic of the motoring public and the tourist industry. He worked for the National Park Service as a seasonal park ranger near Moab in southeast Utah for several years. In his book, *Desert Solitaire* (1968) he discussed his idea of what national parks would be like without motorized vehicles. He indicated that if we took the vehicles out of the parks that the parks would suddenly grow in size.

> No more cars in national parks. Let the people walk. Or ride horses, bicycles, mules, wild pigs—anything—but keep the automobiles and the motorcycles and all their motorized relatives out. We have agreed not to drive our automobiles into cathedrals, concert halls, art museums, legislative assemblies, private bedrooms and the other sanctums of our culture; we should treat our national parks with the same deference, for they, too, are holy places. An increasingly pagan and hedonistic people (thank God!), we are learning finally that the forests and mountains and desert canyons are holier than our churches. Therefore let us behave accordingly. (Abbey, 1968, p. 60)

Abbey felt that cars as a means of touring the park prevented the park visitor from really seeing anything intensely. He felt that a view from a car

Cars lined at the Wawona Hotel. (Photo courtesy of Irene M. Herremans.)

Cabins at Curry Village. (Photo courtesy of Irene M. Herremans.)

One of many waterfalls in Yosemite Valley. (Photo courtesy of Irene M. Herremans.)

Gates of the Valley. (Photo courtesy of Irene M. Herremans.)

really only gave the visitor a superficial, quick overview of the beauty of the park. Instead, national parks should be places where visitors engage themselves with nature and its beauty. Abbey felt that it is better to experience a small area of the park intensely than to see the entire park superficially.

> A man on foot, on horseback or on a bicycle will see more, feel more, enjoy more in one mile than the motorized tourists can in a hundred miles. Better to idle through one park in two weeks than try to race through a dozen in the same amount of time. Those who are familiar with both modes of travel know from experience that this is true; the rest have only to make the experiment to discover the same truth for them. (Abbey, 1968, pp. 61-62)

Abbey also realized the difficulty of changing behavior and that visitors, used to viewing the parks' beauty from their cars, would complain if asked to give up their old ways. However, if motorized tourists could be convinced to give up their cars, he felt that existing roads could be used for walking and bicycling. Buses would be used to shuttle people, and trucks would be used to haul supplies. Funds allocated for new roads would be reallocated for trail building. He felt that once people were liberated from their automobiles, they would find enjoyment in hiking, camping, and exploring.

He made particular reference to Yosemite National Park, located in California in the United States (see Figures 12.1 and 12.2).

> Consider a concrete example and what could be done with it: Yosemite Valley in Yosemite National Park. At present a dusty milling confusion of motor vehicles and ponderous camping machinery, it could be returned to relative beauty and order by the simple expedient of requiring all visitors, at the park entrance, to lock up their automobiles and continue their tour on the seats of good workable bicycles supplied free of charge by the United States Government. (Abbey, 1968, p. 60)

In 1968, at the time Abbey's book was written, many of us might have thought that his ideas were rather extreme. Today, many of us might still think that his ideas are extreme. However, park officials have watched the degradation to the Yosemite environment from traffic in the valley area since 1980. Unfortunately, until recently they were not very successful in implementing a plan to stem the problem and are still facing some barriers.

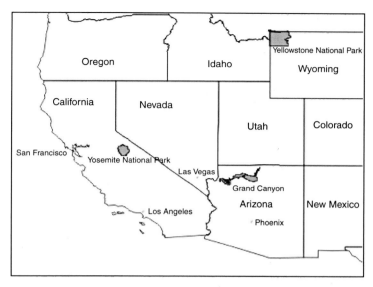

FIGURE 12.1. Yosemite National Park location in the United States. (Map prepared by Hanako Saito.)

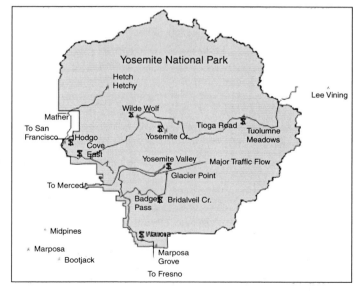

FIGURE 12.2. A detailed map of Yosemite National Park. (Map prepared by Hanako Saito.)

YOSEMITE NATIONAL PARK

Yosemite National Park is located in California approximately 3.5 hours east from San Francisco and 7.5 hours northeast from Los Angeles. Abraham Lincoln designated Yosemite as California's first state park in 1864, and in 1890 it became a national park. The park is comprised of 1,169 square miles; however, the seven miles of Yosemite Valley are the most popular area for visitors. Situated on the western slope of the Sierra Nevada, the park provides visitors with many scenic views. Tourists enjoy beautiful, cascading waterfalls of which two are the world's ten highest waterfalls. Yosemite Falls is the highest waterfall in North America and the fifth highest in the world. In addition, the largest single granite rock on earth, El Capitan, is located in Yosemite. Other interesting attractions near the valley include Glacier Point, Badger Pass, Wawona, and the Mariposa Big Trees Grove.

In 1997, nature took its course in aiding the park officials in their progress toward environmental planning when the largest flood in the park's history caused it to be closed. The flooding of the Merced River destroyed two campsites and many employees' tent cabins. In addition, the river's flooding washed out part of Highway 140 and created problems with the sewage systems, drinking water, and power lines. The closing of the park gave the Park Service an opportunity to discuss how to implement a visitor plan that would be more environmentally friendly.

As early as 1980, the National Park Service, with public input, undertook a comprehensive planning process to determine how to balance preservation of resources with resource availability for people's enjoyment. The General Management Plan, developed out of the planning process, suggested reducing traffic, removing buildings and other facilities that were not essential, restorating natural areas to their original state, and relocating accommodations for employees and visitors away from environmentally sensitive areas.

Issues for development of the GMP were congestion in the park, and environmental impact and the quality of experience provided by the park for the visitors. Little was accomplished in the next few years. Then, in the early 1990s, a crisis in the park moved stakeholders to act. The gates of the park had to be closed due to a traffic jam in Yosemite Valley. Essentially, the valley was lined with cars from one end to the other. The outlying communities were unaware that the park gates were closed and continued to send visitors to the park. Shortly thereafter, Yosemite Area Traveler Information (YATI) was formed to update visitors and others on travelling conditions in the park. Something had to be done. However, some major hurdles had to be overcome to make progress on implementing the GMP. The various stakeholders lacked trust in each other and the plan needed both state and federal monies to carry out implementation.

To handle the reduction in traffic congestion, the Yosemite Area Regional Transportation System (YARTS) was formed in 1992.[1] Primary participants in developing and implementing the system are the surrounding counties of Mariposa, Madera, Merced, Mono, and Tuolumne. Other organizations involved were Caltrans, the National Park Service, and the U.S. Forest Service. Secondary participants include adjacent counties, business, environmental, and tourism organizations, and state and federal agencies (About YARTS, 1998). YARTS was developed to "propose a transportation system for the Yosemite Region that will enable travel throughout the region, including Yosemite National Park, while safeguarding the area's wealth of natural resources" (About YARTS, 1998).

The goals of YARTS are as follows (About YARTS, 1998):

- Enhance the visitor experience and accommodate all visitors
- Improve environmental quality
- Improve accessibility in Yosemite Valley and to major park destinations and enhance travel to and through Yosemite and to other attractions within the region
- Enhance tourism economies
- Be affordable to all visitors
- Complement the objectives of Yosemite's General Management Plan and Valley Implementation Plan

Public input was essential if the plan was to be accepted. The YARTS study team knew that there would be resistance to change. Consequently, the team devised a plan to receive input through a variety of means. Public meetings, postings to the Internet, and regular mailings helped elicit opinions. Stakeholder interviews ensured that each group affected by the plan had an opportunity to provide input before the plan was implemented. This stakeholder input was useful in the formulation of the plan itself.

Some of the stakeholder dialogue from the interviews follows:

YARTS INTERVIEWER: (speaking to a group of stakeholder representatives) We need to gain support for YARTS. What questions do you feel that your stakeholder groups would want answered before they will be convinced that YARTS should be implemented?

FREQUENT PARK USER: I would not be opposed to using YARTS, but I would like answers to some questions. A lot of other people I know simply want to know how the system will work. For example, would YARTS operate year-round or only during the peak summer months? Can I still use my car if I would like? What geographic region would be covered by the bus service? Only the valley? The whole park? Outlying regions? What if I want to enter one gate and leave through another gate? Will that be possible or do I need to make a round-trip? It seems I am giving up the opportunity to be spontaneous and that is important to me. Will the YARTS system still allow that?

TOURISM ASSOCIATION MEMBER: I would like to address the issue of visitor threshold. The GMP suggests a maximum number of day-use visitors of 10,500. It is unclear to me if that is based on car capacity or people capacity. If cars are removed, is it possible that more people would then be allowed to visit the park each day?

COMMUNITY REPRESENTATIVE: I don't understand if the YARTS system is an alternative to using the private vehicle. Or is it attempting to service a market that is not currently served by the private vehicle? I am not really clear on the objectives of the system.

YOSEMITE PARK OFFICIAL: The busy months in the park are July and August. Because there are so many visitors during that time, the quality of the experience for the tourist is lessened. I truly believe that use of private vehicles must be severely restricted during this time. Another way of addressing the problem is to devise a plan to encourage tourists to visit the park throughout the year rather than just during the peak season. What economic incentives might be possible to get more visitors during the shoulder season?

TOUR BUS COMPANY: To what extent does the plan encourage use of existing private bus and tour operators to help with alternative modes of transportation or does the park plan to run its own bus company? Perhaps some of the services could be outsourced. If existing bus services were used, it would not require the huge staging areas that appear to be necessary otherwise. Private bus companies could either pick up people from their homes or pick them up at the bus depot. Their vehicles could be left at home or the bus depot, eliminating the need for additional parking areas. From where do most of the visitors come? Does it make sense to start a route from some of the major cities and airports in California, such as San Francisco and Los Angeles? What is the portion that comes from out of state? How many drive? How many fly?

YARTS INTERVIEWER: What is your biggest fear about YARTS?

FREQUENT PARK USER: The perception is that the system is designed to make it difficult to get to the park. Some people feel that the system has a hidden agenda to reduce visitation. If the system has a hidden agenda or even if people believe that the system has a hidden agenda, it has a high probability of failure. My fear is that YARTS will not be a positive alternative. In other words, will it cost more than taking my private vehicle? Will it take more time? Will it offer the convenience and flexibility of my private vehicle? If YARTS is to be successful, it must be a positive experience for the traveller; it must add value. The vehicles should be comfortable and of high quality; it makes sense that they use alternative fuels such as propane.

OAKHURST CHAMBER OF COMMERCE: We don't simply want to be a parking lot for the park and are concerned with the implementation of YARTS. Over the past five years, the community of Oakhurst has been able to make available a significant number of visitor services including restaurants, lodging, grocery stores, and other services. We are also planning to construct sidewalks through the commercial area to facilitate both resident and visitor pedestrian access. We would hope that the system would be designed to encourage tourists to visit our town as well as the park. Our lodges should be bus stops for those visitors going to the park. Our schools could probably accommodate some cars for "day-use" visitors or those with accommodations in the park. I believe existing parking should be used as much as possible. Of course, there would be additional maintenance costs if more vehicles were using the existing parking lots. The school, for example, would need to be compensated in some way for the additional "wear and tear" to the existing lot if it were to be used as a staging area. Will there be a fee for parking in the staging areas to cover this additional cost?

MERCED COMMUNITY REPRESENTATIVE: We feel it is important that the system use existing parking as much as possible and not destroy prime agriculture land and turn it into parking lots for staging areas. To some extent, huge parking lots for staging areas simply create another environmental problem outside the park that the surrounding communities must then solve.

GROVELAND BUSINESS REPRESENTATIVE: I see a bit of a conflict within the communities themselves regarding implementation of YARTS. Local businesses rely heavily on tourist dollars. Some communities have developed infrastructure to accommodate tourists. If staging areas are chosen away from these communities, they will be hurt economically. However, too many tourists also create problems. We have a Wayside Park that is currently a rest stop for many tour buses. Local residents sometimes complain about noise and smoke from diesel bus engines and overflowing trash containers. If too many buses park there, then there is no room for parking for local residents. Some equitable solution will need to be worked out.

LEE VINING COMMUNITY REPRESENTATIVE: We are interested in making sure that a transportation system does our area justice. As you know, our community borders the park and we overlook beautiful Mono Lake. John Muir described the Mono Basin area as a "country of wonderful contrasts, hot deserts bordered by snow-laden mountains, cinders and ashes scattered on glacier-polished pavement, frost and fire working in the making of beauty." Our Visitor's Center provides exhibits and special activities.

AREA CHAMBER OF COMMERCE MEMBER: It is going to be difficult to treat each community fairly in determining staging areas. If the main concern is the valley, then perhaps parking areas should be located just inside the park entrance. Would this alternative address the goals of the GMP or is it simply moving the problem to a new area in the park? What is the "real" concern—that land is covered with parking lots, or that there are too many emissions from vehicles, or both?

GATEWAY COMMUNITY: I am not convinced that YARTS is solving its transportation problem. In some ways I see YARTS as simply pushing the transportation problem out to the local communities surrounding Yosemite—the gateway communities of Merced, Mariposa, and the others.

TRANSPORTATION EXPERT: As I see it, the strategy must address how comprehensive the regional transportation system will be. By that I mean, there are two key elements that will drive or determine the cost of implementing the strategy. What will be the geographic coverage of the transportation system? and, What will be the frequency of the service during each day and throughout the year? Costs will expand as geographic coverage expands and as frequency increases. It will be much more expensive to provide service to the outlying areas of the park and the surrounding counties than it will be to limit service to Yosemite Valley. To estimate the total costs, you need to look at both capital costs and operating costs, or fixed and variable costs. For example, for a staging area located close to the park, one bus will be able to make several return trips during the day. Of course, the number of buses that will be needed at any one time will depend on when most visitors enter and leave the park during the day. For a staging area located farther away from the park, it will not be possible to make as many return trips; therefore, it will be necessary to have more capital investment in buses in order to carry the same number of passengers from those areas. Of course, operating costs will be higher also. The price of the transportation ticket purchased by the visitor will need to reflect that increased cost. At the same time we are thinking about costs, we need to concern ourselves with customer service and the convenience factor necessary to motivate visitors to take public transportation. Buses that used to pick up visitors in staging areas near the park will be able to travel the distance nearly as quickly as a car because there will not be very many stops in between the staging area and the park. However, when buses pick up visitors in staging areas further away, the bus might take as much as two to three times longer than a car to cover the same distance. Some outlying areas are in mountainous regions. Buses cannot travel as fast as cars over these roads. Also, buses must stop at several places to fill seats before coming to the park. These additional stops will lengthen the necessary travel time and make public transportation a less attractive alternative.

I have gathered some individual costs. Can we figure out how much the price of a ticket would be to provide transportation service within the valley area or a town close to the valley? For example, El Portal, which is only fifteen miles from the valley versus one of the outlying counties, let's say Mariposa, which is approximately forty-five miles from the valley? We would need to make some assumption about the number of private cars we would like to displace with the bus service. How about starting with 1,000? I went through some of the visitor documentation at the National Park office and talked to some of the local bus companies.

- The average auto entering the park carries 2.9 passengers.
- Most buses carry forty-five passengers.
- A standard practice in the transportation industry is to add 20 percent to the required fleet number for spare vehicles.
- Most guests enter and leave the park during the day and during the year. Here are some charts that show park arrival and departure patterns by time of day during the peak travel season (see the Appendix, Figures A.1 and Figure A.2).

ENVIRONMENTAL CONSULTANT: I am just trying to think this through. If one of the objectives is to reduce environmental degradation and most of the problems are caused by cars, then 10,500 cars multiplied by emissions per vehicle equals emissions per day. We need an estimate of CO_2 emissions per vehicle. Emissions will vary depending whether the vehicle is an SUV or a small car, but we could take an average. Then, if we could transfer that into the amount of environmental impact, we would have a measure of impact with cars. If we reduce cars to, let's say, half the maximum capacity or 5,250 cars multiplied by emissions per vehicle, then we need to account for the emission per bus or shuttle or alternative modes of transportation. We need some additional information in order to make an informed decision.

- What is the average amount of car emissions over an eight-hour day with starting and stopping approximately ten times?

- How many buses will be used?
- What is the average amount of bus emissions over an eight-hour day with starts and stops?
- What else might we need to know? Oh yes, the cost to maintain a parking lot in the park has been estimated at $1,000 per year. Under which alternatives could this cost be eliminated?
- Are their any other costs that will be saved if cars are not driven in Yosemite and can those savings to passed on to those that do use the public transportation system?

As the YARTS interviewer reviewed the transcripts and prepared the material to present to the YARTS Project Committee, she couldn't help but wonder if Edward Abbey foresaw all the issues that would need to be addressed if private vehicles were eliminated from national parks. She hoped that the YARTS Project Committee was ready for the challenge.

APPENDIX:
PARK VISITATION STATISTICS

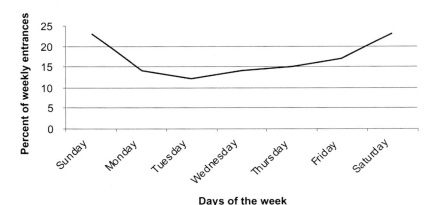

FIGURE A.1. Park visitation by day of week.

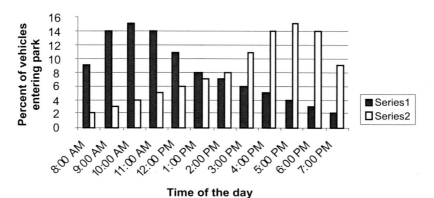

Time of the day

FIGURE A.2. Park summer weekend visitation by time of day. **Series 1: Entrances; Series 2: Exits** (*Source:* Nelson/Nygaard Consulting Associates, 1998. *Yosemite Regional Transportation Strategy. Working Paper #5: Cost and Phasing Issues.* Reprinted with permission.)

NOTE

1. The passing of two regulations in California requiring employers to be more attentive to clean air issues did not help much as the regulations were invalidated by the state legislature in 1995. However, the process made both employees and employers more aware of their responsibility for clean air and the impact that their activities were having on air pollution. Given that emissions from private transportation are the major cause of pollution, the regulations required that all employers with over 100 employees have an Employee Transportation Coordinator (ETC). The responsibility of the ETC was to help employees determine the best way to get to work considering all modes of transportation. After the regulations were invalidated, some employers continued to work on assisting employees in choosing more environmentally friendly modes of transportation to and from work. (Nelson/Nygaard, 1998c, p. 7). (Regulation 13 of the Bay Area Air Quality Management District Clean Air Plan and Regulation 15 of the South Coast Air Quality Management District Clean Air Plan.)

BIBLIOGRAPHY

Abbey, Edward (1968). *Desert Solitaire.* New York: McGraw-Hill Book Company.
About Yarts (1998). YARTS Fact Sheet. <http://www.yosemite.com/yarts/about.httm>.
Grossi, Mark (2000, May 24). Environmental Legend Criticizes Yosemite's Bus Plans. *The Fresno Bee.* <http://www.yosemite.org/newsroom/htm>.

Nelson/Nygaard Consulting Associates (1998a). *Yosemite Area Regional Transportation Strategy.* Working Paper # 5: Cost and Phasing Issues.

Nelson/Nygaard Consulting Associates (1998b). *Yosemite Area Regional Transportation Strategy.* Working Paper #6: Stakeholder Interviews.

Nelson/Nygaard Consulting Associates (1998c). *Yosemite Area Regional Transportation Strategy Major Investment Study.* Working Paper #9: Employee Transportation Strategies.

Newton, Jerry (1999). YARTS Booted by Supervisors. *Sierra Star,* February 19. <http://www.sierrastar.com/past/2-19-99/219yarts.htm>.

Yosemite National Park/California U.S. Dept. of the Interior National Park Service. *General Management Plan* (1980). Yosemite National Park.

Yosemite National Park (1998). Web Site Fact Sheets 1-13. <http://nps.nps.gov/yosemite>.

Chapter 13

Grand Canyon National Park: Tourists by Land, Tourists by Air

Irene M. Herremans

TOURISTS BY LAND

Katie and Sam are very good friends. They met while they were both studying prelaw at a university in the Midwest. After Katie completed her undergraduate degree, she decided that law was not for her. Instead she decided to enter an MBA program to obtain her graduate degree in business administration. She wanted to run her own business and was excited about the opportunities associated with voice-activated software. Katie received her MBA degree and has been working hard to make contacts and do networking to get started in her new venture.

In the meantime, Sam decided that he would enjoy corporate law. So, after completing law school, he landed an internship with a major law firm.

Even though Katie and Sam chose different paths, they both live in the same city and attended the same university for their advanced degrees. Now they were both in their early years of career development. They work long hours each day, and sometimes they even work on Saturdays or Sundays. Although they both enjoy their work immensely, Katie and Sam know the importance of taking time off. As they both enjoy the outdoors and work at staying in fairly good shape physically, they decide that a trip to the Grand Canyon would give them the tranquility and solitude they need in order to come back to the city with a fresh start.

Both of them commute to the city center each day. Even though the noises of the traffic, the crowded buses, and the commuter trains have become a part of their daily routines, they really looked forward to being away from the hustle and bustle of the city and the demands of work. They knew they would enjoy the contrast that the "natural quiet" of the national park would offer.

During the Christmas holidays, Katie and Sam meet to plan their trip to the Grand Canyon in April. They research information booklets and

Grand Canyon Airlines. (Photo courtesy of Irene M. Herremans.)

Helicopter providing an overflight of the Grand Canyon. (Photo courtesy of Irene M. Herremans.)

Trail to Hermit Rapids in the Grand Canyon. (Photo courtesy of Irene M. Herremans.)

Monument Creek in the Grand Canyon. (Photo courtesy of Irene M. Herremans.)

Colorado River through the Grand Canyon. (Photo courtesy of Irene M. Herremans.)

Internet information about the Canyon in order to determine which type of vacation might be most appropriate. They even rent a couple of videos about the Canyon to get some idea of what to expect on their adventure (see Figure 13.1).

During their planning they uncover more facts about the Grand Canyon that help to build the excitement about their trip.

GRAND CANYON NATIONAL PARK

One night as Sam and Katie were looking over books, pamphlets, and guides about the Canyon, they discovered interesting facts and information.

Grand Canyon National Park includes over 1.2 million acres of land. Another way of conceptualizing its vastness is to think of the Canyon as 277 river miles (446 km) stretching along the Colorado River. The 1,450 miles (2,333 km) of the Colorado River has carved two other canyons that are also spectacular sites: Cataract Canyon and Glen Canyon. If one thinks in terms of the width of the Canyon, it is

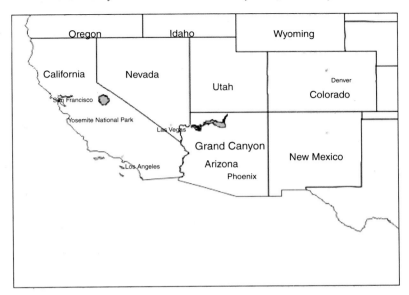

FIGURE 13.1. Grand Canyon National Park. (Map prepared by Hanako Saito.)

7 to 18 miles (11 to 29 km) from the South Rim to the North Rim, depending on where the measurement is taken. At first thought, walking rim to rim might suggest a long day in the park; however, when one considers that the walk involves an elevation gain and loss of approximately 5,000 feet (or close to a vertical mile), it adds a few days to the trip. Visualizing its beauty and stunning colors through its enormous mesas, unusual rock formations, and fascinating geology can be done in many different ways.

Some want to view its beauty from the rim, taking short walks or driving to points that provide wonderful overlooks of the Canyon. Others will hike one of the popular, well-traveled trails down to the bottom of the Canyon, such as the Bright Angel or Kaibab. Still others will choose to ride a mule or horse into the interior of the Canyon. A few will don backpacks and spend their time in remote areas, not seeing another person for several days and venturing off into areas unknown to the vast majority of the Canyon's visitors. Some will spend days rafting on the Colorado River. Others will choose to see it by air, taking one of the many daily flights that are offered. Currently under construction is the Grand Canyon Greenway. The first two segments of the Grand Canyon Greenway on the South Rim were opened to the public in 2001 (Grand Canyon National Park, n.d.). Construction on the next phase, from the Canyon View Information Plaza to the Tusayan Ruins, is expected to begin soon. Visitors will have an opportunity to use the Greenway to enjoy the Canyon's beauty and spectacular views. The Greenway will accommodate those that wish to experience the Canyon in a slow and deliberate manner rather than whizzing by in a car, bus, or airplane. The Greenway is an interconnected set of trails, both on the North and South Rim that can be used by those on foot, on bicycle, or in a wheelchair.

The Canyon attempts to provide something for every type of tourist "experience." Choosing to view the Canyon from an aerial flight provides a feel for its vastness and how it fits into its surrounding environment. The aerial flight is perfect for the traveler who wishes to see as much as possible in a short period of time, has only a few days vacation, and wishes to enjoy a whirlwind tour of the Canyon, and then enjoy some other activity. This type of traveler wishes to get as much out of his or her vacation time as possible.

Now, consider the traveler that chooses a backcountry trip that is strenuous, requires considerable advance preparation and backcountry skills, such as map reading and in some cases rock-climbing skills. The backcountry traveler can become intimately familiar and knowledgeable about a small section of the Canyon. This traveler will not see as much as the one choosing the aerial view but what the backcountry hiker does see will be much more intense and detailed.

Katie, a bit overwhelmed, looked at Sam and said: "There are so many choices. What do you want to do?"

Because both Katie and Sam like physical exercise, they decide that a backpacking trip to some of the more remote areas of the Canyon would be ideal for them. During the next few weeks, Katie would occasionally daydream about falling asleep listening to the refreshing waters of the Colorado River and the sounds of the animals scurrying from place to place that she would encounter on their Canyon vacation. Sam suggests in addition to the backpacking trip that they should plan some extra time to spend on the Greenway. Katie agreed. They hope to enjoy the beauty and spectacular views from a different vantage point than they would experience on their backcountry hiking trip. Sam and Katie make plans for the route they will follow. They decide that a three- or four-day trip below the South Rim of the Canyon would be just about right and still give them time to view some of the Canyon from above the rim.

Katie happened to be in the library one day while doing some marketing research for her company when her eye caught a small book titled *Mountains*

Without Handrails (Sax, 1980). She flipped through a few pages of the book to discover that it was about national parks. She read a few paragraphs.

> When the tourist of an earlier time came to the parks, he inevitably left the city far behind him. He may not have been a backpacker or a mountain climber, but he was genuinely immersed in a natural setting. He may only have strolled around the area near his hotel, but he was in a place where the sound of birds ruled rather than the sound of motors, where the urban crowds gave way to rural densities, and where planned entertainments disappeared in favor of a place with nothing to do but what the visitor discovered for himself.
>
> Tourism in the parks today, by contrast, is often little more than an extension of the city and its life-style transposed onto a scenic background. At its extreme, in Yosemite Valley or at the South Rim of the Grand Canyon, for example, one finds all the artifacts of urban life: traffic jams, long lines, waiting in restaurants, supermarkets, taverns, fashionable shops, night life, prepared entertainments, and the unending drone of motors. The recreational vehicle user comes incased in a rolling version of his home, complete with television for amusement when the scenery ceases to engage him. The snowmobiler brings speed and power, Detroit transplanted, imposing the city's pace in the remotest backcountry. (Sax, 1980, pp. 11-12)

Katie was surprised to read such strong criticism of the national parks. She assumed that the author, Joseph L. Sax, was perhaps going to the extreme to prove his point. She rationalized that even if there were a considerable number of cars and recreational vehicles in the park, that she and Sam would be on backcountry hiking trails and would not be bothered by all the shopping crowds, the restaurant goers, and others that were trying to bring the comforts of the city to the national park. However, her interest was sparked, and she decided to sign out the book and read further. If she couldn't find the time to read the book before her trip, she knew she would have some lazy nights sitting by her tent in camp when she could spend her time reading more of Sax's thoughts and thinking about what they meant, as she listened to the natural quiet of the Canyon.

TOURISTS BY AIR

Jake and Jenny live in New Jersey and have two children, ages seven and nine. Jake commutes to New York City each day to his job with the airlines. Jenny is an administrator at the local hospital. Each year the family tries to take a vacation together. It is sometimes difficult for Jake and Jenny to get vacation time together. However, this year, with some advanced planning, they were able to schedule some time for a vacation for the whole family in April. Even though the children are still in school during this time, they were able to pick a long, extended weekend in April. Jake and Jenny decide that they would like to spend the long weekend in Las Vegas. Although neither is too fond of gambling, they both enjoy the entertainers in Las Vegas. In addition, because the winter had been long and cold, it would give them and their children a chance to enjoy some nice warm weather. They made arrangements to fly out on a Wednesday night and return on Sunday night, giving them almost four full days in Las Vegas.

A few months later, upon arriving in Las Vegas and settling in their hotel room, Jake was looking over some of the tourist information provided. Jake happened to notice that it would be possible to take an aerial flight over the Grand Canyon from Las Vegas and return on the same day. This same company offered an optional intermediate stop at the Hoover Dam for a short rafting trip down the Colorado River. He mentioned this to Jenny and the children. None of them had ever seen the Grand Canyon and thought this would be a great opportunity to see it on the same trip without having to return another time. The rafting trip sounded exciting also. The fact that they could do it all in one day was attractive, as their time was precious. Jake investigated further and found that the four of them could book a trip for what they felt was a reasonable cost. When they compared this cost to the cost of doing a separate trip to the Grand Canyon in the future, they decided that it would be a good idea to book the trip now as they could not only enjoy the excitement of Las Vegas but also the natural beauty of the Grand Canyon and the Colorado River—all on the same vacation.

TWO BY LAND, FOUR BY AIR

Sam and Katie arrived at Flagstaff, Arizona, by air, and from there took a bus to Grand Canyon National Park. They had reservations to camp at one of the park's campgrounds for their first day and would start their hiking trail below the rim bright and early the next day. After a hearty breakfast, they took one of the Canyon's shuttle buses to a trailhead. They were excited about getting started on their four-day journey. They had chosen the Hermit Trail and knew it would take them almost the full day to get to the Colorado River, the site of their camp for the night. They did notice quite a number of people milling around the Canyon rim early in the morning. Daybreak is an excellent time to view the interesting forms of light and geological colors of the Canyon. They were a little surprised to see quite so many people.

Katie had remembered to pack *Mountains Without Handrails.* Consequently, she was looking forward to a long day hike in the tranquility of the Canyon while enjoying the magnificent scenery. Then, toward late afternoon after arriving at the campsite, she would sit by the Colorado River and read more about the ideology of the national parks while listening to the rushing waters at Hermit Rapids.

As they started down the Hermit Trail, they reminded themselves that they had 4,300 foot vertical descent to the Colorado River over about nine miles to reach their campsite for the night. They found themselves switching back through the Kaibab, Toroweap, and Coconino geological formations and were elated to find fossil reptile tracks along the way.

Their first rest stop was at Santa Maria Springs, a natural spring, where they found a wooden shelter covered with greenery. They discovered that the shelter was built in 1913. As they sat in the shelter and rehydrated themselves, the sound of an airplane flying over brought them out of their relaxed state of mind. However, they paid little attention until they heard the sound of a helicopter shortly thereafter, and another shortly after that. They knew that tourists often viewed the Canyon from airplanes and helicopters but were a little surprised to hear the noise from quite so many overflights.

As they started down the trail again, they were enjoying the geology of the Supai and Redwall formations when they noticed a constant buzz of noise from overflights. They decided to keep track of how many they heard within an hour.

Sometimes it was difficult to tell when the noise from one aircraft stopped and another began and, of course, their objective was to enjoy the Canyon rather than to count planes. Checking notes later in the day, Sam and Katie discovered that they had heard between six and ten aircraft each hour. Ten aircraft per hour would mean a flight every six minutes. Furthermore, the noise did not stop until about 5 p.m. that evening when they were in a small canyon leading down to the Colorado River.

At this point, the beauty of waterfalls and greenery instantly reenergized Sam and Katie. Before arriving at their evening's destination, they stopped frequently to take in the immensity of the boulders in various formations in this small canyon and the interesting colors and geology that could not be matched anywhere else in the world. Yes, they were tired but felt accomplished, and even though they were fatigued, they felt exuberant all at the same time. The glorious nature around them brought a renewed energy to their tired bodies. The day's hike took them through flora and fauna that they would never see around their homes in the Midwest. They were able to become intimate with nature and felt the intensity and emotions of their surroundings even while getting their camp ready for the evening. Katie and Sam decided to take a break and enjoy the wildness of the river before they prepared their dinner.

Katie read a few more pages of *Mountains Without Handrails*. Sax discussed Frederick Law Olmsted's philosophy of the existence of national parks and what activities are appropriate for them. Olmsted was the first chairman of the board of commissioners that managed Yosemite Park. Olmsted suggested that the majority of our time is spent in fulfilling the demands and expectations of other people and dealing with petty details that are a means to some other goal. He further suggests that we need an opportunity to remove ourselves from getting things accomplished and to participate in "contemplative faculty" which removes us from the confinement of duty and achievement. He believed that the scenery of the national parks is excellent for clearing our minds of thoughts of our responsibilities. Olmsted believed one of the reasons for preservation of the scenery in national parks was to provide a place for this "contemplative faculty." Although he felt that some structures in national parks were acceptable, he was opposed to those that would occupy the visitor without allowing him or her to be engaged by the beauty of the scenery. He felt that too many artificial structures would provide a distraction to the intensity and emotions of the natural beauty of the scenery—of nature itself.

Katie discussed Olmsted's ideas with Sam. Sam agreed that the backpacking trip provided distraction and that Katie and he were taking full advantage of the opportunity to "disengage their minds." But he also wondered how people who were physically challenged could enjoy this natural beauty if there weren't any artificial structures in national parks.

In the morning they discovered a whole new Canyon with interesting combinations of light and shadows providing a totally different view of the geology than they had enjoyed the night before. After a relaxing breakfast, they broke camp and got their backpacks ready for another day's travel. They enjoyed about an hour of "natural quiet" before they were once again disturbed by the whirling sound of helicopter blades overhead. Katie quickly pulled her binoculars from her pack to get a closer look at the helicopter. It was really too far away to see very much, but the noise certainly was disturbing.

Without speaking to each other, they knew each other's thoughts. They truly understood Olmsted's comments about distractions from the natural beauty of the park and distractions from their own thoughts. They had hoped that they would not experience these helicopters and airplanes every day during their hiking trip. They also wondered what effect the noise was having on the animal habitat in the Canyon.

Finally, Katie said to Sam, "We came here to experience the natural quiet of the Canyon. I can't believe there is so much noise in a national park. I am going to write the National Park Service about this situation after our trip. There must be some regulations that prevent these planes from flying through the Canyon any time of the day. I am going to investigate this further."

For the rest of their trip, they learned to block out the noise as much as possible and enjoy the trip. When they reached the South rim of the Canyon on the last day of the trip, they left the rest of their stove fuel with the backcountry office, as they could not take it back with them on the plane. They commented to the park ranger about the noise from the overflights. The ranger sighed and agreed that it was a problem and that Congress was working to pass laws that would allow the Park Service to restore at least part of the Canyon to its "natural quiet." The ranger indicated that the area over the Hermit Trail and the nearby Boucher Trail is one of the flight corridors for the overflights; therefore, the noise was worse there than in some of the other areas of the park. Sam and Katie thanked the ranger for the information and got ready to leave.

As they were leaving, they noticed signs to the Grand Canyon Airport. The airport was only about a mile from the park entrance; therefore, they decided to stop in. As they entered the airport, they were surprised to see line after line of helicopters. They parked and walked over to the takeoff and landing area. There they saw about five small planes loading tourists for overflights. Each plane would hold about twenty passengers. They noticed one couple with two small children climbing the stairs to board the airplane. While they were watching the planes get ready for takeoff, two helicopters flew over within about ten minutes of each other.

Sam looked at Katie and said, "I am glad that we chose the vacation that we did. These tourists will not experience the intensity of the Canyon in the same way that we did. They will never hear the rushing water or the noise of the wildlife over the sounds of the aircraft or see the beautiful flowers or interesting cactus. By taking a whirlwind tour lasting about a half hour, these tourists are missing so much of what the Canyon really is."

Katie replied, "I agree fully, but did you notice the couple with the two small children? Do you think they could have enjoyed the same adventure we did or should alternatives be available for those whose situations require a different experience?"

BIBLIOGRAPHY

Alexander, Brenton (1998). The National Park Service and the Regulation of the Air Tour Industry at Grand Canyon National Park. *Natural Resources Journal* 38(Spring), 277-295.

Flightseeing Controversy: Sierra Club: <www.sierraclub.org>.

Grand Canyon Explorer (2005). <www.kaibab.org>.

Grand Canyon National Park (n.d.). <www.grandcanyon.org>.

International Standards Organization (2005). <www.iso.ch>.

National Parks Overfights Act of 1987, An act to require the Secretary of the Interior to conduct a study to determine the appropriate minimum altitude for aircraft flying over national park system units. Public Law 100-91. *Stat.* 674.

National Park Service (NPS) (1994). *Report on the Effects of Aircraft Overflights on the National Park System.* Report to Congress Prepared Pursuant to Public Law 100-91. The National Parks Overflights Act of 1987. National Park Service, September 12.

Noise Pollution Clearinghouse (n.d.). <www.nonoise.org>.

Right to Quiet Society for Soundscape Awareness and Protection (n.d.). <www. quiet. org>.

Sax, Joseph L. (1980). *Mountains Without Handrails.* The University of Michigan Press and John Wiley & Sons Canada, Limited.

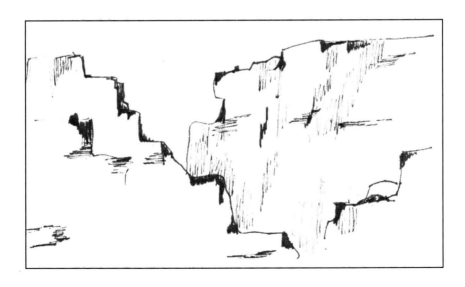

Chapter 14

Addressing Tourism Conflicts in Banff National Park: The Banff Bow Valley Round Table Process

Marcus Eyre
Tazim B. Jamal

CONTEXT: BANFF NATIONAL PARK'S TURBULENT HISTORY

The management of protected areas must increasingly contend with the timeless philosophical debate of preservation versus use being transformed into more direct stakeholder conflicts. Among the current concerns frequently expressed are those of destination image in the marketplace, impacts on ecological integrity, and "sustainable development." The history of the national parks and the issues described in this case reflect the traditional tension and interdependence between development and preservation found in protected areas worldwide.

In 1883, the track-laying crews of the Canadian Pacific Railway (CPR) reached the site of Banff. Two workers came upon a hot spring (see Figure 14.1). Two years later, with the backing of the CPR, the Canadian government reserved an area around the Banff hot springs which was later expanded to become Banff National Park (BNP). In 1886 the town site of Banff was laid out and two years later the CPR opened its first hotel in the Canadian Rocky Mountains. The Banff Springs Hotel and the marketing of tourism for the wealthy was seen to be a means of financing the construction of Canada's transcontinental railway, which was vital to the building of the nation. Thus, the origin of Canada's first national park was intimately linked with economic interests. Indeed, it has been argued that the emphasis on the economic potential of the scenery for tourism entrenched a system and philosophy of "parks for profit" (Bella, 1987).

Early conservation struggles and growing awareness of the need to protect the natural landscape led Canada to enshrine the protection of national

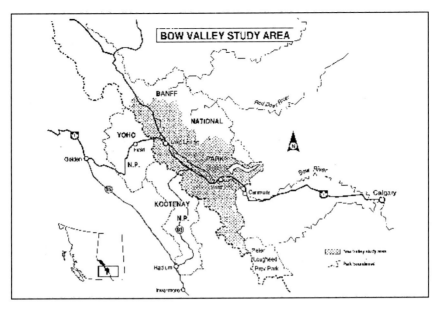

FIGURE 14.1. Location map of Banff National Park and BBVS study area. (*Source:* Reprinted with permission. Newsletter, Issue 1, May 1995. Banff Bow-Valley Study, 1996. Banff-Bow Valley: At the Crossroads. Technical Report of the Banff-Bow Valley Task Force (Robert Page, Suzanne Bayley, J. Douglas Cook, Jeffrey E. Green, and J. R. Brent Ritchie). Prep. for the Honourable Sheila Copps, Minister of Canadian Heritage, Ottawa, ON).

Young elk wander freely in the Banff township. (Photo courtesy of Marcus Eyre and Irene M. Herremans.)

The view south of the Bow Valley immediately east of the Banff township, with the Trans-Canada highway's Cascade interchange and part of the Cascade Wildlife Corridor in the foreground. (Photo courtesy of Marcus Eyre and Irene M. Herremans.)

The Trans-Canada highway through Banff National Park. The fence prevents wildlife from entering the highway. This reduces both accidents and wildlife mortality; however, it also significantly impacts the natural patterns of wildlife movements. To mitigate this, a system of wildlife underpasses and overpasses were built. Their effectiveness is being monitored. (Photo courtesy of Marcus Eyre and Irene M. Herremans.)

parks in legislation. This signaled the winding down of activities such as mining and logging in national parks. Canada's 1930 National Parks Act states that the national parks are dedicated "to the people of Canada for their benefit, education and enjoyment . . . and shall be maintained and made use of so as to leave them unimpaired for the enjoyment of future generations." This is often interpreted as a dual mandate. A 1988 amendment to the Parks Act adds that ecological integrity shall be the first priority in parks management.

Today, visitation to Banff National Park has grown to around 5 million annually, up from 459,000 in 1950, and could reach 10 to 19 million by the year 2020, depending on projected growth rates (BBVS, 1996). Thus the future of BNP, as is the case with many other parks, continues to be influenced as much by tourism as by any desire to preserve a legacy of natural heritage. Most of this human and economic activity occurs in the main watershed of BNP, the Bow Valley. The town of Banff, a railroad and highway corridor, contains ski resorts and other infrastructure and services situated within the Bow Valley. However, the valley is also ecologically significant because it includes most of the park's montane ecoregion, a critical habitat for some species that is rich in biodiversity. Having suffered from a range of environmental impacts due to development and growth (both visitation- and population-related), it is arguably the most controversial area in Canada's national parks, to the extent that the Park's status as a UNESCO World Heritage Site has been called into question.

For years, there has been dispute as to the nature and severity of specific problems. The issues surround the extent of visitor activities and tourism developments, their growth, and the impacts they have on a legislatively protected environment. At the same time, the historically entrenched tourism industry is often uncritically viewed as the economic sector most compatible with sustainable development and the use of protected areas (Butler, 1991), while the interdependence between the natural and the social domains remains largely unacknowledged or inadequately addressed.

THE BANFF BOW VALLEY STUDY AND ROUND TABLE

The need to address persistent conflicts in the park, at least between "environmentalists" and "developers" finally led the federal government to initiate the two-year-long Banff Bow Valley Study (BBVS, 1996) in 1994, at a cost of more than $2 million. The purpose of the study was to "integrate environmental, social and economic considerations in order to develop management and land-use strategies that are sustainable and meet the objectives of the National Parks Act" (p. 2).

To conduct the study, the then Minister of Canadian Heritage, the Honourable Sheila Copps (responsible for Parks Canada) also appointed a five-member task force (Banff Bow Valley Task Force—BBVTF) of experts in ecology, tourism, public policy, and management. Almost immediately, the task force's legitimacy, independence, and objectivity were questioned, as well as the need for another government study. Consequently, the task force had to establish its credibility, and reach out and draw its constituents into the process. The Minister of Heritage also required that public involvement and feedback be incorporated into the study (public input through various mechanisms is established in parks policy as well). The task force used several approaches to elicit input, most notably a high-profile, multisectoral round table facilitated by a formally appointed mediator. This round-table process faced an immediatel setback due to media articles in the national press and reactions to it. Indeed, over the span of the process, the attention surrounding the study, including that in the international print media, took the issues into public spheres beyond the local level.

This complication in the launching of the round table reiterates the need to take time, at the onset, to negotiate rules of procedure, including media relations, and to ensure a means to manage conflict and differences within the process. The first meeting of the Banff Bow Valley Round Table (BBVRT) eventually convened in February 1995 with fourteen sectors, each representing somewhat related interest groups and individuals. These included four commercial sectors, local and national environmental sectors, culture and social/health/education sectors, a park users sector, the federal government, the municipalities of the region, and the BBV Task Force (see Table 14.1). The provincial government sat as an observer and the two First Nations sectors dropped out early in the process.

Because each sector represented a number of organizations and individuals, maintaining a smooth flow of information between the grassroots constituents and their sector representatives was a constant challenge. The initial role of the Round Table, with respect to the study's mandate, was to identify issues, provide public input toward a coordinated strategy for the region, develop a vision, and possibly develop specific action plans (BBVRT, 1996). Although consensus-based, shared decision making was the mechanism selected by the task force for the BBVRT, the Round Table was only an advisory body and was one source of input (though a major one). Its recommendations were considered and incorporated in the final report by the task force. The decision to not only include the main interest groups in the study, but to place them centrally in this negotiating and consultation process also reflects both a method to integrate different considerations and the need to resolve stakeholder conflicts.

TABLE 14.1. Banff-Bow Valley Study—Round Table Representation.

Sector	Participating stakeholders
Alberta Provincial Government (observer only)	Representatives from Alberta Environmental Protection and Alberta Economic Development and Tourism
Banff-Bow Valley Study Task Force	Dr. Robert Page (chair), Dr. Suzanne Bayley, J. Douglas Cook, Jeffrey E. Green, and Dr. J.R. Brent Ritchie
Commercial Outdoor Recreation	Skiing, biking, touring, guiding organizations, etc. (e.g., Ski Banff/Lake Louise, Holiday on Horseback)
Commercial Visitor Services	Accommodations, restaurants, retail services, etc. (e.g., Alberta Hotel Assoc'n, Moraine Lake Lodge)
Culture	Local and regional organizations and individuals
Federal Government	Parks Canada (Banff National Park), Environment Canada, Western Economic Diversification, etc.
First Nations—Siksika	Members of Siksika
First Nations—Wesley	Members of Wesley
Infrastructure/Transportation	Transportation, utilities, etc. (e.g., TransAlta Utilities, Canadian Western Natural Gas, CP Rail, Banff Flying Club)
Local Environment	Bow Valley Naturalists, Trout Unlimited, etc.
Municipal Government	Town of Banff, Town of Canmore, Lake Louise Advisory Board, M.D. of Bighorn, I.D.#9, etc.
National Environment	Canadian Parks and Wilderness Society, Canadian Nature Federation, etc.
Park Users	Steering Committee of over 20 individuals and groups (about 28 listed at some point), including the Alpine Club of Canada, Banff Flying Club, Hostelling International, Rocky Mountain Ramblers Cycle Club, etc.
Social/Health/Education	Community Services and Hospital Advisory Board, residents, etc.
Tourism/Marketing	Association for Mountain Parks Protection and Enjoyment (AMPPE), Banff/Lake Louise Tourism Bureau, Lake Louise Ski Club, etc.

The Round Table started its work by creating sectoral interest statements and conducting an extensive visioning exercise. In the subsequent negotiation phase, the sectors' concerns were reduced down to three broad issues agreed on by all sectors: ecological integrity, appropriate use, and community health (including socioeconomic factors). Along with being descriptive these also imply desired goals. Ecological integrity was the first subject area discussed and on which the most time was spent. Appropriate use was mostly discussed in the context of developing a framework to evaluate future proposals in the park. Community health and the broader socioeconomic context received only limited time in the last meetings. The environmental groups had extensive scientific information to support their arguments, but commercial and visitor use data were limited and not well organized, despite the traditional economic power of business interests in this domain.

In the end, participants in this multistakeholder process formulated a joint vision, participated in a range of activities, including goal setting (e.g., strategic ecological goals), and developed a compendium of information and facts related to the study area. The BBVS and round-table process also contributed to an existing initiative to develop a heritage tourism strategy for the park's tourism stakeholders. All of these were influential to the task force's final report, aspects of which were subsequently incorporated into the 1997 Park Management Plan.

The BBVRT multistakeholder process, which brought together environmental, political, economic, social, and cultural interests to address tourism and ecological-related concerns in the park, presents some useful insights for managers and stakeholders addressing park-based tourism conflicts.

IDEOLOGICAL CONFLICTS IN THE PARK
AND IN THE PROCESS

Public concern and controversy in the park were perceived by many respondents to be major drivers for the initiation of the BBVS. For different participants, the town of Banff and the rest of the park's ecological integrity constituted different realities. For one participant, the overriding concern was "the issue of preservation versus development" (note the use of *versus,* implying one or the other).

For one government participant involved with the park, human presence and ecological integrity were both realities included in the park's policy document creating a "degree of tension." Some business and environmental stakeholders preferred to ignore one or the other, depending on their interest. Many didn't understand the park's policies or plans, or the issue of limits. The contradictions between two coexisting realities arising out of the ongoing evolution of the national parks also creates tension for those assigned to administer the parks. Perhaps not surprisingly, Parks Canada bears the brunt of criticism and disgruntlement. The participant noted that in previous public forums "everyone kicks at the cat here all at once and nobody has to compromise their values. . ." A process like the BBVRT, he went on, forced developers and businesses (for example) to work out some mutual goals before "coming to the table," rather than the usual scenario of approaching park authorities with demands that sometimes conflicted with other business and tourism interests in the park.

In an area where multiple realities conflict, the government agency is in the uncomfortable position of managing a park that is a contested terrain for ecological and human needs. As one respondent noted, its governance did not reflect the ecological knowledge possessed by park managers. This often took second place to administering business, political, and environmental pressures related to tourism development and protection of the park's ecology. For park managers, control becomes a key issue: controlling visitor impacts on the park, and controlling the park from an ecosystem management perspective that considers human presence and needs.

Also caught in the conflict are the local inhabitants in the park, including those in the town of Banff, which serves as both a community for local residents and a service provider to visitors. For a number of the residents who live in and adjacent to the park, documenting and cherishing the culture and heritage of the park was important, as was the small community "feel" and interdependence with the natural environment. One park resident expressed the sentiment that, "It's linking business practices to the environment. It's linking our lives to the environment. It's linking our whole lifestyle, consumption patterns to understanding the consequences of what we're doing" (personal interview, November 1995, Banff resident and BBVRT participant).

As an ideological contest, the BBVRT demonstrates how ideological practices served to construct and legitimize social reality in the process. The following reflects the tone of the "profound conflict" between different stakeholders and their values.

> The fact that there's a whole bunch of dollars produced in this park doesn't threaten my values and my way of looking at the world in any way. I understand that there are decisions made that are based on that because that's important to other people who see the world as something to be consumed. But when you start saying, because we've grown up thinking that the world is something that we can and should consume, and when somebody comes along and says well, wait a minute there's, you know, if we're willing to accept that there are other values, then there are things that we have to do to accommodate those other values. That's a terrifying prospect for people to even think about let alone act on and that's where the most profound conflict exists, I think, at the table and in society generally. (Personal interview, December 1995, BBVRT environmental participant)

Conflict in the park lies in the reluctance of any group with a particular set of values and ideology to accommodate another group with a different set of values. To the previous respondent, businesses see the park as something to consume, yet other values also exist and need to be accommodated, such as valuing wildlife intrinsically. A subtle ambiance of positional bargaining between the business and development groups—a win-lose scenario as indicated in the following quote—its historic pattern throughout the process, though cooperative efforts were demonstrated by most sectors.

> A national park is a perfect example of choosing options, which is what decision making is about, and if we're looking at choosing between preservation and development. If we choose to preserve, the development option remains. If we choose to develop, the option to preserve disappears . . . we're not going to win. We're never going to win. (Personal interview, December 1995, BBVRT environmental participant)

Repeatedly, the sense of competition was felt, because business and environmentalists each perceive the other as holding different values as foundations to their existence. Environmental values included administering the park "with love and respect" and "celebrating the wonder" of the national park through reflective or contemplative recreation. However, such values were never meaningfully discussed.

Instead, the win-lose discourse persisted. The environmental sectors presented a well-knit and strong presence at the table. They were (and still are) exasperated with the lack of attention paid to the deteriorating ecological conditions in the park, and with the long hours spent contesting development proposals in court and public meetings. Political pressures, they felt, influenced the park's administrators to favor development despite existing policies and "what we've seen happen in Banff in the past is the business community has a very strong voice" (environmental respondent, BBVRT). Hence, their strategy at the round table was to focus on providing scientific evidence to legitimize the "crisis" in the park. For the business and tourism stakeholders, it was a struggle to try and understand the science being presented, and to bring forward their own interests. They did not have the social and visitors statistics of the park at their fingertips. This information was not easily available as the tourism facilities, services, and other related agencies in the park tended to perform their own visitor surveys and market research. No central data bank existed on the historic use, economic, and social impacts, visitor use, and activity patterns, etc. Backcountry use statistics (e.g., overnight stays in the backcountry) were available from Parks Canada, but day-use patterns and impacts were not available or not easily accessible. Hence, when it came to setting ecological goals and strategies, it was difficult for the business sectors to understand the implications of the environmental sectors' suggestions. The following dialogue was part of the Round Table discussion on developing ecological strategic goals:

TASK FORCE EXPERT: We need from the table as many descriptors of the desired state. We can provide you with some information.

CHAIR, MUNICIPAL SECTOR: I'm not a scientist; I'm a historian. To write something [I] have to have adequate knowledge . . . the concept here is best available knowledge. From my understanding of the indicators listed here there isn't enough knowledge to do a good job. . . . Jeff said I don't need to understand current state to get an idea of future state. Well, I think I do.

CHAIR, COMMERCIAL OUTDOOR RECREATION: Ted [Chair, Municipal Sector] has discussed most of what I wanted to discuss; we don't know (our sector), we don't know what science knows. . . So its not clear for us what the starting point is.

TASK FORCE EXPERT: We don't need to know current state. We want to know what your sector wants to see, e.g., tourists want to see elk, bears, etc.

MEDIATOR: You've done a lot already; I am confident that you know more and can contribute . . .

CHAIR, TOURIST SECTOR: To some extent I [also] have a great fear of adopting these strategic goals because I don't know where I am and where I'm going.

Later that day, the tourism sector representative repeated his fear of not understanding the potential implications of the strategic goals on tourism interests in the park:

CHAIR, TOURIST SECTOR: I am repeating myself for the umpteenth time. . . [I am] concerned that goals are coming out in black and white. . . [I] don't want to be hemmed in. (Round Table meeting, January 13, 1996)

Not surprisingly, one business respondent felt it was more important to manage the practical implications of specific problems, such as the difficulty of bears and humans vying for the same space in a specific habitat area, than focusing on whether there was a "crisis" in the park or not. For this respondent, not getting the tourism business agenda on the table was partly related to not having access to technical data on human use and visitation aspects of the park. Hence, one outcome of the process was his group asking for the development of a database on the social science aspects of human and visitor use.

The rhetoric surrounding the round table consensus processes is that it seeks to "accommodate rather than compromise" everyone's interests (BBVRT, 1996). The idea of the BBVRT, or any consensus process, being different from bargaining or politics may be debatable. Though a consensus-based round table can help to even out power imbalances, it may also undervalue some interests while overrepresenting others. This problem occurred with the BBVRT. Despite agreement by all BBVRT sectors on the need for open governance, some sectors still attempted to lobby the minister after the process was over.

The BBVRT process was an attempt to resolve and manage an ongoing conflict of great concern to the Minister of Canadian Heritage, due to threats to both the World Heritage Site status of Banff National Park and to the important role of the park to Canadian tourism and the regional economy. Criticisms by environmental advocacy groups and conflicts over use and development reported in the international media were detrimental to the image of Banff as a world-class tourism destination and as Canada's flagship national park. In convening the Banff Bow Valley Study, it was evident to the Minister that managing this space was going to be a difficult task, given the multiple interests and contested mandate of the national parks.

BIBLIOGRAPHY

Banff-Bow Valley Round Table (1996). Banff Bow Valley Round Table Summary Report. Banff, Alberta. (The Summary Report is Copyright Minister of Supply and Services Canada. Cat. No. R63-219/1996E. ISBN 0-662-25091-5.)

Banff Bow Valley Study (1996). *Banff-Bow Valley: At the Crossroads. Technical Report of the Banff-Bow Valley Task Force* (Robert Page, Suzanne Bayley, J. Doglas Cook, Jeffrey E. Green, and J.R. Brent Ritchie). Prep. for the Honourable Sheila Copps, Minister of Canadian Heritage, Ottawa, ON.

Bateson, J.E. (1992). *Managing Services Marketing.* Second Edition. Orlando, Florida: The Dryden Press.

Bella, Leslie (1987). *Parks for Profit.* Montreal: Harvest House.

Butler, R.W. (1991). Tourism, Environment and Sustainable Development. *Environmental Conservation,* 18(3).

Canada's National Parks Act (1930). An Act Respecting National Pars, s.c. 1930, c. 33 s.4.

Darier, E. (Ed.) (1999). *Discourses of the Environment.* Oxford, UK: Blackwell Publishers.

Eagleton, T. (1991). *Ideology: An Introduction.* London: Verso.

Eyre, M. (1997). The Role and Limitations of Indicators in Environmental Decision Making; With an Evaluation of the Banff Bow Valley Round Table Process. Master's degree project, faculty of Environmental Design, The University of Calgary, Alberta.

Freeman, R. E. (1984). *Strategic Management: A Stakeholder Approach.* London: Pittman.

Gray, B. (1989). *Collaborating: Finding Common Ground for Multiparty Problems.* San Francisco: Jossey-Bass.

Gunn, C.A. (1988). *Tourism Planning.* Second Edition. New York: Taylor and Francis.

Harrison, P. (1993). *The Third Revolution: Population, Environment and a Sustainable World.* Second Edition. London: Penguin Book Ltd.

Jamal, T. (1997) *Multi-Party Consensus Processes in Environmentally Sensitive Destinations: Paradoxes of Ownership and Common Ground.* PhD dissertation, Faculty of Management, University of Calgary, Calgary, Alberta, Canada.

Mitchell, R.K., Agle, B.R., and Wood, D.J. (1997). Toward a theory of stakeholder identification and salience: Defining the principle of who and what really counts. *Academy of Management Review,* 22: 853-886.

Murphy, P.E. (1985). *Tourism: A Community Approach.* New York: Methuen.

Murphy, P.E. (1988). Community-driven Tourism Planning. *Tourism Management,* 9(2): 96-105.

Pacas, C., Bernard, D., Marshall, N., and Green, J. (1996). *State of the Banff Bow Valley: A Compendium of Information.* January 1996 draft. Prepared for the Banff Bow Valley Study. Department of Canadian Heritage, Ottawa, Ontario.

Parks Canada (1994). *Guiding Principles and Operational Policies.* Ottawa, Ontario: Department of Canadian Heritage, Minister of Supply and Services Canada.

Saul, J.R. (1995). *The Unconscious Civilization.* Concord, Ontario: House of Anansi Press Limited.

Sax, J.L. (1980). *Mountains Without Handrails: Reflections on the National Parks.* Ann Arbor: The University of Michigan Press.

Searle, M. (2000). *Phantom Parks: The Struggle to Save Canada's National Parks.* Toronto: Key Porter Books.

Chapter 15

A Journey to Define Sustainability: Waterton Lakes National Park

Robin E. Reid

This case study was created from the author's master's thesis. The circumstances surrounding Waterton Lakes National Park are factual. All names have been changed to protect the confidentiality of those involved.

INTRODUCTION

It was a clear, sunny day in late August. Julienne was enjoying the last few days of her vacation in Waterton Lakes National Park, a small destination park in the southwest corner of Alberta. The park is characterized by the mountains of the continental divide to the west, the rolling prairies to the north and east, and Glacier National Park in the United States to the south. As a symbol of international peace and friendship between the people of the United States and Canada, Waterton and Glacier Parks were united in 1932 as the first international peace park in the world and is now referred to as Waterton/Glacier International Peace Park. In 1995, Waterton-Glacier International Peace Park was also designated as a World Heritage Site (see Figure 15.1). Waterton was also one of the first national parks in Canada to be designated as a Biosphere Reserve through UNESCO's Man and the Biosphere program (MAB). Areas selected for designation have a protected core. In this case, Waterton Park is the protected core and the landscape surrounding the park is designated as a "zone of cooperation" in which human impacts are monitored. Waterton is geographically situated "where the prairies meet the mountains" and the unique combination of prairie and mountain landscapes generates a rich variety of flora and fauna, some of which are rare both nationally and provincially. Because the terrain in the Waterton Park town site is relatively low-lying and relatively sheltered it is not unusual to see deer and sheep in the town site.

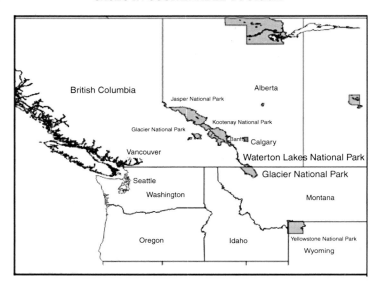

FIGURE 15.1. Waterton-Glacier International Peace Park. (Map prepared by Hanako Saito.)

A scenic view of Waterton Lakes National Park. (Photo courtesy of Paul Gray.) Reprinted with permission.

Bull elk roam freely in Waterton park. (Photo courtesy of Paul Gray.) Reprinted with permission.

Waterton view. (Photo courtesy of Paul Gray.) Reprinted with permission.

Waterton's steep inclines provide a dynamic visual experience. (Photo courtesy of Paul Gray.) Reprinted with permission.

Waterton National Park contains Cameron Falls, a visitor favorite. (Photo courtesy of Paul Gray.) Reprinted with permission.

Ranching is a way of life for some residents of Waterton. (Photo courtesy of Paul Gray.) Reprinted with permission.

While walking from the shore of Upper Waterton Lake to the candy store, Julienne came upon two teenagers offering crackers to a young buck deer in exchange for an opportunity to touch the velvet of his horns. The young buck did not seem to mind this exchange and appeared content to follow the teenagers down one of the few main streets in the Waterton town site. At the time, Julienne wondered why this sort of behavior (feeding wildlife) appeared to be acceptable in national parks. The more she thought about it, the more it began to bother her. So, she stopped at the entrance of the campground and asked a park employee about the park's role in prohibiting people from feeding wildlife.

JULIENNE: Does Waterton Park's management attempt to educate visitors to the park about feeding wildlife?

PARK EMPLOYEE: Park employees do spend considerable energy on personal and nonpersonal messaging about wildlife feeding. However, we don't always have time to cover all the wildlife issues in the park. We have to let people know where to park their vehicles and where the restrooms, cook shelters, and other infrastructure and services in the park are located. We cannot tell visitors about everything in the park because they would suffer from information overload and not remember everything anyway.

Julienne pondered this response and came to the realization that information appears to be prioritized according to visitor needs and demands as opposed to educating visitors about the importance of maintaining the environmental integrity of the park landscape. Julienne decided this situation required more investigation into the purpose of national parks and visitors' behavior toward wildlife in park settings. Her inquisitive nature was developed in part from her present career as a journalist for *Travel Insight Magazine,* based in Calgary. When she returned to Calgary she reviewed the Parks Canada mandate. She found out that the first amendment to the National Parks Act of 1930, in 1988, recognized that "maintaining ecological integrity" through zoning in the Park Management Plan was first priority. In accordance with this priority, the 1994 National Parks policy statement stresses the ecological role of national parks.

INVESTIGATING THE ROLE OF NATIONAL PARKS

If the primary focus is to maintain the environmental integrity of national parks, Julienne wondered why people were still feeding wildlife and not being penalized for their actions. She phoned the Parks Canada office in Calgary and spoke with Jeoff about her concern.
According to Jeoff:

> Fining people for feeding wildlife is a money-losing proposition. For example, there are different levels of penalties that are associated with fines. First, there are major offenses such as poaching that are penalized with heavy fines. Then there are minor offenses such as picking wildflowers and feeding wildlife. At present, feeding wildlife is a summary conviction offense under the National Parks Act. If someone is "found committing," a park warden can give them a warning or issue an Appearance Notice which constitutes a charge and a mandatory court appearance to enter a plea. Now, let's say a fine for feeding wildlife is $150, but it costs taxpayers more than the $150 to have the person appear in court. It becomes economically unfeasible to take people to court over a fine of $150. Furthermore, how do you think a judge with a busy caseload is going to respond to a court hearing over picking wildflowers in a national park? The judge is going to regard the whole process as a waste of time and would probably throw it out

of court. Another option that is presently under consideration is a "voluntary payment ticket" whereby an accused person can plead guilty and pay a preset fine through the mail. However, there is presently no mechanism in place to issue a "voluntary payment ticket." Given this scenario, the most common response by park personnel is to issue warnings to people about feeding wildlife in the parks.

Julienne found this interesting but sad. However, before she could form an opinion about visitor behavior in national parks she felt she needed to gather some more information. She decided to turn her attention toward the tourism industry as a possible avenue for changing human behavior or at least mitigating some of the impacts visitors have on the environmental integrity of parks.

After a few days of rigorous research Julienne became more familiar with the characteristics of tourism. Internationally, tourism is a growth industry and is approaching $3.4 trillion in terms of gross output worldwide. Furthermore, tourism accounts for 10.9 percent of all consumer spending, 10.7 percent of all capital investment, and 6.9 percent of all government spending. Based on these figures it is no wonder that governments, developers, and tour operators are looking for opportunities to build more facilities to attract more visitors to some of the world's natural areas. Furthermore, Julienne began to realize that tourism has traditionally been regarded as a relatively benign industry compared to other industries such as energy and forestry. However, during Julienne's research, she stumbled upon an author named McKercher (1993) who described tourism not as a benign industry but rather as an industrial activity that consumes resources, creates waste, and has specific infrastructure needs. McKercher (1993) further asserts that tourism is a private-sector-dominated industry, and short-term profit maximization is predominantly the basis for tourism investment decisions. Given these characteristics, Julienne had to wonder why tourism as an industrial activity is allowed to operate in national parks at all. Essentially, parks and protected areas are the only places legislated to legally achieve the goals of environmental sustainability. At the same time, tourism continues to be the only exploitative industry permitted in parks and protected areas. The irony of the situation began to irritate Julienne.

Also, Julienne was surprised at how little effort appears to be taken on the part of the tourism industry to make tourism sustainable despite the terminology that has emerged to suggest otherwise. For example, "alternative," "green," "responsible," and "eco" are terms presented to the traveling public as forms of tourism that have the potential to benefit both tourists and host destinations by minimizing ecological and social impacts to local landscapes. Julienne could not find any examples of tourism that actually accomplish ecological sustainability. To her disappointment, she also learned that the term "ecotourism" was being used as a marketing tool by tour operators, governments, and tour agents to capitalize on a growing segment of environmentally conscious travelers. Julienne wondered if this misuse of the term was because the concept of sustainability is not well understood in terms of tourism or human development. In an effort to understand the relationship between tourism and the environment, she began to compile information on the concept of sustainable tourism.

Julienne was aware that the World Commission on Environment and Development's (WCED) Brundtland Report is the first document to stimulate international dialogue and large-scale discussion on the environmental limitations of human growth and development (Bruntland, 1987). The Brundtland Report defines sustainability as "development that meets the needs of the present without compromising the ability of future generations to meet their own needs."

In defining sustainable development, two significant concerns challenged the WCED: first, the deterioration of the earth's environment; and second, the commitment to feed, clothe, house, and deal with the waste of an increasing human population (Rubenstein, 1994). Unfortunately, as the human population continues to increase, the demand for natural resources increases also. Given the present rate of destruction and depletion of the world's ecosystems, the demands of the human population appear to be greater than the earth's ability to sustain human development.

From the dictionary Julienne learned that the word *sustain* means to "bear weight of or support, especially for a long time." The distinguishing characteristic of sustainability then is the "ability to be continued." However, the concept of sustainability is relatively new and is open to various interpretations of what exactly is to be continued. In an effort to clarify what is to be continued, Julienne decided the term "environmental" should be introduced as a modifier of sustainability (Brown et al., 1987; Shearman, 1990). An environmental modifier introduces the underlying assumption that it is important to sustain the earth's environmental processes which make development possible. By adding the term "ecological" to "sustainable tourism" there is a clear message that the environmental integrity of the landscape is to be continued. Consequently, within a tourism context, environmental sustainability refers to the levels of tourism development that do not exceed or destroy the ability of ecosystems to retain their basic structures or functions over the long-term (Grumbine, 1992). Given that many forms of tourism rely on the condition of the landscape for their long-term success, Julienne was concerned that tourism developments and activities still manage to exceed the ecological limitations of local areas.

Julienne went to seek the advice of an old friend of hers, Sam, who was very familiar with the writing of Wilson.

JULIENNE: Why is it so difficult to achieve a common ecological focus for sustainable tourism?

SAM: Because a common focus is dependent upon how we value the natural landscapes that support human activities and development such as tourism. According to Wilson, "Humans and nature construct one another and our ability to shape, transform and control the physical environment determined our relationship with nature" (Wilson, 1991:14). Ultimately, human values determine our relationships with nature.

JULIENNE: At one time tourism was considered an acceptable activity in national parks.

SAM: Wilson had a colleague, Arwal, who pointed out that by pushing nature back to accommodate tourist demands for infrastructure we have essentially created a cash generating type of nature shaped to meet urban and industrial needs. Banff National Park is a case in point.

JULIENNE: Recent public concern for the destruction of the natural world has stimulated dialogue about the type and rate of development that is ecologically sustainable in national parks and protected areas.

SAM: Yes, but as Wilson (1991) pointed out, achieving tourism that is ecologically sustainable is still dependent upon human values. So until society is willing to change its behavior toward nature, tourism activities will probably continue to impact wildlife and degrade the ecological integrity of park landscapes.

As a journalist, Julienne wondered if there was a story here that could reveal the way in which human values shape the tourism environment. She felt strongly that her subject matter was timely given the recent public discourse about Alberta's natural spaces and protected areas. She decided to approach her boss, Robert, about the idea. Robert was receptive to the story idea, but had some concerns. Julienne explained that her story would be based on an investigation of how human values ultimately determine if tourism is sustainable or unsustainable.

Julienne explained further how she planned to approach the story:

JULIENNE: The concept of sustainability has emerged as a clear message that something should and can be done to address the environmental, social, and economic conditions of human development. However, there appears to be some confusion regarding the term sustainability and further misinterpretations about how to achieve the goals of sustainability. For example, in the literature, the economic, social, and environmental are common perspectives from which to view sustainable development and sustainable tourism.

Julienne used the following diagram while talking with her boss.

JULIENNE: From an economic perspective, sustainability refers to the acquisition of wealth and continued expansion of economic activity. However, economic growth and the rising material standards of industrialized countries accelerate resource consumption and depletion of natural resources (Wackernagel and Rees, 1996). From a social perspective, sustainability refers to "the continued satisfaction of basic human needs—food, water, and shelter as well as higher-level social and cultural necessities" (Brown et al., 1987: 716). Within an environmental context, sustainability represents "the continued productivity and functioning of ecosystems" (Brown et al., 1987: 716). Difficulty arises in achieving a common perspective toward the tourism/environment relationship because each stakeholder will have a different perspective toward the concept of sustainability. Consequently, there are misinterpretations of what is meant by the term. From the preliminary research I have conducted I have come to the conclusion that the environmental perspective should be the primary focus of sustainability. After all, it is the earth's environmental processes that make human development and progress possible in the first place. In other words the diagram should look something like this.

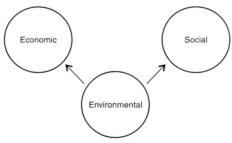

To achieve sustainability, Julienne explained that the environmental perspective should be established first before the social and economic demands are placed on the landscape. The problem is that a common environmental perspective toward tourism is dependent upon human values. Robert listened to Julienne's approach but was unsure how human values could be explored. He asked Julienne to explain how she intended to investigate human values. Julienne explained that she had decided to interview local stakeholders in the Waterton area. These interviews would provide insight into some of the difficulties that arise in achieving a common environmental focus toward tourism that is sustainable. The interviews also could help her to understand the different perspectives between human values and sustainability within a tourism context.

ROBERT: Who are the stakeholders in the Waterton area?

JULIENNE: I am focusing on four major groups—ranchers, the Municipal District of Pincher Creek, representatives of the First Nations people, and Parks Canada.

ROBERT: Why have you selected these particular groups of stakeholders?

JULIENNE: Because the First Nations people and the ranchers have historical ties to the area that extend beyond that of WLNP [Waterton Lakes National Park]. Also, an interesting aspect of WLNP is that it was established in 1895 at the request of local residents and was called Kootenay Lakes Forest Park at the time. Though Banff, Jasper, and Yoho Parks were developed primarily as stopovers for rail and automobile travelers, Waterton was established for the recreational and social opportunities it provided to local residents. Of course, the Municipal District of Pincher Creek will have its own perspective toward tourism development in the Waterton area, as will the representatives of WLNP. By interviewing different stakeholder groups I am attempting to see if there is a common ecological perspective toward tourism development and activities. In other words, is ecologically sustainable tourism a realistic goal in the Waterton area?

ROBERT: I don't know if there is a story here Julienne, but I will agree that it could be an interesting exercise, nonetheless.

Within a few days Julienne was back in Waterton interviewing Gerald Crow, a representative of one of the local native tribes in the area.

GERALD: When we go back to our creation stories, we have a strong tie to the land and to the animals. The native culture is therefore structured by the intrinsic and spiritual value of nature. In the native traditional view, the creator gave all living things (humans, animals, plants, and minerals) authority to exist first in the abstract before they existed in the physical world. Once the physical world was created it was put together with the abstract to create an entity. Every living thing (rocks, plants, animals, and humans) are entities. So everything is equal; the equality starts at that point of becoming an entity. Within this traditional native worldview our culture is integrated with nature at the level of an ecosystem where humans are not placed above nature; rather humans are part of nature. In terms of tourism, the natural draw of tourists to the Waterton Lakes National Park area is the abstract concept of the land that is there . . . the beauty of it all. That's what draws tourists, but they haven't looked deep enough, spiritually, at the land. Consequently, they don't understand how their activities affect the land. Our tribe has historical ties to the Waterton landscape and Waterton Park. Therefore, we can play an important role as interpreters of the past. In this role there is an opportunity for us to educate tourists and build awareness about the spiritual connection to the landscape.

In the sustainable tourism literature, Julienne remembered reading about the importance of including the local community in tourism development decisions and activities. She asked Gerald one final question based on the information she had gathered about the social dimension of sustainability.

JULIENNE: Do you think tourism has a positive impact on your local native community?

GERALD: Fragmentation of cultures such as the native culture can occur when tourism interests focus only on certain aspects of a culture. The Canadian Indian is a large part of the Canadian mosaic of cultures coming together and of the history and heritage that belongs to Canada. In the context of tourism, the spiritual concepts and ceremonies that are part of the native culture have become tourism attributes. However, these cultural resources can be depleted by tourism. For example, Westerners take our native symbols and tipi designs and paint them on their own tipis. Tourists come and sleep in the Westerners' tipis and pay for the experience. So this is one way that our worldviews and our symbols are being eroded by tourism.

Julienne came away from the interview with two important insights. First, the historical ties of local residents to the landscape can shape local perceptions toward the purpose of WLNP and tourism in the area. Second, tourism can fragment natural and cultural resources by assigning value only to certain aspects of the cultural or natural landscape while at the same time ignoring other aspects. Julienne's first insight was reconfirmed in her next interview with a local rancher named Ted Black. Ted explains the historical significance of WLNP as a recreational and social setting for local residents:

TED: Locals used to like to go camping in Waterton and the park did not have nearly the restrictions that it does now. You could go and throw a tent under a tree and camp out in the park area. But now it's a lot different . . . and there really isn't that much night life, the whole damn place [WLNP] closes down. The park used to center on the dance hall. I mean, there is no question about that.

. During Julienne's stay in WLNP she had the opportunity to speak with a number of local residents informally at the local coffeehouse. From these conversations Julienne realized that many of the local residents maintain the perspective that parks are for people and the primary purpose of WLNP is to provide opportunities for people to enjoy a number of recreational activities and amenities. Although the ranchers with whom Julienne spoke are supportive of infrastructure in the park they do not want to see Waterton Park turn into another Banff National Park. However, given the geographic location, physical boundaries, weather, and accessibility of WLNP, Julienne soon realized that it is unlikely that WLNP will evolve into a majestic backdrop for shopping malls, large-scale facilities, and retail stores as has occurred in Banff. Both the geographic location and the physical constraints of WLNP appear to contribute to the slow development of the town site. Specifically, the entire Waterton Park town site is located on the Cameron Creek alluvial fan that spills into the north end of Upper Waterton Lake. It is bordered also by high mountains and avalanche slopes, further limiting the development that can take place within the park town site. Given these physical and geographical characteristics, WLNP has managed to retain its charm as a small, quaint village within a unique wilderness setting.

Also, WLNP has a Biosphere Reserve designation. From a tourism perspective, Julienne thought this designation implied that the park should be used in ways that conserve the environmental features of the ecosystem as well as the cultural heritage of the area. Julienne wondered if the local landowners were proud of this designation. She decided to ask Dot, a waitress at the local coffeehouse, about it.

DOT: UNESCO's Man and the Biosphere Program is one attempt to bridge the gap between park management strategies and the local interests of adjacent landowners. However, many of the local ranchers don't have any idea what the Biosphere program is all about. All they know is if you have land bordering the park and you are within the MD [municipal district] of Pincher Creek, you are within the zone of cooperation. However, ranchers who have been here a long time do not take kindly to somebody from the Biosphere telling them how they should be using their land. Actually, some of the ranchers have even asked the MD of Pincher Creek if they could get out of the program because they don't understand what the Biosphere Program is.

Julienne soon realized that the ecological condition of Waterton Park was interconnected with the interests of local landowners surrounding the park's boundaries. Pamela Wight, a tourism consultant and highly recognized author of sustainable tourism issues, stated that it is impossible to separate the human needs of local populations from the ecological needs of forests, wildlife, and national parks (Wight, 1993). With this is mind, Julienne decided to look further into the relationship between the environmental and the social perspectives of tourism in the Waterton area.

From an environmental perspective, the park's unique geographical situation provides a home to species of both the prairies and mountain environments. Waterton and Glacier Park also serve as important migratory routes and necessary habitat for wildlife in southwestern Alberta. The abundance of wildlife is a drawing card for tourism. What Julienne didn't know is how wildlife was regarded by the adjacent landowners. One afternoon, while visiting an ice cream shop, Julienne was introduced to a local landowner named Jack O'Hara. Jack had recently retired from the Canadian Parks Service and was more than willing to spend some time talking with Julienne. Jack gave Julienne an overview of some of the issues.

JULIENNE: Are there any wildlife issues that affect the environmental integrity of the park and the local residents' interests?

JACK: Because Waterton is a small park, the home ranges of many large carnivores such as wolves, cougars, grizzly bears, black bears, and coyotes extend beyond the protected boundaries of the park into adjacent lands. As a result, the survival of Waterton's predator populations such as wolves and grizzly bears will depend, at least in part, on the values local ranchers and landowners assign to maintaining wildlife populations outside the park's boundaries. Now, I would have to say there is a greater tolerance by locals for grizzly bears outside the park's boundaries than there is for wolves.

JULIENNE: Why is that?

JACK: Because ranchers are primarily concerned with wolves killing their livestock. For example, back in the teens [1911-1919] ranchers had to get rid of wolves before they could raise any cattle on the northwest side of the Waterton River. In the Waterton area, ranchers got along fine for the past seventy years without any wolves in the area. But in 1993 wolves started to move back into the area on their own accord. Unfortunately, if this area gets any number of wolves the ranchers will shoot them. There is no question about that, regardless of whether the park wants to keep wolves in the area or not.

JULIENNE: So then the reason ranchers don't want wolves around is because wolves threaten their economic interests. Is that correct?

JACK: Yes, that is the primary reason. However, in 1994 the Southwest Alberta Livestock Predator Compensation Program was established to financially compensate ranchers and farmers in southwestern Alberta for any livestock animal that was killed by a wolf or a grizzly bear. Despite the program, some ranchers are still adamantly opposed to wolves in the Waterton area. Perhaps this approach toward wolves is more historical than anything else.

JULIENNE: Do local stakeholders have a low tolerance in general for predators outside the park's boundaries?

JACK: Many of the local ranchers regard wildlife in the park as an attraction for tourists. However, wildlife outside the boundaries of the park is not valued the same as wildlife inside the boundaries. Outside the park's boundaries, ranchers' concern for livestock is key in determining predator populations.

JULIENNE: Are there any other issues among local stakeholders that affect the ecological integrity of the park?

JACK: Well, there is always potential for conflict when the ecological interests of Waterton Park management conflict with the economic or historical values of local landowners and ranchers.

Next, Julienne went to see a park representative named Paul at the main office in the Waterton town site. She asked Paul to explain how the interests of local residents bordering the park may affect the ecological integrity of Waterton Park.

PAUL: I think, for the most part that the relationship between park management and the local ranchers is compatible. However, differences usually stem from a difference in priorities. For example, I think that the local residents from earlier days used the park more as a regional or local tourism destination. Although they enjoyed the scenic beauty, they were primarily interested in recreational activities. However, we feel some recreational pursuits can be experienced anywhere and do not necessarily require a park setting.

JULIENNE: I understand some of the locals are disappointed that the swimming pool in the park closed down. Is this one of the recreational activities you are referring to?

PAUL: Yes. The pool closed down primarily because we could no longer afford to keep it operating. Furthermore, people do not come to the park because there is a pool. The primary focus of Parks Canada has shifted toward maintaining the environmental integrity of the park's landscapes while still recognizing the need to provide recreational opportunities. However, the struggle to maintain the park's environmental integrity and high-quality recreational and educational activities continues to be fueled by different stakeholder groups assigning different priorities to the purpose of national parks in general. When I refer to stakeholder groups I am including tourism developers and visitors as well as local residents.

JULIENNE: So, in achieving an ecological approach toward tourism development in Waterton, the issue of supply and demand appears to be a challenge.

PAUL: Yes; visitors to national parks should be willing to accept the environmental limitations in that particular park. In other words, the supply side (natural landscape and cultural resources) is not altered solely to meet the demands and needs of visitors or tourism developers. At the same time, the environmental conditions of national parks should not be altered solely to meet the demands of local residents. The reality is: not all the needs of all the stakeholders will be met. You are bound to have some disappointment.

JULIENNE: Infrastructure inside the park is one aspect of the tourism-environment relationship. Are there other development pressures that impact the environmental integrity of Waterton Park?

PAUL: Yes. I think any protected area or national park, historically, puts a lot of pressure on the land base, from a land speculation and recreational use perspective. Land surrounding park boundaries becomes of considerable economic value if it is subdivided into smaller parcels. For example, if the land in the Waterton area is subdivided for country-style vacation homes it becomes more difficult to sustain agriculture as a viable economic activity. The national park in some cases creates that economic impact on land values. From an environmental perspective, subdivisions further fragment the landscape making it more difficult for wildlife to survive outside park boundaries.

JULIENNE: So you have explained how the environmental condition of the park can be impacted by social interests and economic interests, are there any other issues that affect the ecological integrity of the area?

PAUL: On a regional level, jurisdictional boundaries governing land use decisions also can compromise the integrity of the natural landscape. This is a reoccurring theme in the literature on ecosystem management strategies. For example, in the Waterton area, the ecosystems that support WLNP are influenced by the jurisdiction of two countries: Canada and the United States, and two provinces: Alberta and British Columbia. Within Alberta the condition of the Waterton landscape is affected by the mandates of Parks Canada, and the Municipal Districts of Pincher Creek and Cardston. From talking with stakeholders in the Waterton area, we found that relationships between the park and MDs of Pincher Creek and Cardston have not been conducive to a landscape approach to ecological sustainability. Specifically, the MDs of Pincher Creek and Cardston are likely to arrive at land-use decisions differently than the park given that their mandates are different and so are their interests in the larger ecosystem.

JULIENNE: So what you are saying is that land use decisions of different jurisdictions can fragment the landscape and affect the ecosystems which support the park?

PAUL: Yes, planning is locally based in terms of jurisdictions, but we had a variety of planning going on within each jurisdiction with no connection to each other. We do our park management plan and the municipalities do their plan for their area. In reality, the only way they are linked is if people have been talking to one another. We don't have any planning structure that integrates a number of jurisdictions in terms of broad planning issues. This causes clear contradictions in terms of land use.

Julienne suddenly realized that she may have missed a dimension of sustainability and may have to draw another circle in her diagram to represent the political perspective. She also realized that there would be an obvious connection between the political and economic dimensions of sustainability. Specifically, economic goals appear to be the prime motivator for provincial and local government decisions regarding land-use and tourism-development decisions. In Alberta, tourism development decisions appear to be driven by the assumption that parks and natural landscapes are economically valueless unless humanmade facilities are provided to enhance visitor experiences. To explore the idea of including the political perspective as a dimension of sustainability, Julienne made arrangements to meet with George Lund, a representative of the MD of Pincher Creek.

JULIENNE: How does tourism affect land-use decisions in the MD of Pincher Creek?

GEORGE: In the long-term, the MD of Pincher Creek is likely to benefit economically from tourism growth. Specifically, rising land values for subdivided parcels contribute to the tax base. Tourism demand for vacation homes also creates short-term employment for builders, land speculators, and real estate agents.

JULIENNE: So is economic stability in the MD of Pincher Creek the primary focus on land-use decisions in the Waterton area?

GEORGE: I would have to say it is an important consideration. However, the aesthetic value of the landscape is also important. Communities have historical resources and natural beauty and this is where the tourism dollars come from. Tourism dollars do not necessarily come from only the two-week vacationer. If you want economic sustainability, you want to keep them coming back with cottages and this type of thing. For example, we have a proposal before us to develop vacation accommodation on eighty acres of land bordering Waterton Park.

JULIENNE: I understand the site of the development is within the Waterton Lakes Park Vicinity Protection Area established at the request of the Biosphere Reserve.

GEORGE: Yes it is. But the land within the Waterton Lakes Park Vicinity Protection Area can be rezoned in accordance with the zoning bylaws. Also, the Biosphere Program does not have legal description or political authority.

JULIENNE: Has the MD of Pincher Creek developed a vision or strategy for tourism development in the Waterton Lakes Park Vicinity Protection Area?

GEORGE: Planning is a difficult task because you don't have any idea how much development there will be in the long-term. Planning is more of trying to hold things off long enough to decide what's good and what's bad. That is where the problem comes in long-term planning in the park.

CONCLUSION

At the conclusion of her discussion with George, Julienne returned to Calgary and began sorting out the information she had gathered from her research in Waterton. First, she drew two circles to represent the economic and social dimension of sustainability. Beside these two circles she drew a third circle to represent the political dimension. At the base of the diagram she drew another circle to represent the environmental dimension of sustainability.

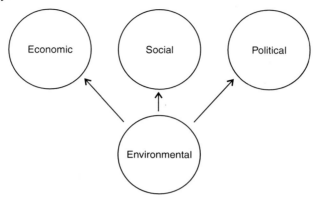

As she was doodling, Julienne realized that the economic, social, and political dimensions of sustainability were all human constructed. The only dimension that was not a human-based system was the environmental dimension. Based on this conclusion, Julienne began to understand why achieving a common environmental focus toward tourism development is a difficult task. As a final exercise Julienne identified issues that highlighted the relationships between human values and sustainability. As she fell asleep that evening, she thought about the information she had collected and the insights provided by the local residents she interviewed. Julienne realized that the journey to define sustainability in Waterton Lakes National Park had raised more questions than answers.

BIBLIOGRAPHY

Banff-Bow Valley Task Force (1995). *Banff-Bow Valley Study, Ecological Outlook: Cumulative Effects Assessment and Futures Modelling, Workshop 1 Summary Report.* Prepared by Coopers and Lybrand Consultants, Canada.

Brown, L., Hanson, M.E., Liverman, D.M., and Merideth Jr., R.W. (1987). Global Sustainability: Toward Definition. *Environmental Management* 11(6), 713-719.

Bruntland, G. (Ed.) (1987). *Our Common Future: The World Commission on Environment and Development.* Oxford: Oxford University Press.

Budowski, G. (1976). Tourism and Environmental Conservation: Conflict, Coexistence, or Symbiosis? *Environmental Conservation* 3(1), 27-31.

Butler, R.W. (1993). Tourism—An Evolutionary Perspective. In J.G. Nelson, R. Butler, and G. Wall (Eds.), *Tourism and Sustainable Development: Monitoring,*

Planning, Managing (pp. 27-44). Ontario, University of Waterloo: Department of Geography, Publication Series Number 37.

Dearden, P. (1993). Cultural Aspects of Tourism and Sustainable Development: Tourism and the Hilltribes of Northern Thailand. In J.G. Nelson, R. Butler, and G. Wall (Eds), *Tourism and Sustainable Development: Monitoring, Planning, Managing* (pp. 165-178). Ontario, University of Waterloo: Department of Geography, Publication Series Number 37.

Dowling, R. K. (1991). An Ecotourism Planning Model. Presented at the Inaugural International Ecotourism Symposium. University of Queensland, Brisbane, Australia, September, pp.1-14.

Grumbine, R. E. (1992). *Ghost Bears: Exploring the Biodiversity Crisis.* Washington, DC: Island.

Inskeep, E. (1991). *Tourism Planning: An Integrated and Sustainable Development Approach.* New York: Van Nostrand Reinhold.

Jones, A. (1992). Is there a real alternative tourism? *Tourism Management,* March, 102-103.

Kreutzwiser, R. (1993). Desirable Attributes of Sustainability Indicators for Tourism Development. In J. G. Nelson, R. Butler, and G. Wall (Eds.), *Tourism and Sustainable Development: Monitoring, Planning, Managing* (pp. 243-247). Ontario, University of Waterloo: Department of Geography, Publication Series Number 37.

Krippendorf, J. and Andrassy, V. (1987). *The Holiday Makers: Understanding the Impact of Leisure and Travel.* London: Heinemann.

McKercher, B. (1993). Some Fundamental Truths About Tourism: Understanding Tourism's Social and Environmental Impacts. *Journal of Sustainable Tourism, 1*(1), 6-14.

Naisbitt, J. (1994). *Global Paradox.* New York: William Morrow and Company, Inc.

Reid, R. E. (1996). *An Investigation of Human Values: Building a Foundation for Indicators of Ecologically Sustainable Tourism.* Master's thesis, University of Calgary, 1996. Ottawa: National Library of Canada. Microform TJ-18698.

Rubenstein, D. B. (1994). *Environmental Accounting for the Sustainable Corporation.* Westport, CT: Quorum Books.

Shearman, R. (1990). The Meaning and Ethics of Sustainability. *Environmental Management, 14*(1), 1-8.

Wackernagel, M. and Rees, W. (1996). *Our Ecological Footprint: Reducing Human Impact on the Earth.* British Columbia, Canada: New Society Publishers.

Wight, P. (1993). Sustainable Ecotourism: Balancing Economic, Environmental and Social Goals Within an Ethical Framework. *Special Edition of Tourism Recreation Research, 16*(2), 1.

Wilson, A. (1991). *The Culture of Nature: North American Landscape from Disney to the Exxon Valdez.* Toronto: Between the Lines.

Woodley, S. (1993). Tourism and Sustainable Development in Parks and Protected Areas. In J.G. Nelson, R. Butler, and G. Wall (Eds.), *Tourism and Sustainable Development: Monitoring, Planning, Managing* (pp. 83-95). Ontario, University of Waterloo: Department of Geography Publication Series Number 37.

Part V:
Land Development
and Governance Issues

Environmental and social concerns are sometimes about more than recycling waste, reducing energy use, and eliminating pollution. Some situations involve the management of an entire region of a country. The decisions made affect the livelihoods and behaviors of the individuals living in the region. Diverse stakeholder interests and required changes in behavior make these situations more complex and difficult to govern. The term, "domain governance," is sometimes used to describe the decisions that are made to determine the future and ongoing management of a region in which the governance responsibilities do not fall clearly on one group or institution.

In these situations, stakeholder involvement is essential. As well, coming to an agreement which will serve the needs of many requires an awareness and acknowledgement of the values that are important to each stakeholder group.

The cases in this section involve such complex situations. The Costa Rica case is structured as a role play with various stakeholders, from a banana plantation owner to a biologist, deciding what, if any, development is appropriate for an area of land adjacent to a national park. The CAMPFIRE case involves a transition from centralized to local governance and the decisions that were made to preserve the African elephant. The Extractive Reserves case is based in Brazil and attempts to transition the people of a region to more sustainable ecotourism activities in the Amazon Rain Forest.

None of the cases has a simple, right answer. To come to an acceptable solution or acceptable options, the decision makers must recognize the interests, positions, rights, and values of other stakeholders as well as their own.

As our world becomes more complicated and the parts become even more intertwined, the decisions become more difficult. These cases provide a setting for developing complex decision-making skills that will become even more necessary in the future as the tourism industry grows and touches the lives of every citizen of the world and his or her village, town or city, no matter how remote the location.

Chapter 16

Costa Rica:
Banana Plantations or Ecotourism?

Mary Jane Dawson
Tazim B. Jamal

The purpose of this case is to help develop an understanding of multi-stakeholder conflict resolution in environmentally sensitive areas (see Figure 16.1). The cultural setting for the case, the diversity of stakeholders, and the environmental context is based on information and historical material obtained from a Leadership for Environment and Development (LEAD) 1996 International Session in Costa Rica. The case study itself is fictitious (including the name of the national park). Characters and events have been fictionalized in order to convey concepts in a learning context, and any resemblance to actual persons, living or dead, or events is entirely coincidental. Information on consensus processes has been added from various sources, including *Building Consensus for a Sustainable Future,* published by the Round Table on the Environment and Economy in Canada.

BACKGROUND INFORMATION:
COSTA RICA

Costa Rica is a country in Central America with a population of approximately 4 million. A small minority (approximately 5 percent) of the population consists of blacks from the West Indies and Native Americans. The majority of the population is of Spanish origin. The main language spoken is Spanish.

Although it is a small country with an area of only 51,000 square kilometers, it is estimated to have nearly 5 percent of the earth's species. The Costa Rican government has committed to the protection of this wealth of biodiversity.

FIGURE 16.1. Tortuguero National Park, Costa Rica. (Map prepared by Hanako Saito.)

Tourists take a leisurely hike in Costa Rica. (Photo courtesy of Costa Rican Specialities.) Reprinted with permission.

Costa Rica dontulio. (Photo courtesy of Costa Rican Specialities.) Reprinted with permission.

Nature surrounds the group engaging in a forest canopy tour. (Photo courtesy of Costa Rican Specialities.) Reprinted with permission.

Brave individuals can try a cable ride. (Photo courtesy of Costa Rican Specialities.) Reprinted with permission.

Costa Rica Marenco Station. (Photo courtesy of Costa Rican Specialities.) Reprinted with permission.

Visitors enjoy the ambience at an outdoor party in Costa Rica. (Photo courtesy of Costa Rican Specialities.) Reprinted with permission.

Almost 30 percent of the national territory is under one of the following protection categories: Biological Reserves (6), Indigenous Reserves (21), National Parks (18), Absolute Natural Reserves (1), National Forests (9), Wildlife Refuges (8), Protected Zones (29), UNESCO Biosphere Reserves (2), Natural and Cultural Monuments (2), all grouped in 8 Conservation Areas. (Calderon and Umana, 1996, p. 33).

Agriculture is a significant component of the Costa Rican economy. Major products include coffee, bananas, beef, and sugar, along with ornamental plants and flowers. Bananas provide approximately 35 percent of the agricultural gross domestic product, and comprised 26 percent of Costa Rica's exports in 1994.

Forestry, mining, fisheries, and tourism also contribute to the economy. Tourism has increasingly become a significant portion of the economy, exceeding the sale of bananas and coffee in the generation of foreign dollars. From the period of 1984 to 1994, the number of international tourist arrivals increased by approximately 200 percent. The national parks system is recognized as one of the main reasons for tourism growth in Costa Rica and is included in the marketing of Costa Rica by the Ministry of Tourism.

Although currently facing concerns with inflation, unemployment, and a sizeable national debt, Costa Rica's standard of living is relatively high for Central America. All Costa Rican citizens are provided free elementary and secondary education as well as access to a state-supported health care system.

In the early 1990s the government of Costa Rica supported expansion of banana plantations as a means of solving economic problems. One of the sites considered for expansion was near Turtle National Park (also known as Tortuguero National Park). Although some viewed this initiative as beneficial from an economic perspective other stakeholders were concerned about the environmental and social impacts of banana plantation expansion.

Banana production is impacted by a number of national government organizations including the Ministries of Economy and Finance, the Ministry of Agriculture, and the Ministry of Environment and Energy. Though the Ministry of Environment and Energy is responsible for environmental protection, overlap between jurisdictions administering the same land area means that competing or contradictory goals and plans may be present among some public sector administrators. For instance, the environmental protection mandate of the Ministry of Natural Resources, Energy and Mines can conflict with the agricultural expansion goals of the Ministry of Agriculture.

Other groups involved in banana production include CORBANA, which is a corporation owned by banana producers, and the Comisión Ambiental Bananera (The Banana Growers Environmental Commission) whose members include banana producers and the Ministries of Health, Agriculture, and Environment and Energy. The commission's objectives include making banana production sustainable and researching options that reduce the environmental impacts of banana production.

Various environmental nongovernmental organizations are involved in environmental research in Costa Rica. The research includes finding sustainable uses for the biodiversity found in Costa Rica and for conservation programs. (See the appendix for a list of laws that pertain to the issues in this case.)

DEVELOPMENT CONFLICT IN TURTLE NATIONAL PARK

The owners of a banana plantation located near Turtle National Park are proposing to expand their plantation by one hectare onto privately owned land adjacent to the park. The park is world famous and known for the nesting grounds of the green turtle.

The owners of the ecotourism lodge located adjacent to Turtle National Park oppose the expansion of the banana plantation as they would prefer to put another ecotourism lodge on this property. They also think that there could be negative environmental effects resulting from the banana plantation which could impact on their business.

In addition, the surrounding communities are also interested in whether the land will be used for banana plantations or tourism because both have the potential of increasing employment but can also impact negatively on the natural and cultural environment.

Because Turtle National Park is an important site for biodiversity and has international recognition, and as a first step in resolving the dispute over land use, the president of Costa Rica has appointed a facilitator to work with a multi-stakeholder group to address the dispute within a specified time frame and budget. This form of dispute resolution has been chosen to ensure that all parties potentially affected by the dispute are represented and that solutions can be found which are appropriate to the circumstances of the parties.

The facilitator is from Limon and has had extensive experience both in facilitation and mediation of sustainable development disputes. All of the participants have volunteered to be in the group. Each participant represents a group of stakeholders. According to Freeman (1984), a stakeholder is defined as one who is (or may be) impacted by, or has the potential to impact, the development or action being considered.

It is hoped that joint solutions and general agreement can be achieved within the multi-stakeholder group which are consistent with the principles of sustainable development. The goal is to achieve consensus within the group on a strategy for addressing the conflict. Even though individuals within the group may not agree with all aspects of the plan, consensus can be deemed to be reached if all group members are willing to live with the recommendations proposed.

The multi-stakeholder group includes the banana plantation owner, the region's ecotourism lodge and the raft-ride business owners, the mayor of Turtle Village, a biologist from a conservation reserve, an environmentalist from IIENGO (fictitious organization), an elder from the town, a worker from the banana plantation, a representative from the Ministry of Environment and Energy, a representative from the Ministry of Tourism, and the plant manager representing the multinational corporation who will buy the additional production from the plantation.

The facilitator suggests that the multi-stakeholder group may be more likely to achieve success if the following guiding principles of consensus processes are adopted (National Round Table on Environment and Economy, 1993):

Principle #1—Purpose-driven: People need a reason to participate in the process.

Principle #2—Inclusive not exclusive: All parties with a significant interest in the issue should be involved in the consensus process.

Principle #3—Voluntary Participation: The parties who are affected or interested participate voluntarily.

Principle #4—Self-Design: The parties design the consensus process.

Principle #5—Flexibility: Flexibility should be designed into the process.

Principle #6—Equal Opportunity: All parties must have equal access to relevant information and the opportunity to participate effectively throughout the process.

Principle #7—Respect for Diverse Interests: Acceptance of the diverse values, interests, and knowledge of the parties involved in the consensus process is essential.

Principle #8—Accountability: The parties are accountable to their constituencies and to the process that they have agreed to establish.

Principle #9—Time Limits: Realistic deadlines are necessary throughout the process.

Principle #10—Implementation: Commitment to implementation and effective monitoring are essential parts of any agreement.

The facilitator's key task is to facilitate the discussion and progress of the group as it engages in its various tasks. The facilitator helps the group to develop a process for identifying and addressing the issue(s)/problem(s) which it wants to undertake. In particular, the facilitator is responsible for helping the group develop skills in conflict resolution and interest-based negotiation (IBN) which was a suggested approach to negotiating this conflict.

ROLES IN THE CONFLICT

Facilitator

The government of Costa Rica has committed itself to a strategy of sustainable development. It recognizes that the biodiversity of Costa Rica is one of the highest in the world, and as such is one of its major resources for tourism and for pharmaceutical research. At the same time, the government also recognizes that the banana industry produces a significant percentage of Costa Rica's total exports.

For facilitators, the best outcome of the stakeholder process will be to help the stakeholders to come up with a written proposal that has general group agreement on how the land should be used. Failure to reach consensus could result in a more costly legal process to resolve the dispute. As a facilitator, your assigned task is to facilitate the group on process aspects, but not to mediate the content of the agreement.

You should begin the process by having everyone introduce himself or herself, and then have the group accomplish a number of initial tasks, such as

- establishing the scope and purpose of the process;
- deciding on how the process will work and developing the ground rules;
- agreeing upon the joint decision-making approach and defining consensus;
- establishing representation parameters, including criteria for stakeholder identification and involvement, plus constituent involvement;
- agreeing on a process schedule, including key milestones, time schedules, and budget;
- identifying the negotiation approach (e.g., IBN), and determining how impasses are to be handled; and
- determining what should be suggested if consensus-based agreement is not reached; for instance, should a mediator be brought in, and if so, who, when and where from?

Once ground rules have been established and the stakeholder mix identified (to ensure that key stakeholders are present or have been encouraged to attend), everyone should be asked to state his or her perspective and concerns. From this initial discussion, you will need to help the group identify the issues/problems that need to be resolved and then try to get the participants to discuss these and develop options, and eventually strategies and action plans (depending on the scope of the project identified in the ground rules). You should encourage everyone to build consensus by discussing and genuinely listening to each participant's point of view, as well as by trying to identify the interests underlying the various positions presented at the table. You should try to encourage the participants to consider their Best Alternative to a Negotiated Agreement (BANTA) (Fisher and Ury 1983), and also provide them with enough information to understand the difference between "positions" and "interests," and strive to find "common ground" and common interests, since this is an interest-based negotiation (c.f. Fisher, Ury, and Patten, 1999; Ury, 1993).

Depending on the time available, you may conduct a group exercise that allows everyone to forward their perspectives, and identify common views. You may be able to also use breakout groups and subcommittee structures to deal with some of the issues.

Banana Plantation Owner

As a banana plantation owner, you are trying to expand your plantation because your current operation is barely breaking even. The Banana Company, a multinational company, has agreed to buy all of the extra production you would have from the expansion. You would then net about US $35,000 that you could partly use to bring other businesses to the town. If you go out of business, seventy-five workers will lose their jobs. Although ecotourism could provide some employment opportunities, not all of them will be able to find employment in the tourism industry.

Currently, the land on which you plan to expand is covered by a tropical rain forest. Therefore, expanding the plantation will result in more land being deforested. However, this part of the land is well suited to agriculture. Your view is that Costa Rica should use the prime agricultural land for agriculture. The land on the other side of the plantation is also owned privately. Although it would be possible to expand on this land, if the owner would sell or lease, the land is not as good quality from an agricultural point of view. Also, there would need to be some additional infrastructure costs (i.e., a road would have to be built). You would only agree to expand on this other property if the community or the government agreed to pay for the cost of building the road.

Banana production carries with it some environmental effects. You are willing to try to mitigate them. For example, to reduce the negative health effects on people that could result from chemical spraying from the air, you are willing to provide extra supervision and training to workers for ground usage of pesticides and fertilizers. You recognize that the pesticides may still get into water sources using this approach. If you could get some partial compensation from the government or the Banana Company in the event of a crop failure, you would be willing to try one of the integrated pest management programs currently being studied by Costa Rica as a means of reducing certain pesticide applications. You are also willing to send all of the plastic bags and twine that you can to the new recycling plant in Freehold, near Limon.

You really want this additional property. If all else fails, you will agree to grow the "new" banana developed through funding by Canada's International Development Research Centre. This banana requires little spraying.

However, it has a slightly different taste than the regular bananas. The profit margin may be less for this type of banana.

You are aware of some negative environmental effects to expanding ecotourism in the area. For example, extra garbage will be produced and will have to be transported out of the area. As well, the tour boats used to view the animals use gasoline, some of which ends up in the water. You are glad that the facilitator has been appointed by the president. A message you would like to give the president is that you and your fellow plantation owners would like the president to negotiate with the United States so that you have direct access to its markets. Currently, your access is limited to selling to a multinational (the Banana Company). You suspect that your profits would be much higher if you were able to sell directly to retailers and perhaps a few smaller wholesalers, rather than through one major distributor.

Ecotourism Lodge Owner

As an ecotourism lodge owner, you oppose the expansion of the banana plantation. Your business caters to a "unique" type of tourist. This type of tourist is not interested in a luxurious hotel facility but is instead interested in experiencing nature. Although such travelers seek a unique experience, they try to have minimal negative impact on the area. Critical to this tourist is the ability to be able to view a pristine natural environment. Many are interested in the aesthetics of the environment; the plants and monkeys, in particular, make for very popular viewing. Some are interested in the local communities and ethnic cultures in this area. You are very concerned that the spraying of chemicals may end up in the water system and harm the biodiversity of the forest, thus affecting the attractiveness of Turtle National Park as an ecotourism destination.

Your lodge is small, with only twenty rooms. Currently, garbage is taken out by boat. Workers are mainly from the Turtle community and have an average salary of US $133 per month. Most workers are employed in support positions. Currently there are seven similar types of hotels in the area with a total capacity of 282 rooms. The average length of the hotel season is eight months with an average of approximately 47,000 tourists visiting the park. The total number of employees is eighty-three for all the hotels, with sixty coming from the local community annually. Total sales in 1990-1991 were approximately $4 million. Income earned by employees was approximately $238,000.

You would like to expand your operation up to the average size for such a lodge (forty rooms), in order to increase your revenue stream and your ability to promote your lodge in the highly competitive global ecotourism market. The prime location for expansion would be the land on which the banana plantation owner is planning to expand on. If you expanded the lodge you would need more workers. This would reduce the unemployment in the area. You are glad that a government representative is present from the Department of Tourism. You would like to make the point that your industry needs more help in marketing your services to international tourists.

Raft-Ride Business Owner

As a raft-ride business owner, you oppose the expansion of the banana plantation. Your business caters to "unique" types of tourists, often considered "ecotourists." Critical to these tourists is the ability to experience a pristine natural environment as they participate on the raft ride. You are also very concerned that the spraying of chemicals may end up in the water system and harm the biodiversity of the forest.

You know that the ecotourism lodge owner would like to expand. You would support him in this initiative, as it would potentially result in more business for you. You are very glad that the facilitator appointed by the president, and the representative from the Ministry of Tourism are present. You have heard that the government, in order to increase electrical production, is considering damming one of the rivers in the Turtle region that you use for white-water rafting. This would put you out of business. You want to make the point to the facilitator that you strongly oppose damming this river. There are plenty of other rivers that could be used for hydroelectricity purposes. Also, you doubt that the extra electricity is really required. Another point you would like to make is that you need help maintaining the river. One of the community footbridges has partially fallen down over part of the river where you do the rafting. Portaging delays the trips. You have tried getting customers to bend down to go under the bridge. Recently, two participants were injured using this method. The tour company then canceled its contract. You think that the mayor or the Ministry of Tourism should pay for either the repair of the bridge or taking down the bridge.

Mayor

As mayor of Turtle Village, you would like to encourage increased employment, assuming that there are no serious negative environmental impacts. Approximately 500 people in Turtle Village make their living from fishing, subsistence agriculture, tourism, cattle farming, banana plantations, logging, and forest management.

You campaigned on improving employment in your community. Either an expansion of the plantation or an expansion of the ecotourism lodge will create more employment. More will be created with the plantation expansion. You would prefer expansion of both. You are aware that there is actually another piece of property on the other side of the plantation that could be used to expand the plantation. The owner of this land is a friend of yours and probably could be convinced to sell.

Although you want to encourage employment you also know that you have to ensure that the environment is reasonably protected. Many people in your community are proud of the national park and would be upset if it were negatively impacted by either type of expansion. You are concerned about environmental effects of banana plantations because you know that in some cases in the past some banana plantation workers have had health problems from the pesticides. If the lodge expanded you wonder how the additional waste would be dealt with.

You are glad that the Ministry of Tourism representative and the Banana Company representatives are going to be in the multi-stakeholder group. You think that the Ministry of Tourism should be doing more to promote your area. You would also like to solicit a donation from the Banana Company representative to buy computers for the elementary school. Unfortunately, the community runs on a break-even basis and accordingly, you barely have enough funds to pay the teachers' salaries. You would like to make the point to the facilitator that the president also promised to bring improved economic development to the country, but you have yet to see any in this area. The average monthly salary for an ecotourism employee is US $133. The average monthly salary for a banana worker is approximately US $250.

Biologist from the Conservation Reserve

As a biologist from the conservation reserve, your main concern is to protect the habitat of the turtles. If the plantation can be expanded in such a way that the habitat is not affected, you will be satisfied. In general, you would prefer the ecotourism expansion, but only up to a point. The more people that are exposed to the green turtle in its natural state, the easier it is to raise funds for research and protection. However, too many people in the area, if not monitored properly, could disrupt the turtle nesting.

You are also concerned about employment in the local community. As a result of ongoing unemployment, some poaching of other animals has occurred in the park. You are concerned that the poaching could affect the turtles. You are glad that the representative of the Ministry of Natural

Resources, Energy, and Mines is going to be in the multi-stakeholder group. You would like to make the point to him that the Ministry should be supplying more park rangers to monitor the activities in the park.

Environmentalist from IIENGO

As an environmentalist, you oppose the banana plantation expansion because of the deforestation and the possible effect that this could have on the park. Costa Rica markets itself as an environmentally conscious nation with a larger than average area of protected public and private land. To ensure that the world's ecosystems are protected, you want all countries to follow Costa Rica's example. Now you feel that Costa Rica is starting to backslide by considering this banana plant expansion, which will result in the plantation encroaching upon the park. You must take a strong stance and prevent this from happening. If this project is allowed, other applications will probably be made. The ultimate concern would be that such development, while not currently allowed in the park, could eventually be allowed in the park land area over the next few years. Because of Costa Rica's wealth of biodiversity, even a small loss of park land could impact significantly upon global biodiversity.

Having a banana plantation next to the park will create negative environmental effects. Banana plantations produce pollution such as plastic bags (containing insecticides) and plastic rope. They require large quantities of agrochemicals. Some of the pesticides used have been classified as "extremely harmful" and "very harmful" by the World Health Organization. Some "are very toxic for exposed wildlife like aquatic organisms, birds, reptiles etc." (Center for Environmental Studies, 1996). You have heard rumors that some of the pesticides used are banned in developed countries. You have been advised that many animals and fish have died due to pesticide contamination in river water resulting from a lack of water treatment facilities at certain plantations. There is also concern about health risks for the workers: some don't have appropriate protection equipment when applying pesticides. An example of this risk occurred in the 1970s when 2,000 banana workers were sterilized due to exposure to one of the pesticides used by banana plantations. This health hazard is greater when the pesticides are aerially applied.

You are not particularly in favor of the ecotourism expansion either because it will create a greater garbage problem or because the noise from the boats disturbs the animals. However, you believe that the environmental impacts of a small expansion by the ecotourism lodge owner should not be as significant as the banana plant expansion. Although there is unemployment in the area, you feel that if the government did its job, this problem could be reduced by more production and marketing of traditional crafts.

You will want to do whatever it takes to prevent this land from being used as a banana plantation. You do not hesitate to interrupt other stakeholders while they are speaking if you think that they are providing misinformation. If the banana expansion goes ahead you will mount an international public campaign against the products of the Banana Company. If you see that a consensus is being reached around the banana plantation expansion, you will walk out of the process and not return until the discussion questions are being discussed. You do not really want to do this, but participation is voluntary and you cannot be part of a process that will weaken environmental standards.

Community Elder

As a community elder, you are recognized as being skilled in contributing to community decisions. When you heard from the mayor that this multi-stakeholder group was being established, you volunteered to be on it.

You are in favor of creating more employment as long as there aren't negative environmental and social effects. Unemployment is high, and as a result, there are some associated social problems such as crime. On the other hand, there have been negative environmental impacts associated with banana plantations particularly in terms of contamination of water. During the 1970s, the spraying of certain chemicals resulted in sterility for one of your cousins. In addition, there were some rumors that indigenous people were unfairly treated as employees on certain plantations. Also, banana plant expansion can encourage peasants to sell their land and then become banana workers. This can represent a loss of self-sufficiency and result in significant social and cultural impacts. In the past there have been some negative social impacts with banana plantations. In some cases, liquor consumption has increased along with drug traffic and prostitution. Some plantations were unable to provide sufficient housing for their workers and workers have had to live in poor-quality houses they build themselves called *tugurios* (illegally erected slums).

In your view, the Banana Company should be putting more money into the community because they make millions of dollars from their operations in Costa Rica. In particular they should be helping to provide educational, housing, and medical services. If the banana plantation expansion goes ahead you would want some assurances about how the negative environmental impacts would be reduced, how workers' health would be protected, and how the negative social impacts would be controlled with respect to plantation workers.

Plantation Worker

As a plantation worker, you have been appointed by your fellow co-workers to voice their needs and concerns at the table. You are well liked by your fellow workers, and are articulate and vocal about worker conditions at the plantation. You will make a good leader, but tend to become aggressive when pressured.

You support the expansion because it will create more employment, approximately thirty-five to forty fieldworker jobs. However, you also think that the workers should be paid more and have better training (especially with regard to handling pesticides), as well as better working conditions. Currently, the average salary is US $250 per month. Some workers are hired as subcontractors instead of as employees to avoid labor legislation. Though most of the workers want to live near or on the plantation, there currently isn't enough housing for them. Many of the houses are without permanent potable water or electricity.

You would like the facilitator to raise the issues of subcontracting and the need for increased employment standards to the president. You are also planning to try to organize a workers' union to ensure fair labor practices.

Representative from the Ministry of Environment and Energy

As a representative from the Ministry of Environment and Energy, you are the regional representative for the Ministry and as such are responsible for ensuring all of the laws affecting the environment, including poaching, are enforced in your region. You have a degree in biology.

You are concerned about the natural environment, but as a government official you also have to be concerned about the economy and the social impacts of development. This means you will favor economic expansion, which doesn't appear to have negative social effects, and then seek solutions to minimize negative environmental effects.

Based on your experience with banana plantations, environmental damage could be reduced by using less toxic agrochemicals, and using better trained workers to apply these chemicals on the ground rather than aerially. For you to support the expansion, you will require a commitment from the plantation owner to:

- perform an environmental impact assessment (EIA) of the proposed expansion;
- leave a reasonable allowance of trees near and on riverbanks to prevent erosion;
- implement a monitoring program to prevent the contamination of rivers, and groundwater systems;
- use pest control practices that minimize or eliminate the harm to the environment; and
- prepare a waste plan that will specifically not have any wastes disposed of near or in water bodies.

You know that the ecotourism lodge owner would like to expand. Before supporting this initiative, you would need to understand how the extra waste generated would be handled and how the lodge would ensure that these additional customers would abide by park rules with respect to viewing of turtles. However, in general, you would expect that the environmental impacts of expanding the lodge would be less than that for expansion of the banana plantation.

Poaching in the area is a problem. However, your Ministry only has resources for a small staff in this area. You would like to make the point to the facilitator in hopes that he will raise this issue with the president. You would also like to make the point to the elder and the mayor that the community should be providing volunteer resources to prevent poaching.

Representative from the Costa Rica Tourist Board

You are a representative of the Costa Rican Tourist Board and are located in the capital San Jose. The facilitator asked you to join this multi-stakeholder group because of your expertise in evaluating tourism opportunities and promoting tourism in Costa Rica. You feel that if the lodge is expanded, it will be a commercial success because demand for facilities currently exceeds supply. You would prefer the lodge expansion over the banana plantation expansion because the lodge expansion may increase tourism in the region, and it fits well with your tourism promotion efforts and goals. You are concerned that unless the environmental effects of the banana plantation expansion are controlled, expansion could cause contamination of water in the Turtle National Park thus causing death of animals and fish. If this was to occur and was observed by tourists, this could ultimately be very damaging to the whole tourism industry in Costa Rica.

The lodge is owned by an individual from Limon. It would be preferable if more lodges were owned by community members around Turtle Village.

Currently, many of the residents work as support workers for the lodge or as plantation workers. In addition, some work in fishing, subsistence agriculture, cattle farming, and logging. You would like to speak to the elder and the mayor about trying to get some locally owned and operated tourism businesses established in the community. This would help to retain some of the tourist expenditures within the local area, rather than see them leak out due to foreign investment, external management and control of operations, and even through imports (if local resources are not used). You would like the facilitator to make the point to the president that to increase the number of community tourism businesses, the national government will need to provide some technical and financial support.

General Manager of the Multinational Banana Company Corporation

As general manager of the Banana Company, you really want the banana plantation expansion. You have had problems getting enough bananas to make your plant have a reasonable rate of return in terms of "first world" standards. Generally, the margins in the food business are very small. Your company makes money when it has sufficient sales volume and therefore market share. The food business is very competitive with expensive marketing and transportation costs.

Your company made $168 million in profits last year, $149 million of which came from Latin America. However, your company has significant amounts of capital assets ($2.4 billion), which it has to maintain and periodically upgrade. Your company has significant debt as well. Last year the company was able to pay only a US 29 cent dividend/share which was a 20 percent decrease from the year before. As a result, the share price fell.

You have to watch this situation carefully. You have heard that the IIENGO representative, if not happy with the final results reached by the stakeholder group, will coordinate a boycott of the Banana Company products. That could be very costly for the company. Within reason you would like to find a solution that is agreed upon by the whole multi-stakeholder group, preferably one involving the banana plantation expansion. You have already provided some financial support for the community. In addition, the company guarantees some of the plantation owners' debt. You may be able to provide some additional financial support for pesticide research, community education programs, and possibly for worker housing, in order to show that you are a good corporate citizen. But you would like additional support from the government for any additional roads that are needed to transport the bananas from the plantation.

BIBLIOGRAPHY

Abell, B. and Winig, B. (1997). Ecotourism. . . Where's the ECO? Costa Rica As a Case Study. <http://www-personal.umich.edu/~eca>.

Baez, A. (1996). Chapter VI. Ecotourism/Responsible Tourism: The Case of Costa Rica, Background Material for The Costa Rica Case Study, Lead I International Session Cohort V, Costa Rica, July 12-22.

Baez, A. and Fernandez, L. (1996). Chapter VII. Ecotourism: The Case of Tortuguero, Background Material for The Costa Rica Case Study, Lead I International Session Cohort V, Costa Rica, July 12-22.

Calderon, P. and Umana, A. (1996). Chapter II. Natural Resources, Background material for The Costa Rica Case Study, Lead I International Session Cohort V, Costa Rica, July 12-22.

Center for Environmental Studies (1996). Chapter IV. Banana Production in Costa Rica, Background material for The Costa Rica Case Study, Lead I International Session Cohort V, Costa Rica, July 12-22.

Cormick, G., Dale, N., Emond, P., Sigurdson, S.G., and Stuart, B. D. (1996). *Building Consensus for a Sustainable Future: Putting Principles into Practice.* Ottawa, Ontario: National Round Table on the Environment and the Economy.

E.T.C.—Meritxell Serrano, The Costa Rica Supersite, 1997-1999 La Nacion S.A. <http://ssite.nacion.co.cr/docs/economy/>.

Fennell, D. A. and Eagles, P. F. J. (1990). Ecotourism in Costa Rica: A Conceptual Framework. *Journal of Parks and Recreation Association,* 8(1): 23-34.

Fisher, R. and Ury, W. with Patton, B. (Ed.) (1999). *Getting to Yes: Negotiating Agreement Without Giving In,* Second Edition. Boston: Houghton Mifflin.

Freeman, R. E. (1984). *Strategic Management—A Stakeholder Approach.* Boston: Pitman.

Hirsch, J. and Aguilar, E. (1996). Chapter V. Banana Expansion in the Humid Tropical Zone, Background Material for The Costa Rica Case Study, Lead I International Session Cohort V, Costa Rica, July 12-22.

Jamal, T. (1999). The Social Responsibilities of Environmental Groups in Contested Destinations. *Tourism Recreation Research,* 24(2): 7-18.

Jamal, T. and Getz, D. (1999). Community-Based Roundtables for Tourism-Related Conflicts: The Dialectics of Consensus and Process Structures. *Journal of Sustainable Tourism,* 3-4: 290-314.

Lumsdon, L.M. and Swift, J.S. (1998). Ecotourism at a Crossroads: The Case of Costa Rica. *Journal of Sustainable Tourism,* 6(2): 155-172.

Menkhaus, S. and Lober, D.J. (1996). International Ecotourism and Valuation of Tropical Rainforests in Costa Rica. *Journal of Environmental Management,* 47: 1-10.

Moore, C.W. (1995). *The Mediation Process: Practical Strategies for Resolving Conflict,* Second Edition. San Francisco: Jossey-Bass Publishers.

National Round Table on Environment and Economy (1993). *Building Consensus For A Sustainable Future: Guiding Principles.* An Initiative Undertaken by

Canadian Round Tables. Round Tables on the Environment and Economy in Canada.

Nelson, J. Gordon. (1994). The Spread of Ecotourism: Some Planning Implications. *Environmental Conservation,* 21(3): 248-255.

Rios Tropicales (1997). The Costa Rica Supersite, 1997-1999 La Nacion S.A. <http://www.incostarica.net/>.

Troeng, S. (1998). Poaching Threatens the Green Turtle Rookery at Tortuguero, Costa Rica. *Marine Turtle Newsletter* 79: 11-12

Ury, William (1993). *Getting Past No: Negotiating Your Way from Confrontation to Cooperation.* New York: Bantam Books.

Chapter 17

CAMPFIRE: A Sustainable Use of Wildlife Resources?

Sandy Hershcovis

Another summer day had come to an end and Musa Abidola sighed as he looked out at the exquisite sunset that cast his farmland in a luminous red glow. The beauty of the Zambezi Valley never ceased to amaze Musa who had grown up in Masoka, a small village located deep in the Zambezi Valley of the Kanyurira Ward in northern Zimbabwe (see Figures 17.1 and 17.2). It was an unusually hot day in December with the temperature reaching 4° Celsius, and Musa had spent the majority of the afternoon fighting off the pests that trampled his land. It had been a difficult afternoon for Musa, who had been experiencing unusually persistent problems with the African elephants. The beasts, who seemed to think that Musa's sole purpose for farming maize was to feed the herd, frequently invited themselves onto his land for an afternoon snack. Unfortunately, a snack for an African elephant equates to approximately 300 pounds of maize. With a herd of eight to ten elephants eating it would not be too long before Musa and his wife Layla would be unable to sustain the meager livelihood that afforded them a modest home and food on the table.

Despite the damage the animals caused to his land the great elephants were a welcome site to Musa, who recalled a time not too long ago when the animals had been threatened with extinction in parts of Africa. Although they had always been plentiful in Zimbabwe, in central and eastern Africa, where poaching had been rampant, the African elephant had been in grave danger. He remembered all too vividly the controversy surrounding the

Thanks to Urs P. Kreuter for his comments and advice regarding the authenticity of this case. Dr. Kreuter is an assistant professor and human dimensions specialist in the Department of Rangeland Ecology and Management at Texas A&M University. He received his undergraduate education from University of Natal South Africa and graduate degrees from Utah State University. Dr. Kreuter's research includes the African elephant.

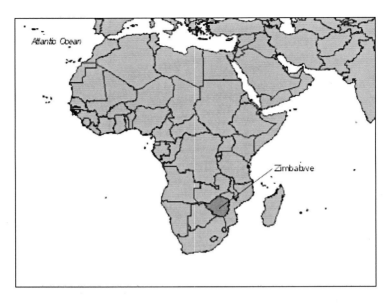

FIGURE 17.1. Map of Africa, including location of Zimbabwe. (Map prepared by Hanako Saito.)

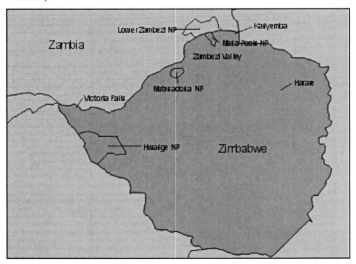

FIGURE 17.2. Detailed map of Zimbabwe. (Map prepared by Hanako Saito.)

Hippos are a common sight in this region. (Photo courtesy of Patti Dolan.) Reprinted with permission.

This Lake Kariba sunset illuminates the evening sky. (Photo courtesy of Patti Dolan.) Reprinted with permission.

A baby elephant looks forward to its regular bottle feeding. (Photo courtesy of Patti Dolan.) Reprinted with permission.

An adult elephant is camoflaged by its surroundings. (Photo courtesy of Patti Dolan.) Reprinted with permission.

Tiger Bay Camp in Zimbabwe. (Photo courtesy of Patti Dolan.) Reprinted with permission.

A lookout stand. (Photo courtesy of Patti Dolan.) Reprinted with permission.

widespread poaching of the African elephant. The controversy had prompted international attention as Western advocates of nonconsumptive conservation demanded that an ivory trade ban be invoked. The proposition had received opposing and equally vehement responses from the various African countries. Some countries, such as Kenya, which had a major problem with illegal poaching, supported an ivory trade ban while other countries such as Zimbabwe, South Africa, and Botswana strongly opposed the ban. Zimbabwe had been experiencing increases in the African elephant population and the local farmers viewed the animals as destructive and sometimes dangerous.

As the ivory trade ban debate waged on, Musa recalled that an alternative solution to the poaching problem in Zimbabwe had emerged. The Communal Areas Management Program for Indigenous Resources (CAMPFIRE) proposed a solution that effectively gave control and benefits of the wildlife resources to those who had to absorb the costs. Although the focus of the program was initially as a wildlife conservation strategy, the program had greater meaning for the people of Zimbabwe. It had been the beginning of a process of democratization, allowing the local people to take responsibility for their wildlife resources and to make decisions about how to allocate the revenues that these resources generated. The two approaches to conservation (ivory ban versus CAMPFIRE) were vastly different and Musa recalled the bitterness that ensued in Zimbabwe after the Convention on International Trade in Endangered Species (CITES) had imposed its Western values on an African problem by invoking an ivory trade ban.

POACHING AND THE IVORY TRADE

Between 1979 and 1989 the population of the African elephant declined from an estimated 1.3 million to just over 600,000 elephants (Heimert, 1995). Musa was saddened by the fact that poaching, as a result of a worldwide demand for ivory, was believed to be the primary cause of the decline in the African elephant population. Musa remembered that the price of ivory had skyrocketed in 1989, to approximately $125 per kg and ivory exports amounted to 770 tons or 75,000 elephants. He knew that the high demand for ivory combined with the poverty found in many African regions motivated poachers to kill elephants for their tusks. In 1989, although the African elephant was not in immediate threat of extinction, CITES put the African elephant onto its highest level of endangered species lists, effectively banning trade on any product derived from the animal. Musa was concerned that the ban, although well-intentioned, would lead to further problems as westerners imposed their own beliefs on an African problem.

CONVENTION ON INTERNATIONAL TRADE
IN ENDANGERED SPECIES (CITES)

Musa had been in his late teens when the CITES ban was invoked, and he decided to look into the program to see what it was all about. He found that CITES, headquartered in Geneva, Switzerland, became effective in 1975 when the declining population of many species began to draw international attention. The function of the organization was to address the threat of extinction among endangered species by controlling the trade of animals. The organization developed three tiers of protection, which were based on the degree to which the animals were in danger of extinction. Musa discovered that an animal could be listed on one of three appendixes. Appendix I, the list on which the African elephant was placed in 1989, provided the greatest degree of protection. Animals on this list are assessed to be at high risk of becoming extinct; therefore, Appendix I requires that imports, exports, or reexports on these species be limited only to specifically approved transactions requiring a permit. The stringent trade rules apply to any of the more than 150 member countries of CITES. Appendix II consists of animals that may become extinct unless trade is strictly regulated. Appendix III consists of species that are subject to regulation within any party's jurisdiction in order to prevent or restrict exploitation, and the party needs the cooperation of other parties to control the trade. Permits for export, import, or reexport are issued only after the advice and consent of both scientific and management authorities of the state.

Musa was curious as to how an animal was determined to be in danger and found that an animal is listed on one of the three appendixes based on criteria developed by the World Conservation Union (IUCN) and based on the proposals made by any CITES party. Any party is able to propose that a species be placed on Appendix I, II, or III but must provide supporting scientific documentation. Based on criteria developed by the IUCN as well as the assessment of the animals or plants committee, the parties vote on whether the species should be placed on the proposed appendix. Two-thirds of the parties must vote favourably in order to place the species on the appendix.

Given the information that he had obtained, Musa was very confused as to why the African elephant had been listed on Appendix I in the first place, since the necessary criteria were not met. In order to be considered endangered, the African Elephant and Rhino Specialist group of the IUCN estimated that 2,000 elephants would be a feasible population size for the species to continue (Kreuter and Simmons, 1995). Although the population was in decline, Musa knew for a fact that there were several regions that had more than 2,000 animals. He found that the pressure on CITES to list the animal came from Western protectionist groups such as the International Wildlife Coalition and the Humane Society of the United States which had conducted extensive "save the elephant" advertising campaigns. These campaigns created a widespread belief that elephants would become extinct if ivory trade was not banned. The result was increased pressure from contributors to wildlife organizations and subsequent pressure from these organizations on CITES (Kreuter and Simmons, 1995).

LIFE IN MASOKA

Musa recalled the anger that had arisen among the local people after CITES placed the African elephant on Appendix I of its endangered species list. He knew intuitively that such measures would not eliminate poaching of the African elephant. The anger had come from the fact that ivory trade provided African communities with a substantial amount of money, which they used to pay for schooling, medical facilities, conservation, and other community needs. With the elimination of all legal means to earn revenue from ivory trade, Musa suspected that illegal ivory trade would become a bigger problem. The lower supply of ivory would likely cause the black market price of ivory to escalate, thereby creating a greater incentive to engage in illegal poaching. To Musa, it appeared as though the Western protectionist groups, while possibly well-intentioned, had made a decision on an issue about which they had little real understanding. Musa felt that the ivory trade ban would aggravate the illegal poaching problem in Africa and preferred community resource management programs as an alternative solution. Such programs served the dual purpose of encouraging a positive shift in attitudes toward wildlife and also teaching the local people how to take responsibility for their own resources.

Over the past few years the government of Zimbabwe had used various conservation efforts as a medium to democratization. Prior to the Parks and Wildlife Act implemented in 1975, the farmers viewed the elephants as nothing more than vermin that ruined their crop and killed local people. The community experienced an average of four incidents of crop damage, a 6 percent injury rate, and a 2 percent death rate from wildlife per year, and the elephant ranked high among the offending animals (Matzke and Nabane, 1996). Musa even had a friend that had been seriously injured by an elephant, so he could understand why the community had not been fascinated or endeared by the elephant; rather, many abhorred the animal and such anger translated into increased incidents of poaching. With the implementation of the Act, however, new efforts at community-based wildlife resource management began to develop, and a new incentive to preserve wildlife had emerged. Although such programs were not immediately successful, people slowly began to view the animal as a potential economic resource for purposes other than just selling ivory.

Musa had never killed an elephant himself. He had a passion for all living things and that included the magnificent elephant whose mere size and strength had mesmerized him as a young child. But most of the farmers, including his father, had little or no tolerance for the animal that had repeatedly destroyed the maize fields. In addition to working his father's land, Musa had worked as a farmhand for another farmer in Masoka as a child. Musa could remember waking up at 5 a.m. each morning and scurrying across the fields of both his father's and his employer's land to warn any elephants or other wildlife that might be feasting on the crop. He had hidden some old iron pots and spoons inside a hollow log on the outskirts of the farm, and whenever an elephant had been in sight he would make as much noise as he could to scare it off. Musa believed that his efforts to frighten away the animals helped to mitigate the spread of anger that farmers, such as his father and his employer, felt toward the animals. Although poaching was illegal, angry farmers who had lost numerous acres of crop to these destructive beasts were more than eager to cooperate with poachers, who helped to rid their farmland of the animals. The death of an elephant would both prevent further destruction to the crop and also, in some cases, provide a small profit. Poaching was therefore a big problem, as farmers sought to illegally sell the lucrative ivory tusks in the underground ivory market. Musa firmly believed that if poaching were to be eradicated, the local people would have to change their perception of the wildlife. Specifically, the community would have to come to view the animals as a benefit rather than a nuisance.

WILDLIFE PROTECTION

Musa knew that, unlike his own country, most of Africa had instituted protective wildlife management strategies that strictly prohibited poaching or otherwise killing the animals. Kenya, for example, took the approach that profit from wildlife should come only from nonconsumptive activity such as viewing safaris. In 1989, Musa had been shocked to hear that the president of Kenya went so far as to publicly burn stockpiles of ivory that had been sitting in a warehouse (Heimert, 1995). With the continued decline in the population of the African elephant, however, protective strategies such as that of Kenya's had proven to be unsuccessful. As Musa suspected would happen, the high prices that poachers could command on the illegal ivory market served as an incentive to engage in illegal poaching and the limited funds for conservation available to the Kenyan government greatly restricted the government's ability to protect the wildlife (Heimert, 1995). Since the elephant population continued to decline and revenues from viewing safaris were insufficient to sustain local conservation programs, Zimbabwe decided to take a different approach to wildlife conservation. Musa took pride in the fact that despite the overall significant decline in the African elephant population during the 1980s, Zimbabwe's elephant population had grown by approximately 43 percent over the same period (Heimert, 1995). The increase in population was primarily attributed to Zimbabwe's unique wildlife management program.

Before the successful implementation of the CAMPFIRE program, Musa held little hope that a wildlife management program could work in his country. He remembered the failed attempts at wildlife management that had come after 1975, when the Zimbabwe government passed the Parks and Wildlife Act. The act had granted private landholders the responsibility for and the use of animals on their land. Landowners were given the authority to manage wildlife resources on private lands and to earn revenues from the "ownership" of such animals. Up until that point, the wildlife in Masoka was considered to be the property of the state. In 1978 Musa had his hopes up when the Department of National Parks and Wildlife Management implemented a program called Wildlife Industries New Development for All (WINDFALL). Musa had been excited because the program was a first attempt at involving local farmers on communal properties in the development of wildlife industries (Peterson, 1991, p. 8). Musa soon realized, however, that although the Wildlife Act had transferred ownership rights to private farmers, most of the private landowners who benefited from the act were white ranchers, while the indigenous people occupied the marginal communal lands. Therefore, there was still no incentive for many of the local people to preserve wildlife resources. Musa had been disappointed because the WINDFALL program had been the first real attempt to provide benefits to the indigenous people who carried the costs associated with living with the wildlife. The program aimed to remit revenues from safari hunts to local district councils and it was also designed to distribute the meat from safari hunts to the local farmers. Although the ideology behind the WINDFALL strategy was potentially workable, Musa identified several reasons why the program had failed.

Prior to independence, district councils were ill-defined and managed. Therefore, revenues from safari hunts did not get back to the people quickly, if at all, and when money was used for community projects, there was little correlation drawn between wildlife protection and the associated benefits. In addition, the success of the program depended upon the direct involvement and decision making of the local communities; however, government officials did not feel the people were ready to take on the responsibility. As a result, local farmers were not given the opportunity to be involved in decision making and therefore did not have a direct stake in the issues to be decided (Peterson, 1991).

Unknown to Musa, the Wildlife Act was the beginning of a trend toward conservation by utilization, which in 1982 led to the beginnings of the CAMPFIRE program. Until independence in 1980, farmers on communal lands were unable to reap the rewards derived from the existence of wildlife on communal property. Therefore, local people had no incentive to protect the wildlife. Rather, as was the case with both Musa's father and his employer, the local farmers often killed any animal discovered to be damaging crops or threatening human life. In 1982, pursuant to the Parks and Wildlife Act, Zimbabwe developed the CAMPFIRE program, which for the first time empowered the local people to manage wildlife resources on communal lands. The premise of the program was similar to that of WINDFALL; however, to Musa's relief, the program aimed to correct the weaknesses found in the WINDFALL program. Specifically, local farmers were to be involved in the decision-making process and in the management of CAMPFIRE. Thus, the program was to be used as a tool to encourage the development of a democratic society. At the same time, if properly implemented, it would provide a real possibility for a sustainable conservation. By shifting control over wildlife to the community, the state gave the local people a direct stake in the conservation of its wildlife. To Musa's delight, the program effectively motivated community members to take an interest in wildlife conservation. Villagers began to see the potential value in their wildlife resources and new programs began to emerge slowly.

CAMPFIRE'S IMPLEMENTATION

At approximately the same time that the ivory trade ban took effect (in the late 1980s), Musa began to hear murmurs about the new CAMPFIRE program. The program was rumored to be a sustainable conservation plan whereby local people would profit from tourism generated by the wildlife found on communal lands. The program, which would operate in the communal areas of Zimbabwe, was meant to allow the people who had to bear the costs of living with wildlife to reap the associated benefits. At first, the local people paid no attention to the program, which appeared to be yet another well-intentioned but futile conservation effort. Musa, however, was always interested in ideas that might help to protect the animals, and so with an open mind, he attended a district council meeting in which program details were provided.

One of the test sites for the program was to be Masoka; and if successful, CAMPFIRE would be implemented in other suitable regions in Zimbabwe. Masoka had been chosen as a test site for two primary reasons. First, its remote location made it home to the most densely populated region of dangerous big game in Zimbabwe. Second, much of the land was not suitable for agriculture. Furthermore, livestock could not be sustained due to the presence of the deadly tsetse fly that inhabited the forests of the Zambezi Valley. These combined factors made it difficult to live in Masoka. The area of land available for agriculture was limited to a small riverine section and was fervently protected by those farming the land (Matzke and Nabane, 1996). These conditions made Masoka a typical poaching community and a perfect location to implement a sustainable conservation program.

The community would first apportion the land between that which would remain available for agriculture and that which would be reserved for wildlife. The community would then lease the wildlife area out to big game hunting safari operators who would charge foreigners who wished to hunt the animals. The cost to a hunter for a typical elephant safari would be approximately $1,200 per day and the trophy fees associated with killing an elephant would range from $10,000 to $15,000. Both hunting and trophy fees would vary based on the type of animal being hunted and the length of the safari. A percentage of the revenues generated from these safaris would then be distributed by the elected district council to the members of the community. The community members would jointly decide whether to use the money to implement community projects, such as schooling, medical and conservation efforts, or to divide it among individual families in Masoka. The key success factor of the program was to be that individuals would decide how the money was to be spent. They could choose to keep the money to compensate for damaged crops or pool the money and spend it on community improvements.

Listening to the organizers explain the CAMPFIRE program, Musa was once again troubled. He was concerned that the program seemed to defeat the purpose for which it was intended, which was to save the animals. He raised the question at the council meeting, and the organizers explained that there would be strict quotas placed on the safari operators restricting the number of each species that could be killed. They explained further that once the revenues were distributed and the community was able to see an actual benefit, they would be encouraged to protect the wildlife rather than kill the animals found on farmland. The animals would be worth much more if they were left to the big game hunters and ultimately, due to the quotas that would be maintained, far fewer animals would be killed. In the long-term, some of the revenue generated could be used to develop the conservation area as a suitable site for viewing safaris and parks in which the animals would not be hunted.

TEN YEARS LATER: CITES

Musa was excited but also concerned when on April 20, 1997, at the tenth meeting of the conference of the parties held in Harare, Zimbabwe, the CITES parties made the decision to move the African elephant to Appendix II in three African range states, Botswana, Namibia, and Zimbabwe. He was excited because the animal was no longer considered to be in grave danger in his country. He was concerned because the decision also provided for a one-time purchase for noncommercial purposes of government stocks of ivory declared by the three African states. The conditions for the sale of ivory were outlined in the decisions from the tenth meeting and repeated in the April 2000 eleventh conference that took place in Gigiri, Kenya. Although strict guidelines as to the use of revenues generated from ivory sales were also outlined in the decision, Musa was concerned about the controversy that was sure to follow. He knew, however, that such restrictions would ensure that the revenues were used for further conservation initiatives.

Musa found that several important conditions had to be met before a range state would be permitted to enter into an ivory trade. Some of the conditions include the following (CITES, n.d.):

- The state has established programs to reinvest trade revenues into elephant conservation initiatives.
- All revenues from ivory trade are deposited into and managed by conservation trust funds.
- An international system is developed for monitoring legal and illegal ivory trade.
- Deficiencies in enforcement and control identified by the CITES panel of experts are remedied.

In 1997, as a result of the CITES decision, limited ivory trade between the range states and Japan reopened. In April of 1999, Namibia, Botswana, and Zimbabwe auctioned almost 60 tons of ivory to Japanese bidders who used the ivory for cultural and traditional purposes. Musa knew that in Japan ivory was used for carving artifacts, making traditional jewelry, and producing traditional hand-carved signature seals (Ndivanga, 1999). He felt that such noncommercial use of the ivory was acceptable, but wasn't sure whether the Western world would agree.

Of great importance to Musa, was that the ivory trade be strictly monitored. When he looked into it he discovered that in order to properly monitor the trade of ivory, CITES had developed two programs, Elephant Trade Information System (ETIS) and Monitoring the Illegal Killing of Elephants (MIKE). ETIS was designed to measure and record trends in illegal trade, to assess whether the down listing of the African elephant to Appendix II was the cause of a change in these trends, and to establish a database to support decision making on remedial actions. MIKE was designed to record trends of illegal hunting in African range states as well as to assess whether there is a causal relationship between the down listing of the African elephant and the change in trends. In addition, MIKE also maintains a database to help with decisions on remedial actions. The primary difference between MIKE and ETIS is that MIKE is concerned with monitoring illegal hunting while ETIS is concerned with monitoring illegal trade (CITES, 1975).

Advocates of CAMPFIRE

As Musa suspected would happen, since its inception, CAMPFIRE received a great deal of attention from both advocates and opponents. Proponents of the program believe that internationally legislated bans such as the ivory trade ban imposed by CITES serves to curb the positive effects of CAMPFIRE. Prior to the Appendix I ban on the trade of African elephants, the Zimbabwean government spent approximately $15 million per year for wildlife protection (Heimert, 1995). Subsequent to the ban, this expenditure decreased to approximately $5 million partly due to the fact that revenues derived from wildlife trade had previously been used to fund such protection programs. With the decrease in revenues earned from trade came a corresponding decrease in expenditure and motivation to protect the wildlife. Because Zimbabwe's management plan purports that African wildlife must pay its way if it is to survive, the ban on trade served to decrease wildlife protection efforts. In 1997, proponents further argued that Zimbabwe should be allowed to sell the stockpile of ivory that was sitting in warehouses. Money generated from such a sale would be partially allocated to communal areas, thereby increasing CAMPFIRE revenues and providing a strong incentive for villagers to protect wildlife (Hess, 1997). Musa could definitely understand this point of view, but he could also empathize with the position taken by the opponents of the program.

Opponents to CAMPFIRE

Opponents to the program, including animal rights activist groups such as the U.S.-based Humane Society, argue that CITES restrictions on the trade of endangered species are sufficient to protect the lives of wildlife and deter poaching. Evidence suggests, however, that increased security and monitoring of poaching activity, and not the ivory ban itself, has reduced illegal killing of elephants (Dublin and Jachmann, 1992). In addition, the Dublin and Jachmann's (1992) report on the impact of ivory trade found no statistical difference in illegal poaching patterns. Opponents further argue that programs such as CAMPFIRE effectively condone big game hunting in contrast to the program's purported mission to protect such animals. Such opponents advocate protectionist views by taking a zero-tolerance stance on killing. In 1997, the U.S.-based Humane Society unsuccessfully sought to outlaw trophy hunting of elephants. The animal had just been moved from CITES Appendix I to Appendix II for the three range states and the bid was made in an effort to prevent organizations and communities from earning a profit by killing a once endangered species.

Musa could understand the opposition to killing expressed by the opponents of the program. He wished himself that they could find another alternative that would entirely avoid animal hunting. But he also knew that this alternative had many advantages over the protective strategies of other countries. He believed that much of the opposition came from value-laden judgments rather than objective evaluations.

TEN YEARS LATER: LIFE IN MASOKA

Musa took a deep breath of the warm evening air and smiled to himself as he watched the silhouette of the herd disappear into the trees. As he slowly made his way across his land back to his home, he thought about the fence that they had just begun to build around the greater agricultural area that included his farmland. The community had agreed to commit the most recent CAMPFIRE revenues to building an electric fence that would ward off the larger wild animals from feeding on the maize. Over the past ten years several community programs had been established with the money generated from the CAMPFIRE program. A school had been built in Masoka that enabled children in the area to obtain an education. Previously, children had to walk great distances through dangerous wildlife territory in order to attend school. During particularly dry years, the CAMPFIRE program had provided revenues to families to supplement the lost crop revenues. During good years the money had been used for social programs and also put back into environmental efforts. The community had transformed from one that loathed the wildlife to one that not only protected the animals but also reported against any member of the community who attempted to harm an animal or otherwise violate the conservation regulations.

Musa was happy with the improvements that had been made in his community. He thought, overall, that his life was better with CAMPFIRE than without. He worried, however, that without funding from USAid and other donor organizations, the program would eventually fail. He thought that perhaps it was time to revisit the issue of ivory trade to determine whether the trade ban was, in fact, in the best interests of conservation. Perhaps, if the community could once again enter into unrestricted trade of wildlife products, the money could be used to ensure that CAMPFIRE would become self-sustaining. Such a question would undoubtedly lead to another values conflict that would garner a new round of arguments from Western protectionists. Musa felt, however, that his community was better prepared to deal with such resistance. Admittedly though, it still bothered him that some of the elephants were killed for nothing more than trophy hunting. He wondered if there was a better way.

BIBLIOGRAPHY

Arica Resources Trust (n.d.). The Wildlife and Development Series. London: International Institute for Environment and Development. Available online at http://www.wildnetafrica.com/bushcraft/articles/document_campfier.html.

Convention on International Trade of Endangered Species of Flora nd Fauna (1975). The CITES Elephant Trade Information System (ETIS). Available online at http://www.environmentabout.com/newsissues/environment/gi/dynamic/offsite.htm?site=; http://www.traffic.org/cop11/briefing room/etis.html.

Convention on International Trade of Endangered Species of Flora and Fauna (n.d.). Decision of the Conference on the Parties—Tenth Meeting of the Conference of the Parties Harare (Zimbabwe), June 9-20, section 10.2c. Available online at http://www.cites.org/CITES/eng/index.html.

Dublin, H. T. and Jachmann, H. (1992). *The Impact of the Ivory Ban on Illegal Hunting of Elephants in Six Range States in Africa.* WWF International Research Report. February.

Heimert, Andrew J. (1995). How the Elephant Lost His Tusks. *The Yale Law Journal,* 104(6), 1473-1506.

Hess, Karl Jr. (1997). Environmentalists vs. Wildlife, *Wall Street Journal,* June 5, pp. 32-42.

Hess, Karl Jr. (1997). Wild Success. Reason Magazine Online. Available online http://www.reason.com/9710/fe.hess.html.

Kluckhohn, Florence and Strodtbeck, Fred (1961). *Variations in Value Orientations.* Evanston, IL: Row, Peterson and Company, USA.

Kreuter, Urs P. and Simmons, Randy T. (1995). Who Owns the Elephants? The Political Economy of Saving the African Elephant. In Terry L. Anderson and Peter J. Hill (Eds.), *Wildlife in the Marketplace: The Political Economy Forum* (pp. 147-165). Lanham, MD: Rowman & Littlefield Publishers Inc.

Matzke, Gordon and Nabane, Nontokozo (1996). Outcomes of a Community Controlled Wildlife Utilization Program in a Zambezi Valley Community. *Human Ecology,* 24(1), 65-85.

Ndivanga, Chris. (1999). Trade in Ivory Restarts. *African Business*, June, 38-39.

Peterson, J. H. (1991). *CAMPFIRE: A Zimbabwean Approach to Sustainable Development and Community Empowerment Through Wildlife Utilization.* Zimbabwe: Centre for Applied Social Sciences.

Sack, Karen (1992). TED Case Studies: An Online Journal. September, 1(1).

Sack, Karen (2002). Trade and Environment Database: Elephant Ivory Trade Ban. American University, TED case studies, 1(1). Available online at http://www. american.edu/ted/ELEPHANT.htm.

U.S. Agency for International Development (1997). Press release: CAMPFIRE. January. Available online at http://www.usaid.gov/press/releases/9700101.htm.

Chapter 18

Ecotourism in Extractive Reserves in Brazil

Marcos M. Borges
Sarah Richardson

INTRODUCTION

Ecotourism initiatives are occurring within a new form of conservation unit in Brazil, called "extractive reserves." These reserves were created in response to land and cultural conflicts within the Amazon Rainforest as a legal mechanism for protecting traditional cultures and natural environments from the outcomes of large-scale deforestation. To this end, extractive reserves are considered places where environmental, cultural, and economic sustainability exist as management priorities. The need to expand economic activity and identify new forms of sustainable development in extractive reserves has generated interest in ecotourism as a potential form of development. Extractive reserves are a unique form of a conservation unit. A process was developed to assess their ecotourism potential and to develop ecotourism opportunities within selected reserves.

ECOTOURISM IN BRAZIL

Brazil is a country rich in cultural and biophysical diversity and thus, tourism potential. It is larger than the continental United States and occupies almost half of South America (see Figure 18.1). It has almost 5,000 miles of Atlantic coastline and five different major ecosystems: Amazonian, Atlantic Forest, Southern Temperate Forest, cerrado (a type of Savanna), and Western Wetlands. Brazil's world share of biodiversity is significant. Twenty-two percent of flora, 10 percent of mammal and amphibian, and 17 percent of bird species reside within Brazilian borders (Gusmão, 1999). The Amazon region, which extends to nine countries and holds approximately 50 percent of the world's biodiversity (Instituto Nacional de Pesquisas Amazônicas, 2000), accounts for almost 60 percent of all Brazilian lands. The Brazilian Amazon

Ouro Preto house. (Photo courtesy of Marcos M. Borges.)

Cajar extractivist family. (Photo courtesy of Marcos M. Borges.)

Cajari family in boat. (Photo courtesy of Marcos M. Borges.)

Cajari rubber tree. (Photo courtesy of Marcos M. Borges.)

FIGURE 18.1. Extractive reserves in Brazil, South America. (Map prepared by Hanako Saito.)

Rainforest, where the extractive reserves are situated, contains approximately one-fourth of all preserved tropical forest in the world.

Brazil is also a country with a rich, diverse culture and history. European, African, and numerous native Indian cultures have shared Brazilian soil for over 500 years, in some places blending their backgrounds through miscegenation, and in others maintaining their cultural distinctiveness and way of life. Together, the cultural, historical, and natural richness of Brazil provide the resource base to support a viable tourism industry that is rapidly growing. In 1999, domestic arrivals were estimated by the Brazilian Tourism Institute (EMBRATUR, 1999a) at 38 million and international arrivals were 5.1 million. These numbers represented increases of 43 percent in domestic tourism and 6 percent in international arrivals over 1998 numbers, which themselves represented a doubling in domestic arrivals and a tripling in international arrivals since 1994 (EMBRATUR, 1998, 1999a). Due to domestic policies encouraging the development of tourism supply in Brazil, and economic and market trends that favor further demand, tourism promises to be an activity and industry of increasing economic, social, and environmental significance.

Recognizing the characteristics of Brazil's tourism resources, and the direction of tourism demand, most of Brazil's government and private industry investments and policies are directed at the development of tourism that depends on natural and cultural resources—often broadly referred to as "ecotourism." EMBRATUR has defined ecotourism as

> the segment of tourism activity that makes use, in a sustainable way, of the natural and cultural heritage, promoting its conservation and seeking to establish an environmental conscience through the understanding of nature, and promoting the well-being of the involved population. (de Barros and La Penha, 1994, p. 19)

Although the mutuality of economic development and conservation goals has been questioned in the tourism literature and by destination examples, many Brazilian policies and initiatives appear to reflect optimism about the economic, social, and environmental benefits that ecotourism can deliver. For example, the Program for the Development of Ecotourism in the Legal Amazon Region (PROECOTUR), financed by the Inter-American Development Bank, is investing US $200 million in infrastructure development that will support ecotourism in the Amazon states. Although this is so far the largest investment in ecotourism in Brazil (EMBRATUR, 1999b), many other government and commercial initiatives to develop ecotourism in Brazil are underway, including an initiative to develop ecotourism in Brazil's extractive reserves.

EXTRACTIVE RESERVES IN BRAZIL

The first extractive reserve was designated in 1990. As of 2000, the Brazilian national government had created sixteen extractive reserves with several others under study or awaiting funding. Extractive reserves are managed by the Brazilian Center for Sustainable Development of Traditional Communities (CNPT), a branch of the Brazilian Renewable Natural Resources and Environmental Institute, the national government agency responsible for environmental policy and regulations. The land contained within extractive reserves belongs to the government and is regulated according to a land use contract with traditional communities who reside within them. For purposes of policy and legislation, "traditional communities" have been defined by CNPT as groups of persons who:

1. have lived and occupied a certain area for several generations;
2. incorporate only low-impact technologies in their uses of natural resources;
3. place strong emphasis on family and community relationships throughout sociocultural and economic activities; and
4. are primarily involved with subsistence agriculture, rubber tapping, and other extractive activities.

Because of this, residents of extractive reserves are referred to as "extractivists."

Extractive reserves are very large tracts of remote and undeveloped land. Each extractivist residing within a reserve is entrusted with a land parcel, only 10 percent of which can be altered for agricultural or other economic practices. The remaining 90 percent of the land parcel can be used only for activities that sustain the resource base, such as rubber extraction and the harvesting of Brazil nuts and the Açaí, a local palm tree. Many people also rely on hunting, fishing, and subsistence agriculture of manioc, rice, beans, and tobacco. Resource-use decisions are delegated to local populations and must reflect sustainable practices. Because of these policies and practices, much of the landmass within extractive reserves remains in a virgin state. For example, in 1998, the Alto Juruá Reserve (one of the reserves included in the ecotourism project) still had 99 percent of its original rainforest preserved (Almeida, 1994).

The lifestyle and living conditions within reserves are primitive by all standards. Residents reside in small villages or enclaves, typically in huts built with local wood and thatched roofs. Homes are dispersed along rivers (the main transportation and communication routes in many reserves), or along rudimentary roads. For example, in the Cajarí Reserve (another reserve included in the ecotourism project) 31 percent of residents live in small villages and 62 percent live along rivers and streams (Filocreão, 1993). Little or no plumbing exists, so old-style outhouses are typical and bathing occurs in nearby rivers and creeks. Power generators or solar panels periodically generate electricity and villagers often share a common television, and some basic appliances.

The majority of the adults residing in extractive reserves are illiterate or semiliterate. Formal education is provided for children through the elementary level (typically the fifth grade), after which they usually contribute to the working life of the reserves or must move to urban centers to pursue higher levels of education. Nonexistent to poor health care has long been a problem in traditional communities, making the creation of community health centers a top priority. Extractive reserves are very sparsely populated areas, some of them with less than one inhabitant for each square kilometer.

The average family size in the Amazon region is 5.3 people, most of whom are children, and people typically live in close proximity to extended family members.

Extractivists descended from intermarriage between European colonizers, Indians, and African descendents. They migrated to the Amazon region from Brazil's northeast region during the rubber "booms" of the industrial revolution and World War II and established their unique way of life, which is rooted in rubber tapping and reverence for the forests. This lifestyle was disrupted in the 1970s when aggressive incentives to develop Amazonia drew ranchers from Brazil's southern regions.[1] The introduction of ranching generated intense deforestation and land conflicts with extractivists whose livelihood depended upon forest products such as rubber and nuts. In 1976, extractivists started a grassroots movement to protect forest resources. *Empates* (peaceful protests) were organized and the fight for land through the legal system began. As the rate of deforestation increased, conflicts between ranchers and extractivists became acute and violent and drew national and international attention. Several members of the extractive community were killed, including, in 1988, Chico Mendes, one of the principle leaders of the extractivists' movement.[2] In an attempt to mitigate the conflict, left-wing political parties, environmental, and local rubber tappers' organizations proposed a sustainable forest management strategy, the cornerstone of which was the creation of extractive reserves (Environmental Defense Fund, 1999). Thus, though the living conditions within reserves are poor and primitive, extractivists are empowered by the legal protection afforded to them through the designation of extractive reserves.

With the creation of extractive reserves, extractivists are represented and governed by reserve associations that work closely with CNPT. Village councils have formed in many enclaves to provide a voice for local concerns. It is a mandate of reserves that economic, social, and environmental practices and initiatives should be locally driven and consensus-oriented. Table 18.1 provides an overview of those entities involved with governing and decision making in extractive reserves.

ECOTOURISM IN EXTRACTIVE RESERVES

In an effort to improve quality of life in extractive reserves, CNPT and several reserve associations have looked to ecotourism as a form of economic development. In 1997, CNPT and several reserve associations initiated a project, funded by the United Nations Development Program, to assess the potential of ecotourism within selected extractive reserves. This

TABLE 18.1. Organizations Involved with the Administration of Extractive Reserves

Organization	Responsibilities
CNPT	Agency of the Brazilian Renewable Natural Resources and Environmental Institute (IBAMA) that oversees extractive reserves. Carries out proposals approved by its council and the reserve associations. Provides technical support for the implementation, monitoring, and evaluation of programs and projects. Assists with securing funding for projects through government, NGO, and private domestic and international sources. Each state with federal extractive reserves has a CNPT regional office.
CNPT Council	Oversees CNPT. Comprised of members from all organizations (governmental and nongovernmental) who work directly with reserves.
National Council of Rubber Tappers	National political organization of extractivists. Chairs the CNPT Council. Lobbies for development projects and public policies affecting the extractivist (traditional) communities.
Reserve Associations	Represent rights and obligations pertaining to extractive reserves, and with respect to the land concession provided by the government. Serve as liaisons between governmental and nongovernmental organizations. Each reserve has its own reserve association. All residents of reserves are considered members of the association. An executive board (comprised of fiscal and elective councils) is elected through direct vote by extractivists.
Village Councils	Councils represent a new and growing form of representation in extractive reserves. They are composed of representatives, elected by direct vote by village residents. Their role in providing village level representation is expected to increase in importance.
Cooperatives (co-ops)	Responsible for the economic management of the reserves. They promote integration of activities and execution of projects specifically directed at income generation.

project, called "Extractive Reserves Ecotourism Project," was facilitated by Grupo Nativa, a nonprofit tourism planning organization in Brazil.[3] All residents of reserves, and those entities involved with the administration of extractive reserves, were considered to be important stakeholders in the project (see Table 18.1). In addition, stakeholders in the gateway communities, which provide points of entry to reserves, included businesses and organizations potentially involved with ecotourism activity. The four reserves that were selected for assessment of their tourism potential were Alto Juruá, Cajarí, Chico Mendes, and Ouro Preto. Table 18.2 provides a comparative overview of these extractive reserves, and Figure 18.2 details their locations.

TABLE 18.2. Extractive Reserves Included in the Ecotourism Project

Extractive Reserve	State	Area (ha)	Distance from near-est urban center[a] (km)	Population	Main extractive products
Alto Juruá	Acre	506,186	400	4,170	Rubber
Cajarí	Amapá	481,650	160	3,283	Brazil nuts, Açaí,[b] copaíba,[c] and fish
Chico Mendes	Acre	970,570	188	6,028	Brazil nuts and rubber, copaíba
Ouro Preto	Rondônia	204,583	300	431	Rubber and fish, copaíba

Sources: Borges et al., 1999.

[a]Urban centers having transportation hubs with airports, lodging, and other services

[b]Açaí is a native palm tree very common in the Amazonian state of Amapá. The extractivists harvest the tree for the palm, which is now manufactured in a small factory in the reserve, and the fruit for juice, which they call Açaí wine.

[c]Copaíba oil is obtained from South American trees in the pea family, used in certain varnishes and as a fixative in some perfumes.

Tourism Assessment Process

A five-step ecotourism assessment process was facilitated by Grupo Nativa for each of the four reserves. These steps included:

1. Analysis of existing data about ecotourism demands in Brazil and characteristics of the extractive reserves
2. Inventory of the natural and cultural attractions, and other components of tourism supply in the extractive reserves and in gateway communities that would serve as important points of entry
3. Identification of potential tourism products available in reserves that would represent the unique natural and cultural attractions within them, and markets for these products
4. Community workshops, held within extractive reserves, to discuss proposed ecotourism products and the potential benefits and costs of ecotourism

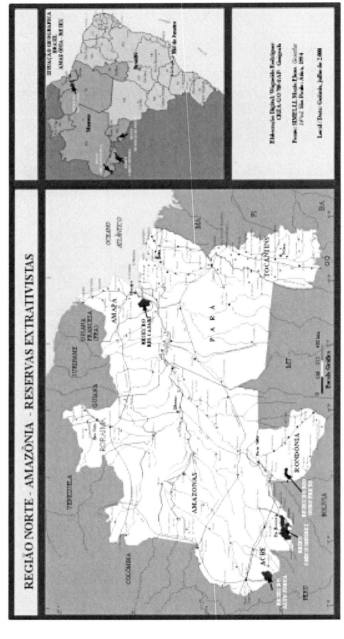

FIGURE 18.2. The Brazilian Amazon Region and the four extractive reserves included in the ecotourism project.

5. A detailed plan for ecotourism development that identified viable ecotourism directions

Critical to this assessment was widespread and representative participation by all stakeholders, including individual extractivists. This participation was essential because:

1. the legal mandate of extractive reserves requires that resource use decisions reflect local consensus;
2. the history and culture of extractive reserves is one that has institutionalized and empowered locally driven resource management decisions;
3. the type of ecotourism likely to have market appeal in the extractive reserves is one that reflects and presents local culture by the active involvement of extractivists in the delivery of the tourism product; and
4. definitions of development, through tourism or other mechanisms, often refer to the strengthening of people's capacity to determine their own values and priorities, and to organize themselves to act on these (Eade and Williams 1995).

Indeed, it is this definition of development that is at the heart of the formation of extractive reserves.

Despite the recognized importance of stakeholder involvement in the tourism assessment process, the characteristics of extractive reserves posed certain challenges. Foremost among these were the very primitive transportation and communication systems that made it difficult for widely dispersed residents to communicate and meet with one another. Announcements about ecotourism workshops were often communicated via shortwave radio to messengers who then traveled up to a day by foot or boat to reach remote villages. When workshops were held within the reserves, residents of these villages sometimes traveled up to four days by foot or boat to attend.

Another challenge was the level of familiarity with ecotourism among residents of extractive reserves. Although many reserve residents are used to interacting with people from "outside" (many have friends and relatives in gateway communities), most are unfamiliar with the requirements of tourism from either a tourist's or provider's perspective. Thus, an important requisite to extractivists' participation in decision making was the development of an understanding of impacts and complexities of tourism. The high rate of illiteracy in reserves posed challenges for achieving this understanding. Tourism concepts had to be depicted in a highly visual form. Videos and photos depicting ecotourism in other Brazilian locations, and potential tourism resources within the reserves, helped to educate residents about ecotourism. In addition, analogies between ecotourism and other economic activities helped to visually communicate challenges and opportunities inherent in tourism. Figure 18.3 depicts one such analogy drawn between a traditional product, Brazil nuts, and ecotourism that helped extractivists picture the nature and realities of tourism.

Tourism Assessment Outcomes

The assessment suggested that three of the four extractive reserves for which tourism assessments were completed had the potential to develop viable ecotourism products that could enhance economic and social conditions in traditional communities, and implementation processes are underway to make this a reality. The ectourism product was defined as the unique opportunity to participate in the extractivists' traditional way of life. It has garnered international attention and respect as the importance of preserving

FIGURE 18.3. Nuts and bolts of ecotourism in Brazil.

the Amazon Rainforest has been recognized and embraced. Ecotourists will be formed into small groups, which will facilitate intimate and educational interactions with extractivists. Ecotourists will be invited into the pristine and natural settings of extractive reserves, where interpretive programs and direct participation will provide information and education about the extractivists' sustainable way of life. Visitors will be introduced to a variety of sustainable activities that occur in extractive reserves, such as agroforestry, rubber tapping and preprocessing, Brazil nut harvesting, production associated with cassava, and uses of medicinal plants.[4] Community members, who will be trained in interpretive techniques, will serve as guides (though some outside translators might be required in the first years of operation).

Market considerations eliminated the Alto Juruá Reserve from further consideration for ecotourism development. As Table 18.3 illustrates, Alto Juruá is poorly linked to market areas via airlines, and does not have strong gateway city services. However, the remaining three reserves were believed to offer access and services necessary to link their products with domestic and international markets. These three reserves are currently the focus of an implementation plan designed to bring ecotourism activity to extractive reserves.

Ecotourism Implementation Plan

The distance of extractive reserves from gateway communities, and the nature of the tourism product, suggest that ecotourism within reserves must be a destination experience. Because of the lack of tourism infrastructure within the reserves, immediate attention has turned to designing accommodations that will house ecotourists and, through their size, capacity, and character, influence the form and function of ecotourism. Several options for accommodations have been considered, and an ecolodge model has been selected as most suitable because of its comfort and market appeal.

Planning for tourism has proceeded with the notion of a single ecolodge within each reserve that can accommodate a maximum of twenty visitors at one time, with the ideal number between twelve and fourteen. It is believed that this occupancy level will maintain the quality of the tourism experience, minimize sociocultural impacts, and address economies of scale— particularly those associated with transportation, including boats and vans (fourteen is the maximum group size for vans and boats). Visitor stays will probably last from one to nine days, since such visits can be accommodated within the more typical trip itineraries of domestic and international visitors and provide for a range of destination experiences.

TABLE 18.3. Criteria for selecting reserves for ecotourism implementation plan.

Reserve	Flight frequency to GC Airport	Air fares high/low season[a]	Trip hours to GC	Lodging in GC	Ecotourism visitors[b]	PROECO-TUR area[c]	Attractions not common to all reserves
Alto Juruá	Poor	815/347	8 h (boat)	Poor	38	No	Impressive primitive forest
Cajarí	Good, including international	553/221	3 h (boat)	Very Good	251	Yes	Cerrado, lakes, and Amazon River
Chico Mendes	Regular	604/242	6:30 h (car + boat)	Good	147	Yes	Chico Mendes' home town
Ouro Preto	Good	565/282	5:30 h (car)	Good	145	Yes	Mountain Range, forest sand patches

Source: Borges et al., 1999.

GC = Gateway community.

aValues in Brazilian currency correspond to a round-trip from São Paulo, a major international airport in Brazil (1998 fares).

bEstimate from existing 1997 data about annual visitors arriving by plane to gateway community.

cPROECOTUR is a government project sponsored by the Inter-American Bank that will invest US $200 million in ecotourism projects in Amazonian states.

Besides providing accommodations, ecolodges themselves should represent and reflect sustainable practices. The design of lodges and other buildings will complement traditional village architecture, and construction will maximize climate comfort, energy use, and impacts on the landscape through features such as the use of local architecture and construction techniques/materials, solar energy, natural gas, and septic tanks with anaerobic filters. In terms of their location, ecolodges will be built close enough to the extractivists' villages to facilitate access for workers but far enough to avoid intrusion by tourists on extractivists' daily life.

Although the ecolodges represent the "bricks and mortor" of the tourism plan, their purpose is to facilate a broader tourism experience that will start and end in the gateway communities and include the unique opportunity to participate in the sustainable practices and lifestyle of extractivists. Other elements of the tourism supply include transportation and tours, and educational and social programs that will provide for the Extractive Reserve tourism experience.

Extractive reserves will not have "mass market" appeal. Instead, they will attract members of environmental groups and tourists seeking "authentic" experiences. Initial strategies will target special-interest markets, which have an affiliation with the Amazon environment and, specifically, extractive reserves. These markets include members of environmental NGOs, Earthwatch volunteer groups, and participants in industries associated with reserves. Because of their existing connections with reserves, members of these groups will be invited to serve the dual role of pioneering tourist and participant in the tourism development process. They will provide important feedback to extractivists and others involved with the Ecotourism Project. After tourism operations experience has been acquired by extractivists within these specialized markets, more general national and international ecotourism markets will be targeted, primarily through environmental organizations that offer ecotourism experiences to their members. For example, the National Audubon Society has over 500,000 members and offers travel programs worldwide. To reach these markets, the Extractive Reserves Ecotourism Project should be commercialized through a Brazilian ecotourism operator with international environmental connections. This operator will place the product in the Brazilian ecotourism market, concentrating on the larger cities in the southeastern region of the country, particularly Rio de Janeiro and São Paulo, and in international markets.

CHALLENGES FOR MAKING ECOTOURISM
A REALITY IN EXTRACTIVE RESERVES

Although the tourism assessment indicated that extractive reserves have the potential to provide a viable tourism product, many challenges are associated with making this a reality. Most of these challenges are related to undeveloped tourism infrastructure and local labor capacity. First, although the primitive nature of extractive reserves is part of the product niche and market appeal, considerable attention must be directed to questions of service quality, hygiene and health, and safety. These questions require the development of accessible and responsive supporting services, including access to available medical care.

Second, the ability to converse in a common language will be critical to attracting an international market. Local residents are not fluent in English or other languages, thus requiring the use of interpreters for visitors who do not speak Portuguese. When needed, these interpreters will be hired in the gateway communities or by the operators from large urban centers such as Rio de Janeiro and São Paulo. The sharing of dialogue and understandings with extractivists is important and central to the intimacy of the tourism experience—an important part of the tourism product—in extractive reserves. The development of language capacity will be a top priority before marketing to an international audience.

Third, start-up financing of the overall tourism project is a critical concern. A feasibility study, based on projections over the five-year operation period, was conducted. These projections were based on variable group types and sizes (for example, ranging from small groups of researchers to larger group tours), and various lengths of stay in the reserves and gateway communities. Costs and revenues were projected over a five-year time period, based on an occupancy rate for the ecolodge of 12 percent for the first year of operation and 48 percent for the fifth year of operation (lower rates than the average occupation rates for Brazilian lodging facilities). Outcomes of the feasibility study indicated a return on investment for the tourism project in approximately eight years. However, the feasibility study identified a low rate of return, meaning that an investor might get more profits from traditional financial investments, such as government bonds, than in an enterprise such as ecolodges. However, the development of ecotourism in extractive reserves represents a pioneer program that actively involves traditional communities with new opportunities for conservation and sustainable development.

Finally, there is a need for the development and implementation of adequate monitoring and management systems, which are needed to guarantee

a quality tourism experience, optimum use of resources, and economic, social, and environmental sustainability.

CONCLUSION

The initiative to assess and develop ecotourism potential in extractive
reserves has received positive evaluations from CNPT and extractivists who
participated in the planning process, from the Brazilian Ecotourism Association, and from gateway community partners. Extractive reserves is an innovative program in which the ecotourism product is the sustainable, traditional way of life of a fiercely proud population. Planning was done in a way
to ensure community ownership. The proposed size, scope, ownership, and
management of the project will permit reserve residents to directly benefit
from tourism's positive impacts, and will help to limit negative impacts.

The success of the ecotourism project described will contribute to the viability of extractive reserves, which provide a new model for conservation
units in Brazil and elsewhere. In Brazil, the majority of conservation units,
such as national parks, require the relocation of people away from park-des-
ignated areas. This relocation incurs high financial cost, and often intense
socioeconomic and upset for the relocated population, who generally be-
long to lower-income populations. Since extractive reserves promote the
conservation of the natural environment and sustainable practices of inhabitants, the reserves not only avoid relocation costs and impacts, but also
improve the quality of life for these inhabitants.

The Extractive Reserves Ecotourism Project is also relevant to other traditional communities, such as Indian populations, who are also considering
ecotourism as an economic alternative. In Brazil, Indian tribes have their
own reserves and are facing challenges in improving the quality of life
within the reserves. These Indian tribes may incorporate the new and appropriate technologies developed within extractive reserves into their own ecotourism initiatives.

The planning process for ecotourism in extractive reserves in Brazil began in the fall of 1997 and recommendations for implementation were completed in 1999. Start-up funding for capital costs for the first ecolodge was
secured through grants from donors in early 2000. Construction for this
ecolodge, located in the Cajarí Reserve, occurred late in 2000. As of the
summer of 2001, implementation of the Ecotourism Project has been placed
on hold due to the requirements of some the funding cycles of supporting
organizations. However, participants involved with the Ecotourism Project are
eager to proceed with its implementation and to evaluate, through ongoing

monitoring, its impacts on the people and resources of Brazil's extractive reserves.

NOTES

1. Ironically, many of these development initiatives were initially sponsored by the World Bank, an entity that is now seeking the transition back to sustainable practices.
2. The movie, *The Burning Season—The Chico Mendes Story,* depicts the conflicts between rubber tappers (extractivists) and ranchers in the Amazon.
3. The first author of this case is a founder and principal tourism planner of Grupo Nativa.
4. Cassava (*Manihot esculenta*): Native to the tropical regions of Mexico, Central America, and South America, cassava is known by many names—manioc, mandioca, manioca, tapioca, Brazilian arrowroot, and yuca. Five hundred million people worldwide rely on the starchy cassava root for a large percentage of their carbohydrate calories (The Food Museum, 2000—www.foodmuseum.com/ hughes/ cassava.htm).

REFERENCES

Almeida, M. W. B. (1994). *Levantamento sócio econômico, reserva extrativista do Alto Juruá* [Socio-economic study, Alto Juruá extractive reserve]. Brasília, DF, Brazil: IBAMA/CNPT.
Borges, M. M., Safadi, M. D. O., Martinelli, F. V., Ferreiro, P. D., and Mourão, R. M. F. (1999). *Programa de desenvolvimento de ecoturismo em reservas extrativistas: Diagnóstico geral* [Proposal for development of ecotourism in Extractive Reserves]. Goiânia, GO, Brazil: Grupo Nativa.
de Barros, S. M. II and D. H. M. C. La Penha (1994). *Diretrizes para uma política nacional de ecoturismo* [Guidelines for a National Ecotourism Policy]. Brasília, DF, Brazil: EMBRATUR: 19.
Eade, D. and S. Williams (1995). *The Oxfam Handbook of Development and Relief.* Oxford, United Kingdom: Oxfam.
EMBRATUR (1998). *Anuário Estatístico* [Annual Statistics]. Brasília, DF, Brazil: Author.
EMBRATUR (1999a). *A indústria do turismo no Brasil antes e depois de Fernando Henrique Cardoso, 1995 a 1999* [The Brazilian Tourism Industry Before and After Fernando Henrique Cardoso, 1995 to 1999], EMBRATUR.
EMBRATUR (1999b). *Institutional Programmes,* EMBRATUR.
Environmental Defense Fund (1999). *Chico Mendes, Ten Years.*
Filocreão, A. S. M. C. (1993). *Sócio-economia da reserva extrativista do Rio Cajari—AP* [Socioeconomy of the Rio Cajarí extractive reserve]. Brasília, DF, Brazil: IBAMA/CNPT.

The Food Museum (2000). Available online at www.foodmuseum.com/hughes/cassava.htm.

Gusmão, M. (1999). As Paisagens Intocadas [The Untouched Landscape]. *Revista Veja:* 66-72.

Instituto Nacional de Pesquisas Amazônicas (2000). *Informações Científicas sobre a Amazônia* [Scientific Information about the Amazon Region], Author.

Index

Page numbers followed by the letter "f" indicate figures; those followed by the letter "t" indicate tables.

EPA (Environmental Protection
  Agency) (U.S.), 47, 134
EPEA (Environmental Protection and
  Enhancement Act) (Canada),
  61
equipment maintenance, 115
ethical issues, 101-103
ETIS (Elephant Trade Information
  System), 258
Evans, Joan, 115-117
Evans, Norman, 7
excess packaging, 67-68
expectations, altering, 35
Extractive Reserves (Brazil)
  administration of, 270
  background information, 267-269
  consensus-based decision making,
    269
  ecolodges, 275, 277
  ecotourism, 269-280
  map, 266, 272
  photos, 264-265
  Reserve Associations, 270
  stakeholders, 270-271, 273
  sustainable development, 263
Extractive Reserves Ecotourism
  Project, 270

FAA (Federal Aviation Administration)
  (U.S.), 47
facilitator in multistakeholder conflict,
  231-234
Fairmont Banff Springs Hotel, 54
Fairmont Chateau, 52
Fairmont Palliser Hotel. *See* Palliser
  Hotel
"fat boy" skis, 119
Federal Aviation Administration
  (FAA), 47
Finnair Catering, 42-44
First Nations people, 211-212
fish, 80-81
Fisher, Bill, 134
Florida Keys (U.S.), 145-150
Freedom Airlines, Inc. (FAI), 9-10, 30,
  41-49
Friends of the Earth, 132
Fry, J., 135

Gadd, Ben, 133
game hunting safaris, 256-257
geological sites, 19-20
Global Code of Ethics for Tourism
  (WTO), 3-4
Global Conference on Business and the
  Environment (1992), 3
Globe 1990 International Tourism
  Conference, 3
glycol, 44
Godfrey, Jim, 138
golf courses, 70
government as stakeholder, 240-241
Grand Canyon National Park (U.S.)
  aerial tourism, 180, 183-185
  Grand Canyon Greenway, 179-180
  Hermit Trail, 182
  introduction to, 13, 178-180
  map, 179
  photos, 175-178
Grand Cayman, 155
Great Barrier Reef Marine Park
  (Australia), 155-156
Green Globe certification program
  (WTTC), 3, 29
Green Leaf Eco-Rating, 29
Green Partnership Program, 51-70
Green Suites International, 68
Grupo Nativa (Brazil), 270-271
guest education, 63, 115

Habitat Improvement Team, 138
Harper, Jack, 34
hazard assessment, 119-120
hazardous waste, 46
Heavenly Ski Resort, 137
helicopters, 24, 183-185
heli-skiing, 109-120
high-density recreational use, 130, 136
historic sites, 19-20
hotel and hospitality industry, 29, 56.
  See also Canadian Pacific
  Hotels & Resorts; ecolodges;
  Palliser Hotel
Hudson, S., 135
Humane Society (U.S.), 252, 259
hunting safaris, 256-257

THE HAWORTH HOSPITALITY PRESS®
Hospitality, Travel, and Tourism
K. S. Chon, PhD, Editor in Chief

THAILAND TOURISM by Arthur Asa Berger. (2007).

CULTURAL TOURISM: GLOBAL AND LOCAL PERSPECTIVES edited by Greg Richards. (2007).

GAY TOURISM: CULTURE AND CONTEXT by Gordon Waitt and Kevin Markwell. (2006).

CASES IN SUSTAINABLE TOURISM: AN EXPERIENTIAL APPROACH TO MAKING DECISIONS edited by Irene M. Herremans. (2006). "As a tourism instructor and researcher, I recommend this textbook for both undergraduate and graduate students who wish to pursue their careers in parks, recreation, or tourism. The text is appropriate both for junior and senior tourism management classes and graduate classes. It is an excellent primer for understanding the fundamental concepts, issues, and real-world examples of sustainable tourism." *Hwan-Suk Chris Choi, PhD, Assistant Professor, School of Hospitality and Tourism Management, University of Guelph*

COMMUNITY DESTINATION MANAGEMENT IN DEVELOPING ECONOMIES edited by Walter Jamieson. (2006). "This book is a welcome and valuable addition to the destination management literature, focusing as it does on developing economies in the Asian context. It provides an unusually comprehensive and informative overview of critical issues in the field, effectively combining well-crafted discussions of key conceptual and methodological issues with carefully selected and well-presented case studies drawn from a number of contrasting Asian destinations." *Peter Hills, PhD, Professor and Director, The Centre of Urban Planning and Environmental Management, The University of Hong Kong*

MANAGING SUSTAINABLE TOURISM: A LEGACY FOR THE FUTURE by David L. Edgell Sr. (2006). "This comprehensive book on sustainable tourism should be required reading for everyone interested in tourism. The author is masterful in defining strategies and using case studies to explain best practices in generating long-term economic return on your tourism investment." *Kurtis M. Ruf, Partner, Ruf Strategic Solutions; Author,* Contemporary Database Marketing

CASINO INDUSTRY IN ASIA PACIFIC: DEVELOPMENT, OPERATION, AND IMPACT edited by Cathy H.C. Hsu. (2006). "This book is a must-read for anyone interested in the opportunities and challenges that the proliferation of casino gaming will bring to Asia in the early twenty-first century. The economic and social consequences of casino gaming in Asia may ultimately prove to be far more significant than those encountered in the West, and this book opens the door as to what those consequences might be." *William R. Eadington, PhD, Professor of Economics and Director, Institute for the Study of Gambling and Commercial Gaming, University of Nevada, Reno*

THE GROWTH STRATEGIES OF HOTEL CHAINS: BEST BUSINESS PRACTICES BY LEADING COMPANIES by Onofre Martorell Cunill. (2006). "Informative, well-written, and up-to-date. This is one title that I shall certainly be adding to my 'must-read' list for students this year." *Tom Baum, PhD, Professor of International Tourism and Hospitality Management, The Scottish Hotel School, The University of Strathclyde, Glasgow*

HANDBOOK FOR DISTANCE LEARNING IN TOURISM by Gary Williams. (2005). "This is an important book for a variety of audiences. As a resource for educational designers (and their managers) in particular, it is invaluable. The book is easy to read, and is full of practical information that can be logically applied in the design and development of flexible learning resources." *Louise Berg, MA, DipED, Lecturer in Education, Charles Sturt University, Australia*

VIETNAM TOURISM by Arthur Asa Berger. (2005). "Fresh and innovative.... Drawing upon Professor Berger's background and experience in cultural studies, this book offers an imaginative and personal portrayal of Vietnam as a tourism destination.... A very welcome addition to the field of destination studies." *Professor Brian King, PhD, Head, School of Hospitality, Tourism & Marketing, Victoria University, Australia*

TOURISM AND HOTEL DEVELOPMENT IN CHINA: FROM POLITICAL TO ECONOMIC SUCCESS by Hanqin Qiu Zhang, Ray Pine, and Terry Lam. (2005). "This is one of the most comprehensive books on China tourism and hotel development. It is one of the best textbooks for educators, students, practitioners, and investors who are interested in China tourism and hotel industry. Readers will experience vast, diversified, and past and current issues that affect every educator, student, practitioner, and investor in China tourism and hotel globally in an instant." *Hailin Qu, PhD, Full Professor and William E. Davis Distinguished Chair, School of Hotel & Restaurant Administration, Oklahoma State University*

THE TOURISM AND LEISURE INDUSTRY: SHAPING THE FUTURE edited by Klaus Weiermair and Christine Mathies. (2004). "If you need or want to know about the impact of globalization, the impact of technology, societal forces of change, the experience economy, adaptive technologies, environmental changes, or the new trend of slow tourism, you need this book. *The Tourism and Leisure Industry* contains a great mix of research and practical information." *Charles R. Goeldner, PhD, Professor Emeritus of Marketing and Tourism, Leeds School of Business, University of Colorado*

OCEAN TRAVEL AND CRUISING: A CULTURAL ANALYSIS by Arthur Asa Berger. (2004). "Dr. Berger presents an interdisciplinary discussion of the cruise industry for the thinking person. This is an enjoyable social psychology travel guide with a little business management thrown in. A great book for the curious to read a week before embarking on a first cruise or for the frequent cruiser to gain a broader insight into exactly what a cruise experience represents." *Carl Braunlich, DBA, Associate Professor, Department of Hospitality and Tourism Management, Purdue University, West Lafayette, Indiana*

STANDING THE HEAT: ENSURING CURRICULUM QUALITY IN CULINARY ARTS AND GASTRONOMY by Joseph A. Hegarty. (2003). "This text provides the genesis of a well-researched, thoughtful, rigorous, and sound theoretical framework for the enlargement and expansion of higher education programs in culinary arts and gastronomy." *John M. Antun, PhD, Founding Director, National Restaurant Institute, School of Hotel, Restaurant, and Tourism Management, University of South Carolina*

SEX AND TOURISM: JOURNEYS OF ROMANCE, LOVE, AND LUST edited by Thomas G. Bauer and Bob McKercher. (2003). "Anyone interested in or concerned about the impact of tourism on society and particularly in the developing world, should read this book. It explores a subject that has long remained ignored, almost a taboo area for many governments, institutions, and organizations. It demonstrates that the stereotyping of 'sex tourism' is too simple and travel and sex have many manifestations. The book follows its theme in an innovative and original way." *Carson L. Jenkins, PhD, Professor of International Tourism, University of Strathclyde, Glasgow, Scotland*

CONVENTION TOURISM: INTERNATIONAL RESEARCH AND INDUSTRY PERSPECTIVES edited by Karin Weber and Kye-Sung Chon. (2002). "This comprehensive book is truly global in its perspective. The text points out areas of needed research—a great starting point for graduate students, university faculty, and industry professionals alike. While the focus is mainly academic, there is a lot of meat for this burgeoning industry to chew on as well." *Patti J. Shock, CPCE, Professor and Department Chair, Tourism and Convention Administration, Harrah College of Hotel Administration, University of Nevada–Las Vegas*

CULTURAL TOURISM: THE PARTNERSHIP BETWEEN TOURISM AND CULTURAL HERITAGE MANAGEMENT by Bob McKercher and Hilary du Cros. (2002). "The book brings together concepts, perspectives, and practicalities that must be understood by both cultural heritage and tourism managers, and as such is a must-read for both." *Hisashi B. Sugaya, AICP, Former Chair, International Council of Monuments and Sites, International Scientific Committee on Cultural Tourism; Former Executive Director, Pacific Asia Travel Association Foundation, San Francisco, CA*

TOURISM IN THE ANTARCTIC: OPPORTUNITIES, CONSTRAINTS, AND FUTURE PROSPECTS by Thomas G. Bauer. (2001). "Thomas Bauer presents a wealth of detailed information on the challenges and opportunities facing tourism operators in this last great tourism frontier." *David Mercer, PhD, Associate Professor, School of Geography & Environmental Science, Monash University, Melbourne, Australia*

SERVICE QUALITY MANAGEMENT IN HOSPITALITY, TOURISM, AND LEISURE edited by Jay Kandampully, Connie Mok, and Beverley Sparks. (2001). "A must-read.... a treasure. . . . pulls together the work of scholars across the globe, giving you access to new ideas, international research, and industry examples from around the world." *John Bowen, Professor and Director of Graduate Studies, William F. Harrah College of Hotel Administration, University of Nevada, Las Vegas*

TOURISM IN SOUTHEAST ASIA: A NEW DIRECTION edited by K. S. (Kaye) Chon. (2000). "Presents a wide array of very topical discussions on the specific challenges facing the tourism industry in Southeast Asia. A great resource for both scholars and practitioners." *Dr. Hubert B. Van Hoof, Assistant Dean/Associate Professor, School of Hotel and Restaurant Management, Northern Arizona University*

THE PRACTICE OF GRADUATE RESEARCH IN HOSPITALITY AND TOURISM edited by K. S. Chon. (1999). "An excellent reference source for students pursuing graduate degrees in hospitality and tourism." *Connie Mok, PhD, CHE, Associate Professor, Conrad N. Hilton College of Hotel and Restaurant Management, University of Houston, Texas*

**THE INTERNATIONAL HOSPITALITY MANAGEMENT BUSINESS: MANAGE-
MENT AND OPERATIONS** by Larry Yu. (1999). "The abundant real-world examples
and cases provided in the text enable readers to understand the most up-to-date developments in international hospitality business." *Zheng Gu, PhD, Associate Professor, College
of Hotel Administration, University of Nevada, Las Vegas*

CONSUMER BEHAVIOR IN TRAVEL AND TOURISM by Abraham Pizam and
Yoel Mansfeld. (1999). "A must for anyone who wants to take advantage of new global
opportunities in this growing industry." *Bonnie J. Knutson, PhD, School of Hospitality
Business, Michigan State University*

**LEGALIZED CASINO GAMING IN THE UNITED STATES: THE ECONOMIC
AND SOCIAL IMPACT** edited by Cathy H. C. Hsu. (1999). "Brings a fresh new look at
one of the areas in tourism that has not yet received careful and serious consideration in
the past." *Muzaffer Uysal, PhD, Professor of Tourism Research, Virginia Polytechnic Institute and State University, Blacksburg*

HOSPITALITY MANAGEMENT EDUCATION edited by Clayton W. Barrows and
Robert H. Bosselman. (1999). "Takes the mystery out of how hospitality management
education programs function and serves as an excellent resource for individuals interested in pursuing the field." *Joe Perdue, CCM, CHE, Director, Executive Masters Program, College of Hotel Administration, University of Nevada, Las Vegas*

**MARKETING YOUR CITY, U.S.A.: A GUIDE TO DEVELOPING A STRATEGIC
TOURISM MARKETING PLAN** by Ronald A. Nykiel and Elizabeth Jascolt. (1998).
"An excellent guide for anyone involved in the planning and marketing of cities and re-
gions. . . . A terrific job of synthesizing an otherwise complex procedure." *James C.
Maken, PhD, Associate Professor, Babcock Graduate School of Management, Wake For-
est University, Winston-Salem, North Carolina*

Order a copy of this book with this form or online at:
http://www.haworthpress.com/store/product.asp?sku=5486

CASES IN SUSTAINABLE TOURISM
An Experiential Approach to Making Decisions

_____in hardbound at $69.95 (ISBN-13: 978-0-7890-2764-1; ISBN-10: 0-7890-2764-X)

_____in softbound at $49.95 (ISBN-13: 978-0-7890-2765-8; ISBN-10: 0-7890-2765-8)

Or order online and use special offer code HEC25 in the shopping cart.

COST OF BOOKS_____

POSTAGE & HANDLING_____
(US: $4.00 for first book & $1.50
for each additional book)
(Outside US: $5.00 for first book
& $2.00 for each additional book)

SUBTOTAL_____

IN CANADA: ADD 7% GST_____

STATE TAX_____
(NJ, NY, OH, MN, CA, IL, IN, PA, & SD
residents, add appropriate local sales tax)

FINAL TOTAL_____
(If paying in Canadian funds,
convert using the current
exchange rate, UNESCO
coupons welcome)

☐ **BILL ME LATER:** (Bill-me option is good on US/Canada/Mexico orders only; not good to jobbers, wholesalers, or subscription agencies.)
☐ Check here if billing address is different from shipping address and attach purchase order and billing address information.

Signature_____

☐ **PAYMENT ENCLOSED: $**_____

☐ **PLEASE CHARGE TO MY CREDIT CARD.**

☐ Visa ☐ MasterCard ☐ AmEx ☐ Discover
☐ Diner's Club ☐ Eurocard ☐ JCB

Account # _____

Exp. Date_____

Signature_____

Prices in US dollars and subject to change without notice.

NAME_____

INSTITUTION_____

ADDRESS_____

CITY_____

STATE/ZIP_____

COUNTRY_____ COUNTY (NY residents only)_____

TEL_____ FAX_____

E-MAIL_____

May we use your e-mail address for confirmations and other types of information? ☐ Yes ☐ No
We appreciate receiving your e-mail address and fax number. Haworth would like to e-mail or fax special discount offers to you, as a preferred customer. **We will never share, rent, or exchange your e-mail address or fax number.** We regard such actions as an invasion of your privacy.

Order From Your Local Bookstore or Directly From
The Haworth Press, Inc.
10 Alice Street, Binghamton, New York 13904-1580 • USA
TELEPHONE: 1-800-HAWORTH (1-800-429-6784) / Outside US/Canada: (607) 722-5857
FAX: 1-800-895-0582 / Outside US/Canada: (607) 771-0012
E-mail to: orders@haworthpress.com

For orders outside US and Canada, you may wish to order through your local
sales representative, distributor, or bookseller.
For information, see http://haworthpress.com/distributors

(Discounts are available for individual orders in US and Canada only, not booksellers/distributors.)

PLEASE PHOTOCOPY THIS FORM FOR YOUR PERSONAL USE.
http://www.HaworthPress.com

BOF06

Due Date	Date Returned
FEB 0 6 2010	FEB 1 2 2010
10 May 2011	MAY 0 1 2014
www.library.humber.ca	